C000018164

A Grim Almanac of
NORFOLK

Interior of
Walsingham
Bridewell.

A Grim Almanac of
NORFOLK

NEIL R. STOREY

The
History
Press

This book is dedicated to Norfolk Constabulary Historians

PC 158 Cecil John Mason.

PC 239 Peter Pilgram.

And all who have trod the beat in Norfolk over the years.

First published 2003, this edition published 2010

The History Press
The Mill, Brimscombe Port
Stroud, Gloucestershire, GL5 2QG
www.thehistorypress.co.uk

© Neil R. Storey, 2003, 2010

The right of Neil R. Storey to be identified as the Author
of this work has been asserted in accordance with the
Copyrights, Designs and Patents Act 1988.

All rights reserved. No part of this book may be reprinted
or reproduced or utilised in any form or by any electronic,
mechanical or other means, now known or hereafter invented,
including photocopying and recording, or in any information
storage or retrieval system, without the permission in writing
from the Publishers.

British Library Cataloguing in Publication Data.
A catalogue record for this book is available from the British Library.

ISBN 978 0 7524 5680 5

Typesetting and origination by The History Press
Manufacturing managed by Jellyfish Print Solutions Ltd
Printed and bound in India by Replika Press Pvt. Ltd.

CONTENTS

Irons and restraints decorate the wall above the old King's Lynn Gaol.

INTRODUCTION

Truth is always strange,
Stranger than fiction.

Don Juan (1823)

There seems to be a sort of fascination in the horrible.

Punch (1851)

From the early nineteenth century, as books, newspapers and periodicals became increasingly available and affordable to greater numbers of people, the accounts of sinister crimes, dark deeds, unexplained phenomena, horrible tortures and strange deaths captured the imaginations of the British public. In the pubs and public meeting places of the day, those who were literate would often read out the news from the papers; but it was always worth a few more drinks when there was a juicy crime to thrill and chill the listeners. As demand for tales of the sinister, the strange and the nasty grew, broadsheets outlining the details of horrible crimes and claiming to record the final death-cell confessions of murderers were published along with small booklets recording the complete story of the more notorious cases, some even including the sermons of ministers about the deed. For the people of Victorian Britain the macabre became as much a pastime as the fictional genre of Gothic Horror – that had grown from Mary Shelley's *Frankenstein* in 1818 to Bram Stoker's *Dracula* in 1897 – and 'penny dreadfuls', with titles such as *Spring Heel'd Jack*, *Sweeney Todd the Demon Barber of Fleet Street* and *Varney the Vampire* tempted the reader and fuelled the desire for more of the same.

In the same period, popular after-dinner entertainments and Cabinets of Curiosities saw finds from the Grand Tour and the Ancients pushed to one side in favour of newer curiosites: sections of used hangman's rope (sold from 2*s* 6*d* per inch, depending on the notoriety of the felon), locks of criminals' hair, buttons and pieces of their clothing, and even sections of their tanned skin. All these vied for position alongside documents associated with the crimes and broadsheets from public executions, every one with its own grim tale to tell. Freak displays were standard fare at passing shows, and in Norwich a popular diversion for those on their Sunday afternoon perambulation of the city was to slip a few pennies to the warden and have a look at the inmates of the Bethel Asylum. A walk around the walls of the prisons would find debtors begging for money at their barred 'gate' or hole; and, if you were feeling generous, you could leave some food at the prison gate for the inmates and hope to catch a glimpse inside.

In museums, old ducking stools, scolds' bridles, instruments of torture and execution (some of them specifically manufactured and 'aged' for this lucrative trade) were put on display in separate rooms or old cells for the titillation of visitors. Typifying the mood of the country and its interest in the macabre, in 1835 Madame Tussaud set up her waxworks on the corner of Baker Street and Portman Square in London – complete with the 'Separate Room' famed from her travelling exhibition. Here were the likenesses of the executed, cast from the actual heads of those decapitated during the Terror, along with life-size figures of the notorious murderers of the day. William Thackeray, writing as Goliath Muff in *The Sights of London* proclaimed of Tussaud's:

Frances Billings and Catherine Frary, 'The Burnham Poisoners', had thousands come to see their 'double on the drop' at Norwich Castle, 10 August 1835.

> Should such indecent additions continue to be made to this exhibition the 'horrors' of the collection will surely predominate. It is painful to reflect that although there are noble and worthy characters really deserving of being immortalised in wax, these would have no chance in the scale of attention with thrice-dyed villains.

Undeterred by Thackeray's typically wry observation, the Chamber of Horrors, as it became known, expanded and developed over the years and is still visited by thousands, who happily stare into the cold glass eyes of the waxen fiends on display there.

Until public executions were abolished in 1868 they formed the highlight of many a grim calendar. The event itself was the culmination of weeks and months of preamble. In the clamour for news, there would be interviews with the people who had discovered the crime, with people who knew the victim, their friends, lovers and families. As the case progressed, from detection, apprehension of the suspect to their trial, the public sympathy or anticipation of a 'deserved' sentence would continue to grow apace as every detail of the hearings, the crime and its circumstances were reported in lurid detail in press and periodical. The culmination of such a build-up was the execution itself. Crowds of thousands filled the open ground in front of the gatehouses (where the scaffold was erected) on Norwich Castle Hill. If the crime had received notoriety like that of James Bloomfield Rush, the Stanfield Hall murderer, special trains were even laid on for parties from London. The gentry paid for gallery seating in nearby houses and shops. Mingling in the crowds were pie and drink and hot-nut vendors, while proclaiming the facts of the case in lurid detail and stentorian voice the broadsheet and long-song sellers plied their wares. Less desirable were the pickpockets, who on some days could steal watches and money far in excess of the goods the poor soul on the gallows was being executed for!

Such was the interest in public executions that a unique vocabulary evolved, some of it lost, but some still known today. Terms for a public execution include a Hanging Match, Collar Day and Scrag'em Fair. The hangman was known as Jack Ketch, Surveyor of the New Drop, Yeoman of the Halter, Topping Fellow, Doomster and The Lord of the Scaffold. To swing, to dance the clink (meaning prison) hornpipe, to be stretched, to be turned off and to die of hempen fever all meant to hang. Hanged men were known as Gallows Apples, and corpses for the surgeon. Even the pies served to the crowds were named 'Greenacres' after a particularly good and crusty batch were served at James Greenacre's execution at Newgate on 2 May 1837.

From 1869 all executions were carried out within the prison walls, with only a few observers from the prison and civic authorities and a few invited members of the press present. The public's interest did not wane, however, so newspapers and periodicals covered horrible crimes and disasters in greater detail than ever before. The grimmest of all publications, and in many ways the first of the 'gutter' press came about at this time. The *Illustrated Police News* had one of the widest circulations of any periodical from the 1870s to the 1890s. This paper was profusely illustrated with artists impressions (often horrific and heroic) of the scenes of crimes, investigating officers, witnesses, suspects and victims, sometimes claimed to be drawn 'in the mortuary,' from all over the country. By about 1910 press members were no longer admitted to the execution chamber, so the crowds outside the prison wall received the notification via black-framed and glazed notices from the Prison Surgeon,

Governor and/or Sheriff displayed on prison gates after completion of the execution.

In later years the media was not made aware of improvements (including the speed of) executions behind prison walls: public executioners like Albert Pierrepoint signed the Official Secrets Act and stuck to it! But the press carried on offering detailed accounts, describing, for example, 'how the executed man took a last slug of drink to steel himself to meet his maker' and 'the priest reading the 23rd Psalm led the procession to the execution chamber down silent corridors'. However, in the light of executioners' memoirs published after the abolition of hanging in Great Britain in 1964, it is evident that for many years execution chambers had adjoining condemned cells, and the full procedure of execution from entering the cell to the drop of the gallows trap-door took a maximum of 25 seconds. Most of the old press accounts were exposed as wide-of-the-mark fiction based on obsolete procedures.

Out of the nineteenth century came two of the greatest influences on my research and interest in the sinister, strange and curious side of history. The first, Charles Hoy Fort (1874–1932), was born in Albany, New York. Sceptical of scientific explanations, he challenged the parameters of scientific knowledge, collecting notes on anomalous phenomena from museum archives, libraries, scientific publications, newspapers and magazines from all over the world. His work amounted to tens of thousands of accounts and annotated cross-referenced notes on topics as diverse as sea monsters, showers of frogs (not rain), spontaneous human combustion, wild people, phantom black dogs, ghosts and stigmata, to name but a few. Fort marshalled his evidence and set forth his philosophy in *The Book of the Damned* in 1919, *New Lands* (1923), *Lo!* (1931) and *Wild Talents* (1932). Today, no self-respecting book of mysteries and anomalous phenomena excludes the work of Charles Hoy Fort. His research into strange phenomena, curiosities, prodigies and portents continues today in the magazine *Fortean Times*.

The second and no less influential figure in matters grim and anomalous is Mr Charles Mackie. A veteran reporter, one of his proudest claims was that (in 1935) he remained the only living journalist who had witnessed a beheading at an execution in Great Britain. The incident to which he alludes was the infamous execution of Robert Goodale at Norwich in 1885, when, despite the experience of hangman Berry, Goodale's head was wrenched from his body at the moment of 'the drop', when the rope should have simply dislocated the vertebrae in his neck. For Norfolk historians, Mackie's greatest achievement was his two-volume reference work *Norfolk Annals*. Long out of print, even today this book is still an indispensable point of reference for local historians. This monumental record of Norfolk in the nineteenth century lists all the significant events of each year in chronological order – theatrical performances, notable lives and significant public occasions, including entries for significant crimes, executions, riots, disasters, hoaxes, unusual funerals and anomalous human behaviour. Many of the 'finds' of these two figures have lead directly to the stories included in this book.

In my research over the years I have often made a note of strange or grim events in the margins of my current work, or hastily scribbled a reference on to a piece of scrap paper. Many of such references have ended up in an old cardboard file marked 'Miscellany'. Bulging at the sides and expanded in the writing of this book into a storage box, inspired by and in the true spirit of Fort and Mackie, this 'Grim Almanac' is the product of many thousands of hours of research by generations of non-fiction writers, journalists, historians, academics and amateurs. Combined with privileged access to coroners' reports, inquest accounts, assize records and police archives I have plumbed the depths of many of the dustiest and most sinister records of the past, scratched the surface of history and squeezed out some of the pus below. In an unashamed investigation into the not-so-good old days, join me on a journey down the darker paths of Norfolk's past, from burning heretics and hanging witches to rebellion, riots and untimely ends up to the last executions in the county – a grim event or theme can be found on every day of this almanac – enter . . . if you dare!

'Spy flap' at
Walsingham
Bridewell.

Neil Storey
North Walsham, 2003

January

A broadsheet for the Denver Common murderers, 1837. *(Norfolk Local Studies Library)*

JANUARY **1783** In January 'an incorrigible youth' by the name of Joseph Beeton was brought before Lynn Quarter Sessions charged with the capital crime of highway robbery. In a trial that lasted six hours it was revealed that

on one Saturday night in October 1782 Beeton concealed himself in a clump of thorn bushes beyond the Long Bridge which crossed the River Nar. When the elderly 'postboy' who had left King's Lynn to connect with the Wisbech coach drove by in his cart Beeton dropped on the coach and stole the mail bags containing cash and exchange bills worth in excess of £1,000 that it was carrying. A high reward was offered for capture of the highwayman. Traced through an informant, Beeton was arrested and incarcerated in Lynn Gaol. Not wishing to resign himself to defeat he escaped and fled to an inn at Castle Acre but the landlord grew suspicious and an armed guard was sent to arrest and bring Beeton back to Lynn in irons.

Being young and attractive, and with this being his first offence he drew considerable local sympathy. The law was the law, however, and young Joseph Beeton was found guilty. A crowd estimated to have numbered about 5,000 gathered near the South Gate to watch his execution, preceded by prayers offered by two clergymen and hymns rendered by the choir of St Margaret's. Rather than wait to be

Richard Beeton, the highwayman in his cell at King's Lynn.

'turned off' by the hangman, Beeton threw himself off the cart when the noose was placed around his neck, breaking it instantly. His body was covered in pitch and gibbeted near the scene of his crime as a warning to others.

1 JANUARY **1814** A remarkable funeral took place at Shelfanger. The body of Mr Smith, a farmer, was conveyed from Fersfield in a wagon drawn by his own team. The coffin was covered by a wagon tilt and sacks of straw served as seats for his children and grandchildren. Behind the wagon walked his riding horse as chief mourner, and the singers of the congregation chanted a funeral dirge. 'He was a person who in habits, manners and opinions exhibited a singularity that was not easily paralleled.'

1649 Following disturbances in Norwich between 22 and 24 April 1648, in objection to mayoral appointments of 'persons in the place of Aldermen' and 'countenancing malignant and sequestered Ministers publicly to preach in the city,' 108 people are prosecuted for riot and mutiny. Petitions of objection were raised, causing about a thousand to riot; the crowd stormed the Sheriff's house and got arms. Following casualties a troop of horses was brought in to restore order, but not before the committee house was blown up and about forty people were slain. Most of those prosecuted were fined, but those adjudged 'ringleaders' at their trial on 25 December (Christmas Day had been abolished) were executed in the castle ditches on this day, namely Christopher Hill, brazier (later judged as executed wrongly!); Anthony Wilsonne, blacksmith; William True, dyer; brothers Thomas and John Bidwell, labourers; Henry Goward, saddler; and Jonas Gray, oatmeal-maker. To complete this hideous spectacle, an old woman of the hospital named Tyrrell and Mary Oliver were burnt nearby for witchcraft.

2 JANUARY

1935 Reported in the *Eastern Daily Press* this day, the inquest of William Neville Carpenter (held in an inquest room noted for its Christmas decorations!) revealed that he was discovered shot in the belly and the small amount from his cash box removed. Mr Carpenter had recently taken in an orphaned lad of 18 named William Waller. Following an ugly exchange between the two of them Mr Carpenter was shot and the money stolen. After a drink binge Waller regretted his action to the extent that he decided to end it all. He was found decapitated the following morning on the railway line at Great Hautbois, his head about 10 ft from his body.

3 JANUARY

1902 A truly tragic event occurred on this day on Happisburgh beach. Young John Davis, aged 11, was playing with his 5-year-old brother on the beach they knew so well. They had spent their short lives growing up in the village: their father Edward was a local man and chief boatman of the coastguard. Both boys had been digging and the elder lad had been attempting to make a tunnel between their holes when the sand collapsed and buried him. After initial rescue attempts failed his little brother ran to a field where he found Ambrose Mason, a farm labourer, who ran to try and help. The lad was trapped: even the strong labourer could not pull him out on his own. All hope was lost – and all that remained was for the inquest to return 'accidental death', and extend sympathy to the grieving parents.

4 JANUARY

1831 Of 205 prisoners, 108 were indicted at Norfolk Quarter Sessions for machine breaking in riots at during November and December 1830. Sixty-seven rioters were found guilty and 41 were acquitted or otherwise discharged. Of those found guilty one was sentenced to 14 years' transportation while the others got 15 months or less. Fifty were charged with rioting. Of these 18 were discharged, 9 acquitted and 23 convicted. One fellow received two and a half years' imprisonment, the rest two years or less.

5 JANUARY

6 JANUARY   **1896**   *The reported capture and arraignment of infamous Norfolk poachers.*
A number of Lord Hastings gamekeepers on his estate at Melton Constable came 'into violent and disabling collision' with notorious poachers Walter Wylie and Charlie 'Shirts' Rudd. Wylie was seized during the fight but Rudd made good his escape. Rudd was not going to get clean away, the local police were determined of that! Inspector Willimott of Holt police, with seven of his men, assisted by Superintendent Grimes and three officers from the Aylsham district, formed a 'task force' to track him down. The trouble was that Rudd 'had no lack of friends amongst the labouring classes, who not mindful of a past share in his spoils, and perhaps a lively sense of future favours, are only too eager to embrace the chance if not of offering their rude hero asylum, at least of conspiring to throw his pursuers off the scent'. After a week of pursuit the police team narrowed their search and, paired with some of Lord Hastings' keepers, surrounded Edgefield. Inspector Willimott heard, possibly in response to a widely placarded offer of £10 reward to anyone who would divulge the whereabouts of Rudd, that the hunted man would probably be found near Thurning Barn plantation. While interviewing Rudd's mother at her home in Crymer's Beck, a hamlet near Briston, a 3-pint jug with hot tea inside was spotted by a small barrow shed in her back garden. Hardly had this been discovered when Rudd bolted. All the pursuers were soon joining the hue and cry of the chase. Rudd was run to ground on Briston Common while running towards Thurning Mill. Standing trial and punished for their crimes, Wylie got three and Rudd seven years' penal servitude. Their popularity did not diminish and they received much local sympathy. This was explained at the conclusion of the report: 'A successful night's poaching means drinks all round and a mug of beer is still a powerful factor in the life of an agricultural labourer.'

7 JANUARY   **1814**   A curious incident occurred at the funeral at Blickling of Benjamin Edwards, coachman for 20 years to Lord Suffield. The corpse was conveyed from the house to the church for interment, followed by 30 servants in their liveries. After the Revd Mr Churchill had retired from the grave an old acquaintance came forward and performed a promise which he had made before everyone present. He took a bottle of rum from his pocket and threw it on the head of the coffin. The bottle broke and the rum splashed on the lid of the coffin, and the dead man's old friend exclaimed: 'God bless him. I have performed my promise as I am sure he would have done had I gone first.'

8 JANUARY   **1907**   A report was made in the *Eastern Daily Press* of the trial of Jane Watts of Stokesby under the leader 'Woman's Alleged Artifice'. She was charged with gilding and colouring two sixpences with the intent to resemble half sovereigns.

9 JANUARY   **1785**   On or about this date was born John Green. An incomer to King's Lynn from his post as 'boots' at the Greyhound Inn, Newmarket, he moved to Lynn to carry on his trade at the Duke's Head Inn. Having 'ruined himself upon

cocks and horses' he became a common 'shoe blacker' to the town. Money did not roll in and the notorious squanderer soon got into difficulties. Green decided to extricate himself from this mess by selling his wife. Placing a halter around her neck he took her to the market-place. Failing to get a bid for her in cash he swapped her for a gallon of beer. Even then he had to 'stand treat' with half the gallon, so that in fact he sold her for the grand sum of one shilling. 'It is but justice to the unhappy creature to state that she was sold no more, but continued with the man who bought her till she died.'

John Green, the 'Old Scallywag' of Lynn.

1910   Henry Briggs, an Attleborough labourer, appeared before the bench at East Harling accused of stealing two fowls (Black Orpingtons), value 14s, from Charles Warren of Morley St Peter. George Duffield, an Attleborough shoemaker, testified that while on his way home he saw a fellow acting furtively near the farm with a couple of dead chickens. Police Sergeant Parsley was called and he recovered one of the fowls' heads, which was positively identified by the farmer. A fair idea of the culprit was ascertained and Sergeant Parsley tracked Briggs to his shed, where he was found with blood on his clothes. His boots were taken and compared with the prints left at the scene of the crime, and matched in every respect. Still vainly defending his corner, Briggs argued that he had been drunk on the night in question and could not remember his actions; he explained the blood as coming from an earlier nose bleed. Finding him guilty, the Bench 'took a lenient view of the case' and Henry Briggs was sentenced to 21 days' imprisonment with hard labour.

10 JANUARY

1805   A murderous poaching affray occurred in Thorpe Woods, near Aylsham, when several game watchers, in the service of Lord Suffield, were severely wounded. At the Norfolk Assizes at Thetford the following March six of the poachers, indicted under the Black Act, were found guilty and sentenced to death. Lord Suffield and the Hon. Edward Harbord pleaded that their lives be spared, and the sentence was commuted to transportation. When the gang was being conveyed by the *Expedition* night mail coach from Norwich to a prison ship at Portsmouth the convicts got free of the chain, and made a desperate attempt to escape – but they were too heavily ironed. They attacked the coachman, and one

11 JANUARY

of the guards presented a pistol which misfired; then Johnson, the gaoler, rushed among them with a cutlass and subdued them. One prisoner escaped, but the others were lodged in the Surrey New Gaol the following morning.

12 JANUARY **1616** Mary Smith was burnt for witchcraft in the Tuesday Market Place, King's Lynn. She was the subject of the rare tract *A Treatise of Witchcraft* by Alexander Roberts BD 'and Preacher of Gods Word at Kings-Linne'. Mary, wife of Henry Smith, who was a glover in the town, occupied herself making and selling cheese but, apparently jealous of the proficiency, quality and success of others in the trade, she was alleged to have set about cursing them through her pact with the Devil. Her wrath knew no bounds when John Orkton, a sailor, struck her son following a misdemeanour. She cursed him that 'his fingers might rotte off', and within nine months Orkton's fingers were so infected that they had to be amputated. Following similar misfortunes visited upon other people that she cursed, her black cat was declared a 'familiar' and she was tried as a witch, and found guilty. Such was her repentance when in gaol while she awaited her fate that when the day came for her execution the crowds sung psalms rather than jeering her to the stake. It is even said that the heart carved above one of the windows in the market-place marks the spot where, when the flames were at their highest, her own heart flew out from her body and smashed onto the wall – a sign, some said, of true repentance and purity, while others declared it a final curse against the magistrate who put her there.

Another poor soul burning at the stake.

A CORRECT ACCOUNT OF THE
Trial, Execution, Life, Character & Behaviour,

Of the unfortunate Man who suffered on the Castle Hill, at Norwich, on Saturday the 9th of April, 1831, with an interesting detail of the manner in which the unhappy Culprit have conducted himself, from the time of his Condemnation, with the affecting separation betwixt Knockolds and his family which will long be remembered as the most heart-rending scene ever witnessed within the walls of a Prison!

The greatest degree of interest amongst all classes of people both in City and County was excited on the trial of R I C H A R D K N O C K O L D S, Thirty-four years of age, who was indicted for maliciously setting fire to the premises of Mr. Ducker, Swanton Abbot, and destroying property to a great amount!—The trial of the prisoner lasted for an unusual length of time, and the Court was crowded to excess.—The crime being of a nature the most diabolical! and the frequent occurrence of which have lately rendered it one of the most terrible and alarming subjects of anxiety that ever occurred in a civilized Country!—The evidence against the prisoner was the most clear and satisfactory ever produced in a court of Justice, and not the least shadow of doubt remained with the Jury of his guilt, and after a most impressive charge from the Judge they brought in a verdict of Guilty! a man named Davison having been admitted as evidence for the Crown.—The prisoner on hearing the awful sentence of death! shewed the greatest dispondence, it being evident from the defence made by Knockolds, and his being cleared the day before from the first indictment he was charged with, that he expected he should be able to evade the ends of Justice in this case also,—but providence had willed it otherwise, and the awful retribution of Justice, put a stop to the existence of a man, who delighted in destroying the blessed fruits of the earth, and causing terror! and dismay! wherever his footsteps led him!—It is difficult to conceive the motives which could induce such a man a Knockolds, an inhabitant of this City, and a weaver, to leave his home his wife and five children, and travel miles into the Country, merely for the pleasure of setting fire to Barns, Stacks, &c. for it does not appear that he always expected to be paid even for his trouble! indeed the character, and conduct of this man, seems altogether inconsistent for that he did not want sense was evident both from the defence he delivered on his Trial, and the account of those who have had opportunities to converse with him, and yet that he should peril his life for that, with which he could have no concern whatever seems to be only the actions of a madman!—For an Agricultural Labourer suffering under the depression of wages in the Country, may though mistaken, imagine he has an interest in destroying machinery, firing Barns, Hay Stacks, &c. but, how a Norwich weaver can suppose himself called upon to leave his loom for such a purpose is most astonishing instance of the folly and inconsistence the spirit of anarchy will lead a man into! It was singular that on the trial of Knockolds on his first indictment, on which he was cleared that his expecting family and friends had so firmly anticipated his acquittal, that preparations were actually made by them for a frolic on the occasion of his return home! what a sad disappointment to his unhappy family! when instead of receiving him in their arms rejoicing at his safety, the result of his next days

trial should bereave them of him for ever!—For it seems with all his crimes the attachment of this man's wife and family of little ones to the unhappy father, and husband, was great in the extreme. And the meeting that took place betwixt them in the Prison was of such an affecting description, that the heart must be hard indeed that could have witnessed it without tears—how heart-rending! to behold five blooming children, taken their last long farewell of a beloved father who 'though a criminal in the eye of the law! their innocent hearts knew only as their father! who though they now beheld him a condemned felon! was dear to them, if unpitied by all the world beside! what were the feelings of the poor disconsolate mother and her unhappy children on entering the cell of her husband! how did they shudder, at the clank of the chains that fettered their poor Father's limbs! what tears of anguish! trickled down the cheeks of his innocent offspring, come to take a last look at his pale and emaciated features, worn down with Grief and remorse for the crimes that have torn him from these dear pledges of his Love!—And when in speechless agony he gave them each a parting kiss! what would he have given to be again restored to their fond Embrace to the Bosom of his Family and Friends! And when the youngest of his Children clung tondly round his Neck, and would not be removed, no Eye could behold the Affliction of the Father in that moment without pity for his fate! however great his crime! who could see a man in the very prime of life torn from the bleeding hearts of his innocent Children! and compelled to leave them to the Scoffs and ill usage of an unfeeling world! and whose memory when dead and Cold! his children for their own credit must learn to forget!—who could at such a scene as this refuse a tear, to the heart struck Criminal, and his sorrowing Family, a weeping Mother! left to struggle though the world with her helpless Offspring! their only Protector! Friend! and Parent! And when at last they took their sad farewell, how did their lingering looks cast back one glance upon the poor dejected Criminal, whose ratling Chains struck like a Death bell Cold upon their hearts! and warned them of their Father's numbered hours, and that they never never more should see the face of him, their lost beloved Father !!!

The interest excited by the fate of this unhappy Man induced such a vast number of Spectators to assemble at the place of Execution, that the avenues to the Castle Ditches were thronged to an excess, and when the unfortunate Man ascended the Platform the Multitude stood with awe struck Silence to witness his last Moments! and when the fatal Bolt was Drawn that Launched him into eternity! a universal Shudder amongst so many who knew the unhappy sufferer, accompanied his Prayers for mercy on his Soul from the Blood of his Redeemer !!

WALKER, PRINTER, ST. LAWRENCE, NORWICH.

Norwich broadsheet for the execution of Richard Nockolds, who confessed to throwing acid in the face of John Wright. (*Norfolk Local Studies Library*)

1830 Vitriol (Sulphuric Acid) was thrown in the face of John Wright, one of the principal master manufacturers of Norwich, on St Faiths Lane. Dreadfully injured Mr Wright discharged his pistol at his assailant but he escaped. The trouble had begun two days before when weavers had rioted in protest at the relief committee of the Court of Guardians' erection of two looms in the workhouse. The riots continued unabated the next day and were only

13 JANUARY

put down when the 7th Dragoon Guards were summoned from the cavalry barracks. Richard Nockolds, who was executed for arson on 9 April 1831, confessed to the outrage perpetrated on Mr Wright.

14 JANUARY   **1837** John Smith (aged 25), John Varnham (aged 23) and George Timms (aged 22), chief suspects in the 'Denver Fortune Teller Murder', were arrested by Constable Wright of the King's Lynn police, who had pursued them to Doncaster. This horrible crime had been perpetrated against Hannah Mansfield, aged about 50 years and 'a woman of eccentric habits', on the night of 2–3 January at her home, her neighbours finding her with her throat cut on the morning of the 3rd. The motive appeared to be theft: an amount of plate and about £20 had been stolen. The three accused were described as bankers and had been seen in the area before and after the crime. After arrest they were committed to Swaffham Gaol to await trial at the next Assizes. On 6 April 1837 they were tried before Justice Coltman. Commencing at 10.30 a.m., the trial concluded at 15 minutes past midnight the next day, when the jury returned a verdict of guilty and the prisoners were sentenced to death. The sentence on Varnham was commuted after an ample confession by the other prisoners. On the 29th large numbers arrived in the city to watch the execution of Smith and Timms, now 'notorious' murderers on Castle Hill. The proceedings began at the doors of the castle at noon, headed by a number of javelin men of the High Sheriff's posse. Smith, who was in the last stage of rapid decline, was assisted to the scaffold. 'After the bolt was drawn and the bodies swung round, a piercing cry rose from the dense mass of people of both sexes. After hanging the usual space of time the bodies were taken down and carried into the interior of the gaol, when all the prisoners were brought forward to view them in the place where they lay.'

15 JANUARY   **1896** A tramp's tale was reported in the *Eastern Daily Press*'s 'In the Police Courts' column. Maria Deekin, a 'woman on the tramp', was charged with being drunk and incapable. PC Amis stated that he saw the prisoner lying upon the pavement in Baker Street, Gorleston. She was 'helplessly drunk', but with the assistance of another man he managed to get her to the police station. The tramp then explained in all seriousness that she had been struck by lightning, and whenever she took a little drink it got hold of her: 'I have only had two glasses and tha's one too many.' She was found to have money, and when she said she was travelling to Ipswich where she was born magistrates adjourned the case, to give her a chance to go to Ipswich by train.

16 JANUARY   **1906** This was the first day of the 'Heigham Murder Trial', a case that in its day caught the imagination and emotions of many in the county. Mrs Rosa Kowen (aged 33) of Railway Street, Heigham, was charged with murdering her husband James between the hours of 10.45 p.m. on 28 and 12.45 a.m. on 29 December 1905. The preceding 12 months had seen the couple quarrelling with increased frequency. On the night of the murder neighbours were roused by cries of 'fire' from the Kowen house. The fire brigade and police were summoned, and

Horrid MURDER

o'

HANNAH MANSFIELD,
THE DENVER

FORTUNE

TELLER

By Three Bankers, John Smith, John Vernam, & George Timms.

On Tuesday, January 3rd, 1837, a most diabolical murder took place at Denver, near Downham, Norfolk, which has excited a sensation of horror in all ranks. Hannah Mansfield a female about 50 years of age, residing on Denver common, of rather eccentric habits, left the house of a friend, in the village, about 10 o'clock on the evening of Monday, and in going to her home called in at the adjoining cottage and stayed a short time, and then retired to her own dwelling, On the morning of Tuesday, the 3rd, her neighbours saw nothing of her, but payed no attention to that circumstance, as she sometimes lay in bed rather late; but about half-past 10 o'clock a female who came to deliver a parcel called, and, receiving no answer, went into the neighbour's house, to ask if the deceased was not up; they replied that they did not know, and their daughter went to see, and immediately called out that there was some blood upon the threshold; upon which they attempted to open the door, and to their horror found the poor woman lying upon the floor in a pool of blood, with her throat cut, having been dead, apparently, some hours. Her body was lying across the doorway, so that the door could not be completely opened without touching it. Some of her clothes were lying on the table, and her pockets also, but rifled of every thing, and a considerable quantity of plate was also taken from the cupboard, together with the money she had about her, supposed to be nearly £20. In consequence of the absence of the coroner, a jury could not be summoned until next morning, when after examining several witnesses, they adjourned until next day. It is rather extraordinary that the neighbour heard a sort of "rumbling" noise, as he thinks, about two o'clock in the morning, and supposing it was some stock got into the small adjourning yard, he arose and opened the window; but finding that not to be the case, and hearing no more he retired to rest. The poor victim was in her night dress only, and had evidently come down stairs on hearing the noise, and appears to have struggled violently.

Three bankers were seen near the unfortunate woman's house, on the evening preceding the murder, and the following morning, so early as three o'clock, were also met close to the spot. These men however, at first eluded detection, and having traversed the country taking the direction of Stamford, reached Doncaster on Thursday evening last, and took up their quarters at a notorious house, called the Bird-in-hand, St. Sepulchre Gate, in that town. The Sessions for the West Riding were going on at the time, any they had the effrontery to attend the Court, in the Town-hall, nearly the whole of Friday. The following morning the Express coach arrived and with it Mr. T. V. Wright, one of the principal officers of the town of Lynn, who lost no time in procuring the assist-rnce of Mr. Tymms, chief officer, and Wheater, of the day police, who, conjointly traced the navigators, and found them as above described at the Bird-in-hand. Five pounds of beef-steaks were cooking for them at eleven o'clock in the morning, and one of them was playing a match at "puff and dart," The three officers alluded to, with firmness and promptitude, grappled and handcuffed their powerful prisoners in a few seconds, who were led, trembling, to the gaol. On searching their persons, a bar of silver was found upon one, evidently melted from spoons, and on the others three sovereigns and some silver. They were strongly ironed, hands and feet, and conveyed on Sunday, at one o'clock, by the Express coach, from the Rein Deer, to Newark, and from thence to Lynn. They gave their names, John Smith, 25, John Vernam, 25, and George Timms, 22. On mounting the coach, Vernam pulled of his hat and huzzaed, which struck terror into the minds of hundreds o spectators who witnessed their depart-ure. The greatest credit is due, to Mr Wright for his exertions during the past fortnight who has traced sufficiently not only the persons of the prisoners, but their undoubted guilt. They were all dressed in new blue smock frocks and new velveteen jackets, with large pearl buttons; and he has discovered that their old ones were burnt on the road. The men were committed to Swaffham Gaol, on Wednesday, the 18th, for trial at the next Assizes.

WM. UPCROFT, PRINTER & BOOK-BINDER, MAGDALEN STREET, ST. CLEMENT'S, NORWICH

A broadsheet for the Denver Common murderers, 1837. (*Norfolk Local Studies Library*)

Mrs Kowen was rescued by neighbours. Searching for Mr Kowen, a neighbour fought through the flames to find his body between two fires – one in the grate, one on the floor: he had obviously been bludgeoned about the head and murdered. A bloodstained hammer was on the mantlepiece in the room and a bloody hatchet was found in the coalhouse. Traces of paraffin and rags to aid the spread of the fire were found in the house.

After Mrs Kowen was arrested and charged with her husband's wilful murder she is recorded as saying 'I did not plan to murder him, nor yet to hurt him in any way', and she pleaded not guilty. The case against Mrs Kowen, before advanced forensics, was based 'purely on circumstantial evidence' – she said she didn't do it and there was no way of proving that she did. It transpired at the trial that Mr Kowan had beaten his wife and children with fists and cane, and Mrs Kowan received much popular sympathy. She twice stood trial at the Assizes, but neither jury could agree on a verdict and she was returned to prison to await a third trial. There was massive popular support for her release: her journey from prison to and from court was met by well-wishers, many of them ladies, who threw flowers along the route and kept vigils at the gates of the prison. A warrant for her release arrived with the prison governor on Friday 6 July. Leaving the prison by carriage she was whisked to Thorpe station and the first train to London's Liverpool Street station, and a blissful return to obscurity.

The scorched and bloodstained 'Relics of The Heigham Murder House' attracted lively bidding when they were auctioned on behalf of the landlord at the Corn Hall on Thursday 19 July.

17 JANUARY **1899** An evening inquest was held at Yarmouth Workhouse into the death of Mrs Hunn (aged 39) of 8 Tyrolean Square, Cobholm, who was found in the river 'under distressing circumstances'. There were eleven children in the family, as well as four of her sisters, a brother, and her father and mother who were all laid up at the same time with fever. Her daughter Ethel testified that the Revd Mr Clissold had just left her mother and asked Ethel to put out the light. Her sister Florrie went into her mother's room the following morning and found her gone. Her little brother Stanley (aged 5) said he saw his mother get up and go to Mrs Chipperfield's next door, after kissing her two other children, Albert and Sydney. Mrs Chipperfield said that Mrs Hunn had come round at 1.00 a.m. to ask her to put some vinegar on her head, as she thought she could get some sleep. She was known to worry a great deal: she couldn't get anyone to look after the children, and because of all the illness in the house very little money was coming in. Dr Youatt was called to the inquest. He had been treating the children, and following a bout of pneumonia Mrs Hunn was diagnosed as suffering from typhoid fever. Asked why she had not been removed to the isolation hospital Dr Youatt replied: 'There is no room for typhoid patients, but there will be a new block opened shortly.' The jury found that the deceased had committed the act in 'an unsound state of mind', and the coroner concluded by saying this was one of the saddest cases he had ever investigated in the borough.

1828 With scares of bodysnatching spreading across the country, watch-houses were built in larger cemeteries, while in more rural areas good money was to be made by offering to keep a vigil over a grave for a night or two, until the body was useless to the resurrectionists. The success of one of these vigil parties was recorded during the pitch-black night of 18 January when a bodysnatcher was shot at Bacton while disinterring the body of James Howlett. Although badly wounded, the snatching scoundrel effected his escape into the darkness.

18 JANUARY

1915 This evening the first German Zeppelin air raid on a civilian target was carried out on Norfolk. Making landfall over Bacton at about 8.30 p.m. the two airships divided, one (L4) heading over North Norfolk and the other (L3) towards Great Yarmouth. The first bomb was dropped without exploding or injury on Whitehall Yard, Wymondham Street, Sheringham. The first casualties, Samuel Smith, a shoemaker, and an elderly lady, Mrs Martha Taylor, were incurred in the St Peter's Plain/Drakes Buildings area of Great Yarmouth; other casualties were caused as the Zeppelin dropped bombs over the town towards the fish wharf. One soldier took shrapnel in his chest. He survived, and the largest piece removed by the local doctor was

19 JANUARY

Pages from *The War Illustrated*, January 1915.

The Coming of the Aerial "Baby-killers"

Futile Zeppelin Savagery on Norfolk Coast

mounted and worn as a tie pin by the physician for years to come. On its coastal journey Zeppelin L4 dropped a number of bombs at Heacham and Snettisham, where it blew out the church windows. At King's Lynn it wreaked havoc in the Bentinck Street area. A 15-year-old lad named Percy Goate was killed and also, tragically, was Mrs Maude Gazely, a widow who had only just lost her husband at Mons. The Germans were described in the British press as aerial baby killers, while German newspapers reported a successful raid on the industrial areas of the Humber region!

20 JANUARY   **1816**   James Clabburn, for many years keeper of the Close Gaol in Norwich, died in the city aged 83.

21 JANUARY   **1860**   Accounts were recorded of the people of Southtown, Great Yarmouth, being alarmed by a report of a 'Spring Heel'd Jack' in the locality for some days. The supposed fiend, who assaulted one of the employees on the East Suffolk Railway, and left him insensible on the ground, was said to be a man clad in white tight-skin dress, with goat's horns fixed to his head.

Spring Heel'd Jack up to his old tricks.

Norfolk beliefs and omens that warn of the approach of the Angel of Death 22 JANUARY

A fire found burning in the grate in the morning, is a sign of a death in the family.

If a clock strikes the wrong hour, it betokens sickness or misfortune to the household.

An open grave on Sunday is said to be the sign of another burial shortly.

If the passing bell gives a double note, it foretells another funeral.

23 JANUARY **1820** Thomas Smith, a shoemaker who died at Ludham, was carried to his grave by six men of his own trade, each with a leather apron tied around him, and stirrups with hand leathers attached slung across their shoulders.

24 JANUARY **1819** Madame Tussaud's collection of 'composition figures representing 90 public characters' was exhibited at the Angel Inn, Norwich. Before choosing a permanent base on the corner of Baker Street and Portman Square in London Madame Tussaud toured the country: in 1819 it was East Anglia's turn. Handbills advertised the characters on display, while 'interesting figures and objects in consequence of the peculiarity of their appearance are placed in an adjoining room and form a separate exhibition': for this, admission was an additional 6d.

The 'separate room' contained displays of the heads that Madame Tussaud (left) and her mentor, Dr Philippe Curtius, cast from the actual bloody guillotined heads of famous aristocrats who had been executed during the Terror. Combined with likenesses of notorious British criminals and items such as hangmen's ropes, model guillotines and engines of torture, this was the original Chamber of Horrors.

25 JANUARY **1776** Adverts appeared in local papers as follows: 'Wanted, a person qualified to act as General Constable to the Hundreds of Loddon and Clavering, particularly for the purpose of apprehending the putative Fathers of Bastard Children, and all fathers belonging to said hundreds, running away and leaving their wives and children chargable to same. All persons willing to undertake the above office, are desired to apply at Heckingham House of Industry any Monday morning between the hours of ten and twelve.'

26 JANUARY **Old Punishments: The Crank**
With the rise of the 'silent' and 'separate' systems in British prisons more devices to occupy the solitary prisoner were developed. The most notorious of these morale breaking devices was introduced about 1840 and could best be described as a minature treadwheel known as 'the Crank.' Operated by a single convict as opposed to a team it comprised a drum on a metal pillar or a handle set into a wall, a dial on the machine registered the number of times the crank handle had been turned – usually about 20 times a minute, culminating in a total of 10,000 revolutions in eight and a half hours. If the set target was not reached on time the convict was given no food until the dial registered the required total. If the prisoner was refractory the screw could be tightened to make the handle harder to turn (hence the warder's nickname of 'the screw' common to prison parlence today).

27 JANUARY **1821** Adverts placed in newspapers and bills posted around the city of Norwich advertising a £100 reward for witnesses to come forward for an assault and theft in Chapelfield Gardens. It was alleged that Mr John Thurtell

The crank.

had been knocked down by three men and robbed of his pocket book, which had contained £1,508 in notes. With no witnesses coming forward a free pardon and the reward was opened to any of those involved with the crime who would inform on accomplices. Tempting though the offers were, nobody volunteered. As a postscript to the case, in the following week it was announced a commission of bankruptcy was issued against John Thurtell and John Giddens, bombazine manufacturers, dealers and chapmen. Soon afterwards Thurtell absconded.

1860 *Yarmouth Hard Man.* With a sheet of convictions Yarmouth shoemaker **28 JANUARY** Albert Jay with his hard, scarred face and broken nose was constantly in and out of Norfolk gaols for almost 30 years between 1860 and 1887. A notorious rogue among the Rows, Jay was convicted of no less than 25 crimes on 25 occasions, his crimes ranged from wilful damage (1 count),

Photograph of Albert Jay and part of a page of his criminal record. *(Norfolk Constabulary Archives)*

assault (6 counts), threatening language (2 counts) and drunk and disorderly (7 counts). Theft was to be his nemesis, on the third appearance of Jay in court on similar charges, in this case of 'stealing from the person,' the judge took direct action to remove Jay from society and hammered down a sentence of 10 years' penal servitude.

29 JANUARY **Norfolk beliefs and omens that warn of the approach of the Angel of Death**

A limp corpse foretells another death in the family before the end of the year.

Two unburied corpses in certain villages at sundown on a Sunday are looked upon as foretelling a third death before the week is out.

It is considered unlucky for anyone, other than the proper officials, to toll the death bell. The stranger is said to ring his own death bell.

If you overturn a loaf of bread in the oven, you will have a death in the house.

A light left burning by accident in a room or cupboard by itself foretells a death in the family.

30 JANUARY **1903** At the previous day's police court at Norwich Private Stephen Hastings of the Cavalry Barracks was charged with using obscene language on Riverside Road on 25 January. When Police Sergeant Rayner said the prisoner was with other soldiers and shouting. Someone told Hastings a policemen was near and he made use of 'a disgusting expression'. An officer from the

MUNICIPAL CORPORATIONS' ACT.

THE BOROUGH OF

KING'S LYNN,

IN THE

County of Norfolk.

I, the undersigned George Hogge Esq. Mayor of the said Borough, do hereby give public Notice, that the Watch Committee, acting under the provisions of the recent Municipal Corporations' Act of Parliament, (6 William the 4th, c. 76.) in relation to this Borough, have appointed the several Constables for the same Borough, and have determined that such Constables shall begin to act on Monday next, the 25th day of January instant.

GEORGE HOGGE,
Mayor.

Dated 20th January, 1836.

The following is a list of the Constables appointed, viz.

Daniel Rolin, *Mayor's Beadle.*

James Dewson
Thurlow Groom
Thomas Valentine Wright } *Day Police.*
James Melton

William Andrews, *Superintendant of the Night Police.*
William Catchpole, *Keeper of the Police Office*
James Blanchflower
Robert Daplin
Samuel Richard Johnson } *Night Police.*
John Cooke Seaman
Dennis Bowles
Benjamin Lacy.

AIKIN, PRINTER, LYNN,

(Norfolk Constabulary Archives)

barracks said the prisoner was only a recruit. The chairman said that a man wearing his uniform ought to know better. He was fined 10s and 4s 6d costs.

31 JANUARY 1826 A large number of weavers rioted in Norwich, destroying a carrier's cart which was conveying materials for manufacturing purposes into the country. On 1 February the mob stopped all country carts and seized any manufacturing materials found on them. They broke the windows at a number of local factories and became so aggressive that the Scots Greys were called out from the Cavalry Barracks to quell the disturbance. Rioting resumed on 13 February. Many citizens were sworn in as special constables to put down the disturbance, and after the Riot Act was read the cavalry cleared the streets.

31 JANUARY 1781 One of the most notable surviving headstones in Norfolk, this memorial marks the last resting-place of David Bartleman, master of the brig *Alexander & Margaret* of North Shields, and tells how he came to be buried in St Nicholas's churchyard, Great Yarmouth. 'Who on the 31st January 1781 on the Norfolk Coast, with only three 3 pounders and 10 Men and Boys, nobly defended himself against a cutter carrying eighteen 4 pounders and upwards of a Hundred Men commanded by the notorious English Pirate Fall, and fairly beat him off. Two hours after the enemy came down upon him again. When totally disabled his Mate Daniel MacAuley, expiring with loss of blood, and himself dangerously wounded, he was obliged to strike and ransome. He brought his shattered vessel into Yarmouth with  more than Honours of a Conqueror and died here in consequence of his wounds on the 14th February following in the 25th Year of his Age. To commemorate the Gallantry of his Son, the Bravery of his faithfull Mate and at the same time Mark the Infamy of a Savage Pirate His afflicted father Alexander Bartleman has ordered this Stone to be erected over his Honourable Grave . . .'

FEBRUARY

A Yarmouth 'Row', *c.* 1905. Nostalgia gives 'the
Rows' a certain quaint charm but this cramped and
unsanitary environment meant hard times and
vulnerability to endemic diseases for the families living
in them. Fights and arguments were frequent here, and
disorderly houses and squalor was well known.
Row 6, off Northgate Street became so notorious for the
nocturnal activities of some of its inhabitants it became
known as 'Bodysnatchers' Row'.

1 FEBRUARY **1906** William Hammond of Row 17 was summoned for keeping a disorderly house and his housekeeper Hannah Barber for assisting him. Detective Inspector Moore stated he had kept Hammond's house under observation for some time and found it 'used by well-known women'; he commented 'Hammond did no work for a livelihood.' The Inspector had visited the house at midnight and found 'proofs of the use to which the premises were put'. Along with Hammond's 12-year-old daughter, young girls of 17 or 18 resorted to the house. The men found in the house admitted making payments to Barber, and Hammond did not deny this when informed of it. Detective Parker mentioned occasions on which he had seen men and women visit the house: 'one of the latter was a married woman'. The Chief Constable said Hammond was fined for a similar offence in September 1900; he did not pay and went to gaol for two months. Magistrates committed Hammond to hard labour for three months and Barber to one.

2 FEBRUARY **1929** The five-minute murder trial of Joseph Reginald Victor Clarke was held on this day at Liverpool Assizes. Born at Hilgay, he was adopted by a Mrs Clarke when he was three weeks old and was raised in her home on Keppel Street, King's Lynn. After travelling in America he returned and set up a wireless business in Lynn until he finally left the town in 1926, believing he could earn a better living as a hypnotist. His scheme also had a darker side. He thought he could hypnotise sensitive, attractive ladies into relationships to keep himself free from financial worries. As incredible as this scheme may sound, it had already duped a number of girls in Lynn who were 'fascinated by his mystic qualities'. When in Liverpool, Clarke chanced to meet a Miss Mary Fontaine and, improving on this casual acquaintance, took lodgings with her mother. In his confession Clarke claimed he just snapped when Mrs Fontaine was enquiring why he had not made good: 'I suddenly put my hands on her throat good and hard for about a minute, and she stopped breathing.' Running into Mary's room he put his hands around her throat and attempted to kill her too, but she put up a fight, screamed and shouted for help. Taken into custody, he made a full confession, was found guilty and sound of mind and was sentenced to death.

3 FEBRUARY **1823** Clearing up and planning for reconstruction commenced at the City of Norwich public house on St Stephens after a floor collapsed in an adjoining function room during a 'Ranters' religious meeting the preceding evening. About 120 people had crammed into the small room, and after the floor gave way 25 injured were removed to the Norfolk and Norwich Hospital, four with fractures. One man had his leg amputated.

4 FEBRUARY **1840** On or about this date was buried John Browne, master of the Yarmouth Bridge public house and for several years turnkey of Norwich Gaol. He was a big fellow: his coffin measured 3 ft across, 6 ft long and 1 ft 9in in height.

1842 Richard Cricknell, the Norwich pugilist, died on this date. A well-respected and accomplished fighter, he had not been well since he had fought in a bout with Cain on 7 January 1840. An injury to his head had deprived him of his reason, and he had spent his declining months in the Bethel Lunatic Asylum.

Artist's impression of the Bethel Asylum, c. 1725. (*Simon Pegg*)

1776 John Howard, the prison reformer, paid his first visit to Great Yarmouth Gaol, where he found six debtors and fourteen felons incarcerated. He recorded the jail as consisting of 'gaoler's house, in which are four rooms for master's-side debtors'; for the rest of the prisoners 'only a small day-room and court; two or three lodging–rooms for such as pay for them: three dungeons or night-rooms down a ladder of 10 steps'. Each prisoner was allowed a penny loaf of 13oz a day and four chaldrons of coal a year, supplemented by the corporation begging basket which was sent round the town three times a week.

1828 Bodysnatching scares were such at King's Lynn that on this date an un-named individual was consigned to his grave with 13 iron loops around his coffin and the lid firmly closed with 50 screws.

1927 Reported today was the sad tale of a very unlucky man. A well-known character in the Brandon area was one-armed Charles Grass, who had lost his limb 19 years before in a tragic accident at George Wood's saw mills. He was last seen going to draw water from his garden well by a Mr A. Rolph, a tree

Engraving of
Yarmouth Gaol or
Tolhouse, c. 1810.
(Johnson Collection)

feller. Mr Rolph's concerns were aroused when he could not recall noticing the return of the elderly Mr Grass to his house. Walking round to investigate, Rolph lifted the lid on the garden well. To his horror he was greeted by a pair of booted feet standing out of the water.

9 February **1805** A woman who had eloped from her home in Kent with a horse dealer was found by her husband in a house in St Peter Mancroft, Norwich, and refused to return with him. The horse dealer offered to buy the woman for £5, and her husband agreed. He went to the market-place, placed a halter around her neck and publicly surrendered all right and title to her for the sum named.

10 February **1886** John Thurston (aged 30), a labourer from Hingham, was executed at Norwich Castle by public executioner James Berry. Thurston had been drinking with fellow labourer Henry Springall on the evening of 5 December 1885. Seeing Springall had changed a sovereign, Thurston determined to relieve him of a few shillings. Following Springall home, Thurston attacked him on Ringers Lane, smashing his skull with a big flint stone. Easily traced, he was arrested and appeared before Mr Justice Hawkins at the Assizes, where he was found guilty and sentenced to death for this 'very cruel murder'.

1885   Arthur Orton (right), 'the Tichborne Claimant' (released from 11 FEBRUARY
Pentonville on 20 October 1884) appeared at Sanger's Circus, Norwich,
and addressed the audience on his life and adventures. A central
character in what was for many years Britain's longest trial,
Orton was a Wapping-born butcher who turned the scales
at 27 stone. In response to the worldwide advertisements
placed by Lady Tichborne seeking her son, Orton hoped to
prove that *he* was really Sir Roger Tichborne, the beloved
lost son. When last seen Sir Roger had been a skinny young
man of 9 stone with a Stonyhurst-educated accent and
the bearing of an ex-Guards officer. Orton had none of
these attributes, but the grief-stricken Lady T. was taken
in. A case was raised against the imposter, Lady T. died
before the trial, and Orton's case totally crumbled when
Lord Bellow, a Stonyhurst schoolfellow of Sir Roger,
recalled the missing man had a tattoo on his left forearm.
In total the case took over 1,025 days, but it took the jury just
30 minutes to find him guilty of perjury and he was sentenced to 14 years
with hard labour. After leaving prison he joined the circus. . . .

1803   Nearly 100 pairs of shoes, the property of 20 different people who had   12 FEBRUARY
been fined for making them, contrary to Act of Parliament, were symbolically
burnt in Norwich Market Place.

1750   The last full day Charles Holditch was on this earth. The following   13 FEBRUARY
day he was to be executed for the attempted murder of his father, a crime
only prevented by a child in the room screaming. Awaiting his fate in his   Charles Holditch in
cell in King's Lynn Gaol, where he celebrated his twenty-first birthday on   his cell at Tales of
3 February, filled with remorse he composed this rhyme and sent it to his   the Old Gaol House,
priest: King's Lynn.

> I, Charles Holditch, vile and base
> Did my own father rob
> But justice had me overtook
> And I die for that job.
>
> Both vile and base O Lord I've been
> Have much offended thee
> But now I do confess my sins
> O, Lord now pardon me.

In the cart at the South Gate of Lynn, where he was
executed, he was asked if he had anything to say. 'I desire
all young people to take warning by me,' he replied. Then
he dropped his handkerchief as a signal, the cart pulled
away, he sprang forward and the rope did the rest.

14 FEBRUARY   **1903** *The Lovers' Tryst.*

Reported on this day the inquest held at the Waterman public house, King Street, into the horrible tragedy enacted in the garden of Mr Read of Rivington on Newmarket Road, Norwich. The bodies of Ellen Baxter and James Everitt Cook, which at the time of the inquest lay in the public mortuary almost opposite the pub, presented a shocking sight when inspected by the jury. The girl's wound was in the back of the neck, near the skull, and the man had three wounds, one under the chin, one on the chin and one through the eye. Ellen had been in service at Mr Read's house for six years; her suitor, Cook, had served in South Africa, where he had been badly wounded. As a consequence their planned marriage had been called off by Ellen, but she said she would always receive him as a friend. Cook kept on calling on Ellen by surprise and no suspicions were aroused by his visit on the Wednesday when they went out with a cheery 'Farewell'. At 10.10 p.m. fellow servant Ethel Payne was in the kitchen when she heard the report of a firearm, quickly followed by a second. About a minute afterwards she heard two more shots in quick succession. William Mack Fisher and a companion were passing Rivington at about the same time and went to investigate the shots. Discovering the bodies about 15 ft from the entrance gates he biked back to the city and summoned Police Sergeant Varley who found the army revolver at the scene. He was soon joined by the Chief Constable and Dr Mills, who arranged for the bodies to be removed to mortuary by police ambulance. At the inquest, wilful murder of Ellen by Cook was declared, and for Cook a verdict of suicide while in a state of unsound mind.

15 FEBRUARY   **1821** By the careless driving of the coachman the 'Morning Star', the Yarmouth coach, was overturned at Scole Inn. Of the three inside and nine outside passengers one, Mr Butterfield of Leeds, was seriously injured and died on April 14th. At the Norfolk Assizes in March 1822 an action was brought by Butterfield's employers against the owners of the coach for the recovery of damages sustained by them by the loss of their servant. The jury found for the plaintiffs, awarding damages of £100, £258 expenses and costs of 40s.

1823 *Bodysnatchers.* Owing to the frequency with which a number of trunks, measuring 28 in long, 13 in wide, and 12 in deep, had been sent from the Rampant Horse Inn, Norwich, by the *Telegraph* coach to London, suspicion was aroused at the coach office. Direction was given that the porter bringing the next be detained and the parcel examined. This was done on 15 February, when it was found the package contained the naked dead body of an old man. The Revd George Carter, vicar of Lakenham, identified the body as that of a man named Brundall, whom he had buried a few days previously. Brundall's grave was examined and it was found that only the coffin and shroud remained. From the information given by the porter two men named Collins and Crowe were apprehended and committed for trial at the Quarter Sessions. On 15 July they were tried, found guilty, and sentenced to three months' imprisonment and a fine of £50.

A little something for
the surgeon.

1888 The recapture of the first escapee from the new Norfolk Prison on
Plumstead Road, Norwich. Two men had got out on 11 February. One was
Robert Annison who was serving 12 months for 'fowl stealing'; he was
captured on this day by Constable Clipperton at Martham. Six days later the
leader of the escape bid, the notorious Norfolk rogue Robert Large, who was
serving three months with hard labour for poaching, was re-taken after a
struggle at his father's house in Lenwade. As Large was a bit of a folk hero,
when news got out of his arrest a crowd gathered to shout abuse at the
arresting officers, a scene repeated at Norwich City Station, where threats
were made to turn over the cab in which Large was to be transported back to
prison.

16 FEBRUARY

NORWICH CITY POLICE.

Photo and description of

ROBERT LARGE,

alias "Seymour," an ex-convict and notorious poacher, wanted on warrant in this City, charged with assault on Police on 13th August, 1904.

Aged 37 years, height 6 feet 1 inch, swarthy complexion, dark brown hair, brown moustache, brown eyes, proportionate build, stoops slightly, long, swinging gait; a native of Gt. Witchingham, Norfolk. Marks :—scar middle forehead, left side neck, scar front left thumb, palm of hand, back little finger, top joint left little finger contracted, scar inside and 2 outside front right wrist, scar right of back and front left shin, mole left shoulder.

Dressed usually in light brown coat and vest, cord trousers, cap, and heavy lace boots.

May be found associating with poachers and thieves, or at low Public-houses.

Please cause every possible enquiry to be made for this man, and if found, arrest and wire me, when an officer shall be sent for him, or any information obtained kindly communicate to

E. F. WINCH,
Chief Constable.

The Guildhall, Norwich,
24th August, 1904.

(Norfolk Constabulary Archives)

17 FEBRUARY

1811 John Thompson, lamp lighter of Norwich, died aged 62 – 'his lamp of life being out, and all his oil consumed'. He was buried as per his request at St Martin at Palace at night, all this brethren of the ladder and torch attending in the funeral procession with their flambeaux, to light him to his long home – in the presence of thousands assembled on the Plain.

1832 *Getting into a pickle.* Thomas Foyson (aged 53) ran a small family vinegar works in Calvert Street, Norwich. On this day in 1832, overcome by fumes from the vat of vinegar he was gauging, he fell in and was drowned before he could be rescued. Thomas Foyson left a widow and nine children. In a typically caustic swipe of the time the newspaper concluded the report: 'it is some consolation to add that his life was insured for a large sum.'

1839 *Stand and deliver!* Mr Hotson, a solicitor from Long Stratton, was robbed of a purse of money by highwaymen at Harford Bridges.

1840 Announced on this day the death of popular local character Richard Pattle of Rudham in his 108th year. Such was the affection of the local people of all classes towards Mr Pattle that even a print of him was published, to acknowledge a great local personality and celebrate the great age he attained.

1889 With a past record for sending threatening letters, Joseph Betts was well known to the Norwich police. On this night he confronted PC 45 James Southgate in Northumberland Street. After mumbling something about false charges by the police Betts drew and fired a revolver, which caught PC Southgate on the inside of his arm. Seeing Betts preparing to fire again Southgate withdrew at speed, returning with PCs Clarke and Holland, but found Betts barricading himself in his house and threatening to shoot anyone who came near him. At noon the next day, having obtained a warrant, Inspector Guiett came to arrest Betts. Not being able to gain entry the Inspector got a ladder, but when his foot was on the first rung Betts appeared at his window and shot Inspector Guiett. He was the second lucky escape: the bullet struck the peak of the inspector's cap and tore the flesh of his forehead, but caused no life threatening injury. Further shots rung out as other entrances were attempted to break the siege, until entrance was negotiated by a detective and a press man under the personal supervision of the Chief Constable. Betts was sentenced to 15 years' penal servitude, and was later removed to Broadmoor Criminal Lunatic Asylum.

1898 At about 7.00 a.m. an attractive but mischievous young lady named Theresa Ann 'Maude' Bensley, who was well known to the Great Yarmouth police for minor offences, was bickering in the early hours with her industrious but insanely jealous partner Samuel Frederick Steel (a carter on the M&GN Railway) at their home in Angel Hotel Row. As the quarrel turned into a furious row Steel lost his temper, seized a razor and came for his mistress in a frenzy. He delivered such cuts across the throat that it was found to be severed to the spinal column: even the vertebrae were found to be gouged to the depth of one eighth of an inch. Flinging up the bedroom window, Steel then threw the woman's body on to the stone paved yard below. Possessed by ungovernable rage, he then ran downstairs and into the yard, and with an engineer's wrench beat her head to a pulp. He then retreated to the winding staircase of his house where he attempted to take his own life with the same razor as had been used to kill Theresa. Children larking nearby discovered the body and raised the alarm. Constables came running. Breaking into the house the they discovered a hellish scene, with blood splashed everywhere. Steel had not succeeded in taking his life but was bleeding profusely and had to be overpowered. Taken to hospital, he recovered from his wounds and eventually stood trial. Found guilty but insane, he was ordered to be held 'in strict custody for the rest of his life'.

The Norwich to London coach. (*Johnson Collection*)

23 FEBRUARY   **1843**   The coach from London to Norwich, driven by Thomas Wiggins, ran into a brewer's dray at Tasburgh during a thick fog and was overturned. Mr Scott of Newton Maid's Head, one of the outside passengers, was jammed between a coach and a tree, which had to be cut down to extricate him. Wiggins was thrown head first off the box seat and severely injured, and Mr Thomas, the guard, was dashed against a tree stump and killed outright, 'his head being completely split open'. It was not until almost a year later on 22 January 1844 that Wiggins returned to the road. So highly was this 'excellent whip' esteemed at each inn where the coach stopped that the landlords had prepared a gala day in his honour.

24 FEBRUARY   **1821**   Following local instances of bodysnatching and in response to the resulting fears of families being deprived of a deceased loved one by resurrectionists, Mr J.M. Murray of Davey Place, Norwich, was proud to advertise himself in local newspapers as 'sole agent for the sale of Bridgman's patent iron coffins as security to the deceased persons'.

1835 Posters were going up across the county and handbills were being pressed on to coaches declaring that Charles Moore of Banham, known commonly as 'Brundell Mure', had escaped from Edmund Bailey, the Constable of Kenninghall, while on his way to Norwich Castle after being charged with highway robbery. Moore was described as 'a strong athletic man about 21 years of age (but has the appearance of being older), stands near six feet high, dark full eyes, bristly dark hair, with a sullen and forbidden aspect, and has little or no whiskers, rather stoop in his walk, has long legs and particular long feet (about 14 inches), had on a drab Fustian Frocks, two Waistcoats, Cord Fustian Trousers split across the knee and an old hat, right and left shoe half highlows, with two rows of nails on each side the soles, and clate off the shoe on the right foot, he had a red and yellow handkerchief loose round his neck with a check lilac-coloured Handkerchief beneath, and had locked on his left wrist a pair of Police Hand-Cuffs.'

25 February

1830 At 3.00 a.m. John and William Brooks, awaiting trial in Norwich Castle Gaol for highway robbery at Middleton, attempted escape. They were confined in Bigod's Tower, from the summit of which William endeavoured to lower himself by means of his blanket and rug. The improvised rope gave way and Brooks fell a distance of 70ft. His thighs, pelvis, left arm and all the ribs on his left side were broken, and a large tumour subsequently formed at the back of his head. Notwithstanding his terrible injuries Brooks recovered, and at the Summer Assizes was borne on the back of a warder to his trial. Despite Brooks being permanently crippled, Mr Justice Parke sentenced him to transportation for life.

26 February

1830 The story of Private Flood of the 7th Dragoon Guards was reported. Tried by court martial for sleeping at his post at Norwich, he was sentenced to receive 300 lashes. The man was, however, in luck. 'His Majesty was graciously pleased, in consideration of the long imprisonment he had undergone, to remit the infliction of the punishment.'

27 February

Old Punishments: The Brank or Scold's Bridle

28 February

One of the perceived scourges of medieval and early modern British life was the scold, nagging wife or village gossipmonger, so the judiciary, with its usual robust approach to such social problems, devised the brank or scold's bridle (left). There were several different designs but the basic construction consisted of a lockable iron framework in the form of a helmet shaped cage that fitted tightly over the head. An aperture was provided for the mouth with a small, flat metal plate protruding into the unfortunate woman's mouth when worn, to hold her tongue down or prevent speech. Such devices were known to have been in use across the country until the late eighteenth century.

29 FEBRUARY   **Strange Beliefs**

In the month when the first cuckoo could have been heard here are some grim Norfolk beliefs associated with the bird.

If the cuckoo alights in front of you, rises and then alights again, it is a sign of sickness or misfortune.

To hear the cuckoo's first note in bed forebodes illness or death to the hearer or one of their family.

If a cuckoo alights on touchwood, or on a rotten bough and makes a noise, it betokens a death.

Canōrus, the Cuckoo.
(Robert Wright)

MARCH

Norwich Castle, March 7th, 1829.

At a Meeting of the Visiting Justices, the following Additional Rules relating to the offices of Turnkey, Taskmaster, &c. were agreed upon; and as it is considered that the good order and discipline of the Prison depends in a very great degree on the strictest attention being paid to them, such attention will be required from all persons whom they may concern, under pain of forfeiting their places for any neglect.

TURNKEYS.

1.

THE Turnkeys must at all times be upon the watch, and take the utmost care to prevent any communication whatever between the Prisoners of the different classes.

2.

Accordingly in passing from one part of the prison to another, they must never leave any door or gate unlocked behind them, even though they may have to come back immediately.

3.

They must conduct every class separately to and from Chapel, and the Mill-yard, and they must not quit them for a moment during the whole of their progress from any one part of the prison to another; nor may they leave any class in the Chapel, unless the Schoolmaster be there to receive and see to them; nor in the Mill-yard, unless the Taskmaster be there.

4.

They are particularly required to see that no prisoner be employed in cleaning any part of the prison, or in any other kind of work, beyond his own ward.

5.

They must be careful also, whenever any new prisoners are brought to the gaol, to put them into separate cells, and to prevent any kind of communication between them and all other prisoners, until they shall have been examined by the Chaplain, Surgeon, and Gaoler, and appointed to some particular class.

6.

They must deliver every morning a list of such prisoners in their respective departments as may have been absent from Chapel, with the reasons of their absence.

7.

Every Turnkey will be held responsible for whatever is done in his own division.

TASKMASTER.

1.

The first object of the Taskmaster must be to take care that the different classes of prisoners be kept distinct from each other, both on the wheel and in their progress to and from labour; and accordingly that the classes be brought to the Mill and discharged from it, separately, and at sufficient intervals of time and distance from each other to prevent the possibility of any communication between them; and that no class at any time be suffered to come or depart without a Turnkey to attend them.

2.

He must be careful to preserve the utmost order and silence among the prisoners, whenever they are at work or assembled in the Mill-yard for that purpose; and therefore to suffer no prisoner at labour to speak to any other prisoner without punishing the offence, by depriving the offender of his next turn of rest, and as occasion may require, reporting him to the Gaoler or the Visiting Justices.

3.

He will accordingly observe that, with a view to the above rules, his own presence in the Mill-yard at all times is absolutely necessary, and that he must not, on any account whatever, leave the Yard for a single moment, while any of the prisoners are there or in the Mill-house, without first calling a Turnkey to supply his place, and see to the preservation of good order during his absence; and even so, he must not leave the Yard except in cases of absolute necessity.

4.

He will be required to attend the Gaol, not only while the prisoners are at work, but two hours further every night after they shall have done work; and also on every other Sunday.

5.

He will further be required to attend the Barber on shaving days, from two to three o'clock, and to see that no communication takes place between him, or any of his assistants, and any of the prisoners. If at any time the labour of the Mill be suspended, he will be required to be with the Barber during the whole time of his remaining in the prison.

SCHOOLMASTER.

1.

The Schoolmaster will be careful, whenever he is attending on his duty in the Mill-house, to instruct only one prisoner at the same time, and on no account to suffer any other to speak. He will be accountable also for the silence of all the rest on that wheel to which he is attending.

2.

He will be required to attend the Barber on shaving days, from one to two o'clock, except when the mill-work is at a stand, when he will be relieved by the Taskmaster.

PORTER

The Porter will be required to attend Chapel once in every Sunday.

MILLER.

The Miller will be required to give his attendance in the Gaol two hours every evening after the prisoners shall have ceased to work, and also every other Sunday, alternately with the Taskmaster.

GENERAL RULE.

No servant of the prison will be permitted, under any pretence, to receive any fee or gratuity whatever from any person who may come to visit any prisoner or to see any part of the prison.

MATCHETT, STEVENSON, AND MATCHETT, PRINTERS, NORWICH.

Rules and regulations sets out for Norwich Castle Prison, 7 March 1829.

1 MARCH **1836** *New police on duty for the first time in Norwich.* Following the Municipal Corporations Act of 1835 the wheels were put in motion for the creation of organised and regulated forces to police the streets of major towns and cities across the country. The Norwich Watch Committee headed by the mayor was soon created, and their intention of a police force for Norwich resolved. On duty for the first time on this day, the force was commanded by Superintendent Wright and consisted of 18 constables supplemented by 32 Night watchmen or 'Charlies' to maintain order across the city.

Norwich Police.

RULES, REGULATIONS,

AND

INSTRUCTIONS,

Prepared by Order of

THE WATCH COMMITTEE.

Norwich:
BACON, KINNEBROOK, AND BACON, MERCURY OFFICE.
1840.

POLICE CONSTABLE.

Every Police Constable must make it his study to recommend himself to notice by a diligent discharge of his duties and strict obedience to orders.

He is at all times to appear neat in his person and correctly dressed in the established uniform; his demeanour must always be respectful towards his officers and the public.

He must readily and punctually obey the orders and instructions of the Superintendent and Sergeants. If such orders appear to him either unlawful or improper, he may complain to the committee, who will pay due attention to him; but any refusal to perform the commands of his superiors, or negligence in doing so, will not be suffered.

When going on duty he is to assemble with the others of his division at the appointed place, if not before, precisely at the prescribed hour, and after inspection and receiving orders he is to proceed immediately to his beat, and will be held responsible during the time he is on duty for the preservation of life and property, and general good order.

It is important that he should make himself perfectly acquainted with all the parts of his beat.

He is not to call the hour, and if at any time he require assistance, and cannot in any other way obtain it he must spring his rattle; but this is to be done as seldom as possible. He must report to his Sergeant every occasion of using his rattle.

When he takes any one into custody, he will immediately repair to the Station House with his prisoner, and speedily return to his beat; when he takes property from any one he should not suffer it to be out of his sight until he has marked it, and delivered it to the Officer on duty.

He is not to quit his beat during his tour of duty (unless under the circumstances already mentioned, or others which may make it necessary), nor enter any house except in the execution of his duty. He shall pay particular attention to all public-houses, beer, and liquor-shops in his beat, and report all such as are not closed at the proper time, or kept in good order.

(Norfolk Constabulary Archives)

The constables were paid 15s a week with 1s stoppage for clothing, despite having to provide their own trousers. The new police were issued with a dark blue swallow-tailed coat, leather top hat, greatcoat, cape, belt, lanthorn, truncheon, alarm rattle (whistles were not issued until 1860) and a pair of handcuffs.

The first crime statistics from 25 December 1837 to 25th December 1838 show that the police dealt with 69 felonies, 56 assaults, 113 disorderly persons and 5 cases of uttering false coins.

An early
Norwich police
constable.
*(Norfolk
Constabulary
Archives)*

2 MARCH **1642** On this day during the English Civil War William Gostlin, Mayor of Norwich, was carried prisoner to Cambridge, where he was confined for three months for refusing to confirm the orders of parliament.

3 MARCH **1821** Going prepared! On or about this date died at Reepham Moor Mr St John Hunt, who was buried at his desire in his best suit of clothes, greatcoat and hat, complete with his well-stuffed tobacco box, short pipe and walking stick beside his coffin.

4 MARCH **1902** *Just to be sure or how did he do that?*
The inquest on the body of George Large (aged 55) was held before the coroner, Mr B.H. Veres, at the Ship Inn, Narborough. A well-known local labourer, he had been found on the previous Monday hanging in an outhouse with his throat cut. Quite how he achieved this feat is not recorded. All the jury returned was a verdict of suicide while of unsound mind.

5 MARCH **1890** Norfolk Assizes heard the case of Elijah Snelling who murdered his mother-in-law at Pulham St Mary Magdalene on 7 January. Found guilty and sentenced to death, his punishment was soon commuted to penal servitude for life.

6 MARCH **1877** Benjamin Daniels, claimed as the last of the East Anglian giants, died on this day aged 54. He stood over 6 ft 6 in tall and weighed 24 stone.

7 MARCH **1898** Harry Dix, a young lad aged 11 of Marlborough Road, Norwich, was summoned for stealing two coquilles, value 2d, and 6d in money. Dix was also summoned for stealing an overcoat, value 10s, on 22 February, another overcoat on the 24th and a third overcoat on 2 March. The lad had already been before the bench a few days before and an order was applied for to send him to industrial school, but the application was adjourned for a month. Adelaide Dix, his mother, now stated that both she and her husband were unable to control the boy. After being before the bench previously he had truanted from school, took a coat from the school and pawned it, 'and that wasn't the first time he had done it'. Witnesses confirmed that all attempts to get Dix to mend his thieving ways had failed. Magistrates ordered the lad to be sent to the training ship *Formidable* until he was 16 years of age.

8 MARCH **1950** James Frank Rivett, a Beccles bricklayer's labourer, was executed by hanging at Norwich Prison for the murder of 17-year-old Beccles schoolgirl Christine Cuddon.

9 MARCH **1904** Before the Norwich magistrates at the Guildhall, Alfred Smith (aged 57), a fisherman of no fixed abode, was charged with refusing to perform his allotted task while a casual pauper inmate of the Norwich Workhouse. William Styles, porter at the workhouse, said the prisoner had been admitted into the casual ward the previous Saturday. When asked to perform the task of breaking stones he refused point blank to do so. The prisoner then complained to the labour master of one of his arms. The Medical Officer saw him but could find nothing wrong with the arm. Smith offered to pick oakum but refused, again, to break stones, saying he had never broken stones in his life. He was given a chance to enjoy this task and others by the bench, as they sentenced him to seven days *with* hard labour.

Norfolk beliefs and omens that warn of the approach of the Angel of Death

10 MARCH

If the cock crows before sunset and dawn, it is a sign of a death in the family.

A failure in ash-keys portends a death in the royal family.

Bats flying in front of the house betokens sickness or death to one of the inmates.

A dog howling under the window of a sick room denotes death or prolonged sickness.

A winding sheet on the candle forebodes a death.

11 MARCH

1789 A handbill was published by a Great Yarmouth printer about Martha Stanniot, 'commonly called Queen Martha, an extraordinary madwoman', who fancied herself Queen of England. She resided in Row 28 and died there in 1788. When at church she would remain quiet, until the prayer for the King, when she shrieked out 'No George!' She sometimes walked to Norwich to call on the bishop. She even walked to London and obtained an interview with Lord North, when he was Prime Minister. With great quickness and pleasantry he sent her home quite happy with the assurance 'that the next cart full of money which should come in to town was intended for her'. She was supported by an allowance from the town, which she treated as a benevolence from her subjects.

Old Punishments: Branding

12 MARCH

Branding, a term from the Teutonic word *brinnan*, 'to burn', was used first by the Anglo-Saxons and until the nineteenth century. The punishment was carried out by the application of a red-hot branding iron to the hand or

Branding irons.

face; the letter you were branded with depending on your crime. The choice of letters provides a veritable ABC of crimes, and gives a good idea of the types of criminal acts which attracted this horrible punishment: 'V' for vagabond, 'T' for thief, 'C' for coin-clipper, 'B' for Blasphemer, 'SS' (one s either side of the nose) for those who sowed sedition, 'M' for malefactors, 'FA' for false accuser. In 1726 prisoners who could demonstrate their ability to 'read like a clerk' were not treated as common criminals but had the right to be cold ironed. On payment of a small sum the branding iron was plunged into cold water before being pressed against the skin.

13 MARCH 1945 LAC Arthur Heys (aged 37), of Colne, Lancashire, was executed at Norwich Prison for the murder of WAAF Winifred Mary Evans (aged 27) of Harlesden, Middlesex, at Ellough, Suffolk. She had been 'outraged, suffocated and found in a ditch'. In a case where the forensic evidence was examined by the famous Dr Keith Simpson, the most damning evidence came from the accused himself. He went to great trouble to smuggle an anonymous letter out of prison, to his CO purporting to come from another who committed the murder, but he tripped himself up with the transposition of events, and by revealing facts that only the murderer could have known. In effect he wrote his own death warrant.

14 MARCH 1900 At Reepham Petty Sessions Sidney Rudd (aged 13) of Hackford and Kirby Woods (aged 13) of Whitwell were charged with stealing about £5 from Frank Cole, the baker and confectioner of Reepham. Rudd, who had been employed by Cole as errand boy, was spotted near the Sun Barn Pit counting his ill-gotten gains with Wood. They went to Norwich and blew the lot on a watch each, a magic lantern and a selection of knives. Mr Gibbs, the Reepham ironmonger, had his suspicions aroused after a number of purchases by the boys and he spoke to Rudd's father. Inspector Shepherd, upon intelligence received, went to Hackford School where he spoke to Sidney Rudd in the presence of the schoolmaster. The young lad confessed all. The punishment for their crimes was 12 strokes of the birch each.

15 MARCH Norfolk Old Dame's Leechcraft

Up to the nineteenth century a visit to the local cunning woman or man was often the only recourse of action for country folk if bleeding persisted. Here are a few treatments for bleeding handed down the generations:

Write Veronica in ink on the ball of the left thumb.
Lay a thick black cobweb over the cut.
Insert a puff-ball into the wound (I remember my grandad using puff ball or 'bulfer' pieces to stave off shaving cuts).

Or say this rhyme over the wound.

> In the blood of Adam death was taken,
> In the blood of Christ it was all to-shaken,
> And by the same blood I do thee charge
> That you do run no longer at large.

1902   *The Bridewell Alley jewel robbery.* Following his arrest and publicised trial for an attempted break-in at a Doncaster jeweller's, John Lane alias Whale, and Aird of Clapham Junction, London, was summoned before the

16 MARCH

Norwich Bench on a Home Office Warrant on 28 January 1903. The charge against him in Norwich was for breaking into Edward Hugh Briggs, jeweller's shop on Bridewell Alley, on 16 March 1902 and stealing a haul including 34 gold watchers, 40 gold alberts, 138 fancy, paste and gold fronted brooches and 275 gold gem rings, a total haul valued at £1,000. The evidence was damning. He was clearly remembered by Mrs Whitrod of the Eastbourne Hotel on Rose Lane. Saying he was off to the Princes Street chapel, suspicions had been aroused when he was seen leaving with a light brown hand bag. The following day, when Mrs Whitrod was cleaning the sitting room, she had to move the same bag and saw a brace bit and candle within. Pawnbrokers came forward to connect Lane with the stolen goods. This case really did have Lane 'banged to rights' and he was sentenced to five years' penal servitude.

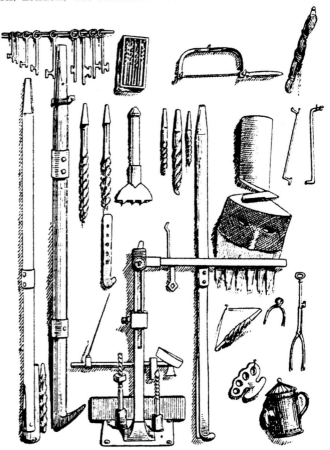

The tools of a burglars' trade.

1825   John Harper, a Norwich auctioneer, stole cloth from Jonas Driver, a roving cloth auctioneer from Leeds, while he was in the parish of North Walsham. Harper, being well known in the town, was employed by Jonas to auction his goods on his behalf. Tricking Driver into signing the goods over to a Mr Dye, because he lacked a hawker's Licence to sell in the town, Harper claimed a policeman had wised up to the scam and was going to serve

17 MARCH

a warrant on the two of them. Driver and Dye were sent to hide out in the King's Arms public house. To his distress Driver was informed by one of the pub's ostlers that large portions of his cloth had been cut off and stashed in Harper's gig. Seized, Driver was taken to the magistrates and eventually the Assizes, where the damning evidence saw him found guilty and sentenced to seven years' transportation.

18 MARCH

A sixteenth-century ducking stool.

Old Punishments: Cucking Stools and Ducking Stools

There is a good deal of confusion between these two punishments, and the two terms have blurred over the years to indicate the same punishment. Both were widely used for the punishment of minor offences, especially in relation to strumpets and scolds. The cucking stool is far older and features in the Domesday Book: its use consisted of simply publicly exposing the miscreant by placing him or her on the seat, often with a sign proclaiming the misdemeanour. There is no evidence to suggest that this original punishment was used for submerging offenders in water. The ducking stool was, however, a punishment to be dreaded. It was used on scolds and strumpets and was probably sixteenth century in origin. A chair or stool was fixed to the end of a long pole. When the culprit was fixed in the chair the pole was lifted by human or mechanical contrivance, and the chair's occupant was ducked in the water – in many cases a specially selected muddy pond or stinking pool near the village green.

19 MARCH **1817** The Revenue cutter *Ranger*, under Captain Sayers of Yarmouth, captured a large lugger with an armed crew of 36 men. In the action the *Ranger* saw casualties of three killed and seven wounded. The cargo consisted of 507 ankers and 945 halves of spirits, 27 bales of tobacco and 47 bales of Bandannas (sic), the whole worth £8,000.

20 MARCH **1899** *A parting shot.* At an occasional court held at Fakenham, Sarah Vyne of Tivetshall, a domestic servant, was brought up under remand in charge of a warder from Norwich Prison, for attempting to poison the Revd Samuel Francis Barber of West Raynham with arsenic. Vyne had been employed as the reverend's cook since the preceding September, Mrs Barber said she had given Vyne a month's notice having found her quarrelsome and an inadequate cook. After this incident the good reverend and his wife started suffering severe cramps, sickness and a burning sensation in the throat. It soon became apparent that the feelings were always more acute when they had highly seasoned soups. By process of elimination pepper was considered

to be the cause, but on investigation the pepper was found to have arsenic mixed with it! Mr Francis Sutton, Public Analyst of Norwich, said the quantity of poison was not enough to endanger the life of an adult but would make one very ill. Vyne was sent to the next Assizes.

1929 As a grim climax to his non-violent resistance on the day before he was to be ejected for non-payment of mortgage interest on his small farm at Tilney St Lawrence, Wallace Benton (right) came across Thomas Williamson, the man who was to have the reversion of tenancy, and shot him dead near the small row of stables adjacent to the farmhouse. Benton, over 70 years of age and partially blind and stone deaf, ignored almost everything said to him in court – insisting on repeatedly re-enacting the circumstances of the case, using the clerk of the Assize as his dummy victim and waving his gun within a few inches of the unfortunate official's head. The death sentence passed on him had to be bellowed by a warder through a ear trumpet, to which Benton replied 'I'm not at all sure of that. I don't see why he should.' Benton's appeal was dismissed but he was swiftly reprieved.

21 MARCH

Wallace Benton. *(Norfolk Constabulary Archives)*

County Bridewells and Gaols visited by Prison Reformer John Howard

22 MARCH

Wymundham (*sic*) Bridewell was visited by Howard in 1776, 1779 and 1782, finding five, five and nine prisoners incarcerated respectively. It was described as a day room, with three closets on one side of it, four night rooms, measuring about 6 ft by 4 ft. Howard recorded: 'A prisoner complained to me of being obliged to lie in one of these closets, with two boys who had a cutaneous disorder.' Howard went on to state: 'There is another room for women, in which at my visit in 1779, there were four dirty and sickly objects at work with picklocks on their legs, though they are never out in the court except on Sundays.' Also found here at the time was a dungeon down eight steps with the stocks in it. Prisoners, although confined to cells most of the time, were still kept in irons. Howard sternly remarked in his report: 'The justices seem to have overlooked a clause in the Act of Parliament to prevent prisoners from being kept underground, whenever they can do it conveniently, as there is abundant room on the premises.'

1841 Charlotte Yaxley, alias Middleton (aged 22) murdered Lavinia Kerrison, the 13-month-old illegitimate child of her husband, by drowning her in a duck pond at Great Yarmouth. Indicted for the murder at Norfolk Assizes on 5 April 1841 she was found guilty and sentenced to transportation for life.

23 MARCH

1838 Reports were recorded of an incident where Mary Maxey, widow of John Maxey, made very public accusations that Mr George Perowe, a vet practising in her parish of All Saints, Norwich, had removed her late husband's body. No exhumation records exist as a result of these allegations, so how she was pacified we can but wonder.

24 MARCH

25 MARCH   **1731**   George Smith was hanged in the Tuesday Market Place, King's Lynn, for the murder by strangling of Mrs Ann Wright, the landlady of the Queens Head in the High Street; 17 yards away stood the stake on which his accomplice Mary Taylor was burnt. The murder had occurred during an abortive attempt by Smith to burgle the pub; he had been let in by the maidservant Mary Taylor, and this act sealed Mary's horrible fate, as such a crime was considered petty treason: betraying the trust granted to her by her mistress, her punishment stood as a stern warning to all. On the execution day Smith was first to his death. As the rope was adjusted about his neck he is said to have kicked off his shoes and exclaimed 'My mother always told me I should die in my shoes. There! Just for a joke I'll make the old woman a liar!' As they set the fire to Mary they hanged Smith. Mary's pathetic cries were recorded as being 'dismal to spectators'.

26 MARCH   **1896**   John Fields, hansom cab driver, of St Mary's Plain was summoned before Norwich Guildhall for furiously driving a horse and cab in Exchange Street. He was estimated to have been driving at up to 12 mph. The Salvation Army, headed by its band, had just left St Andrew's Hall and was turning up Exchange Street, with hardly room for anything to pass. Field was seen to whip up his horses and drive straight at the parade. Josiah Dennington had already shouted 'Go steady man – for God's sake!' by Messrs Randalls' shop. James Taylor, a skilled horseman of Kimberley Street, was at the front of the parade and, crying at the driver to ease off, was seen to 'fly' at the horse, grabbed its head and stopped the cab, averting a terrible smash up. George Hubbard, a dealer from Lakenham, stepped in and held the bridle, only to be struck by Fields as he attempted to whip the horse. Many witnesses came forward to attest to the case, especially those who had experience of horses. These included William Clarke, a blacksmith of Unthank Road, who described the horses as 'smashing along': he had a good vantage point as he was carrying the banner at the front of the parade! Case proved, the driver was fined 10s with 25s costs.

27 MARCH   **County Bridewells and Gaols visited by Prison Reformer John Howard**
Swaffham Bridewell was visited in 1774, 1776, 1779 and 1782; on his last three visits Howard recorded five, ten, and four prisoners plus 'a lunatic'. All male prisoners appear to have been confined in one inadequate 'lodging room' of 10 ft 9 in by 7 ft 9 in. Prisoners were provided with 'a work room 17 ft by 15 ft, but no employment'. The prison courtyard had been enlarged to 28 ft square but there was no pump, and 'the prisoners are confined to their rooms'. The only apparent concession for prisoner welfare was an allowance of 20s a year for straw and a licence for beer.

28 MARCH   **1851**   George Baldry (aged 33) was found guilty at the Norfolk Assizes, before Mr Justice Earle, of murdering Caroline Warnes of Thurlton by striking her on the head with a hammer. Mitigating circumstances were pleaded and the sentence was commuted to transportation for life.

1904 The inquest into the Harleston Artillery tragedy was reported. The 29 MARCH
deceased was Frederick William White (aged 18). On his first turnout with
the local artillery volunteers he was put on the wheeler horse of a four-horse
team pulling an ammunition wagon. Sergeant Dineen gave the order to move
on. John Downing, an experienced horseman, could not get his nearside
leader to move off quickly and White's horse pushed up against him, so he lost
control of the offside horse. They then bolted and ran off down Station Road.
At the corner of the road the two pairs of horses wanted to go in different
directions; this pulled them on to the lamppost and pillar-box. White was then
pitched out of the saddle and his head struck the lamp post. Accidental death
was recorded, with the added comment: 'The jury consider it an extremely
dangerous practice to use ordinary farm horses with government regulation
bridles, which are without blinkers.'

1822 An entertainment was put on for the ensuing nights at Norwich's 30 MARCH
theatre. It was described thus: 'A serio-comic Mill-Dramatic Farcical, Moral
Burletta, called *The Tread Mill* or *Tom and Jerry at Brixton* . . . . An exact
representation of a tread mill with culprits at work made a goodly show
in the lower circle, crowded the gallery and filled the pit to the excess of
squeezing.

1904 During the preceding month legal actions had been taken against 31 MARCH
the 'passive resisters' who had objected to paying the portion of their poor
rate that applied to educational purposes. Many of the protestors were non-
conformists who with the backing of their religious leaders refused to pay.
Orders were given by magistrates, and property to the value of outstanding
monies was auctioned in front of the nearest public building or meeting point.
In front of the County Police Station on Thorpe Road the auction included
property seized from Mr R.K. Juniper, a leading member of the Norwich
Baptist community: it included his kettle and whatnot. Property was seized
at a number of locations across the county; for example, fine items of silver
were sold in front of the Fisher Institute at Gorleston, two family Bibles
were sold at Outwell, and, poignantly, among the items from the Primitive
Methodist community at Aldborough a portrait of Oliver Cromwell from
Mr H.C. Cooke, the local miller was auctioned in front of the village post office.

Parts of Norwich Castle had been used as a prison from the twelfth century, 31 MARCH
a purpose to which the whole building was devoted by the fourteenth
century. By the eighteenth century the old stone of the castle was blackened,
its battlements decayed and overgrown, with the castle ditch becoming a
stinking receptacle for rubbish. Large buildings were added to the east side
of the castle in 1793 at a cost of £15,000 to serve as a new gaol. Greater
improvements were enacted in the early nineteenth century when the old
shire house and these gaol buildings were demolished, and the site cleared
for the new County Gaol and House of Correction, completed in 1828 for
the sum of £50,000. The governor's house contained apartments for his

family and also the prison chapel and committee room. Branching from it were three radiating two-storey wings, each containing double rows of cells. There were 225 cells in these wings, and there were 36 retained in the old keep. The diagonals, crossing the radiating wings at right angles, contained a single row of cells; each had an arcade for the use of the prisoners when the weather would not permit their walking in the yard. The governor's house was octagonal: placed in the centre, it had a commanding view of all the wings and yards. A tread wheel was installed to the right of the entrance; the prisoners employed on it pumped water for use in the establishment. The prison was run on the 'separate system', in which the prisoners could not see or speak to each other. Labours for the prisoners included weaving of matting, and making sacks, clothing and shoes. In 1862 the average daily number of prisoners confined was 134, and 862 throughout the year, of whom 103 were debtors. There were about 20 officers of the Gaol including governor, surgeon, chaplain, turnkeys, matron, warders, taskmaster, engineer, schoolmaster and porter, their total salaries amounting to £1,443. Norwich Castle Gaol finally closed in August 1887 when its last prisoners were moved to the newly built Norwich Prison on Plumstead Road.

Norwich Castle Prison, *c.* 1870.

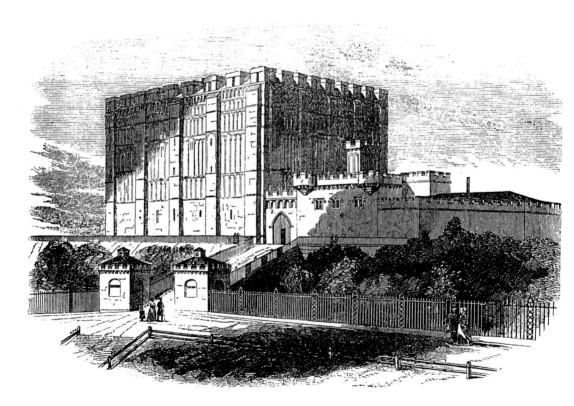

APRIL

Rules and Regulations

TO BE OBSERVED IN THE

House of Correction,

AT

LITTLE WALSINGHAM,

In the County of Norfolk.

THE KEEPER of the said House of Correction shall have power to hear all complaints touching any of the following offences, committed by Prisoners of any description: (that is to say) disobedience of any of the Rules of the Prison, assaults by one person confined in such Prison upon another, when on dangerous wound or bruise is given, profane cursing and swearing, any indecent behaviour and any irreverent behaviour at chapel, and also touching any of the following offences committed by any Prisoner under charge or conviction of any Crime: (that is to say) absence from Chapel without leave, idleness or negligence in work, or wilful mis-management of it; and the said Keeper may examine any person touching the several offences, and may determine thereupon, and may punish all such Offences by ordering any Offender to close confinement in the refractory or solitary Cells, and by keeping such Offender upon Bread and water only, for any term not exceeding three days; and in case any Criminal Prisoner shall be guilty of any repeated Offence against the Rules of the Prison, or shall be guilty of any greater Offence than the Keeper is empowered to punish, the said Keeper shall forthwith report the same to the visiting Justices, or one of them, and any such Justice, or any other Justice, shall have power to enquire upon Oath, and to determine concerning any such matter so reported to him or them, and to order the Offender to be punished by close confinement for any term not exceeding one Month, or by personal correction in the Cases of Prisoners convicted of Felony or sentenced to hard labour.

IF ANY PRISONER shall be of a Religious persuasion differing from that of the Established Church, a Minister of such persuasion, at the special request of such Prisoner, shall be allowed to visit him or her at proper and reasonable times, under such restrictions imposed by the visiting Justices, as shall guard against the introduction of improper Persons, and as shall prevent improper communications.

WARDSMEN shall be selected from such of the Prisoners as are most orderly and best qualified for the purpose. They shall sweep the Cells, Work rooms, Day-rooms, Stair-case, and Galleries of the Classes under their care once every Morning, and shall wash the Day-rooms and Stair-cases, at least once every week, and other parts of the Prison as often as shall be required. They shall in dry weather see that all the Doors and Windows of the night Cells be kept open, and the bedding frequently beat and put out to air. They shall attend to the cleanliness of every part of the Wards and Airing Yards committed to their care, and to the maintenance of decency and good order therein. And shall for the performance of these Duties receive such increased Prison allowance as the visiting Justices shall from time to time direct, and shall be entitled to such share of the earnings of their Classes as the Rules shall respectively prescribe, and they shall not be permitted to receive any fee or gratuity on any account whatever.

NO PRISONER convicted of Felony, or of misdemeanor, and sentenced to hard labour, shall receive any food, clothing, or necessaries, other than the Goal allowance, except under special circumstances to be judged of by one or more of the visiting Justices. And all convicted Prisoners shall be placed in the Wards allotted for them immediately after sentence.

THE SEVERAL persons who shall be committed to the House of Correction to be kept to hard labour, shall be employed, unless prevented by ill health, every day during their confinement, except on Sundays, Christmas day, and Good Friday, and on any days appointed by Public Authority for fasting or thanksgiving, or as many hours as the day light in the different seasons of the year will admit, not exceeding ten hours, being allowed thereout to rest half an hour at breakfast, and one hour at dinner.

THE KEEPER shall adapt the various employments which shall be directed by the Justices at the Quarter Sessions, to each person, in such manner as shall be best suited to his or her strength and ability, regard being had to age or sex.

THE RULES for Labour among Male Prisoners, shall be applied, as far as the Case allows, to Female Prisoners, who shall be employed in washing, needle-work, and other Female occupations under the direction of the Matron.

EVERY PRISONER, unless under solitary confinement by way of punishment, shall be allowed the benefit of fresh air and exercise for the space of one hour at least every day, either altogether or at different times, at the discretion of the visiting Magistrates. Those who are under solitary confinement, from the circumstances of their case, and not especially by way of punishment, such for instance, as persons under charge or conviction of unnatural Offences, shall exercise in Yards, separately, one hour in each day, at a time when such Yards are unoccupied, by other Prisoners.

WARM and sufficient Clothing shall be provided for every convicted Prisoner, consisting of a woollen cap, jacket, trowsers or breeches, linen shirt, worsted stockings, and shoes. No Prisoner before trial, or person convicted of misdemeanor, and not sentenced to hard labour shall be forced to wear a prison dress, unless his or her clothes shall be found insufficient, or improper, or necessary to be preserved for the purposes of Justice.

THE PRISON allowance shall be to each individual, two pounds of white bread per day; and on Sundays, broth made with meat and vegetables; those who undergo severe labour, and those who are committed for trial, or shall be under sentence for capital offences, may be allowed at the discretion of the visiting Justices, one half pound of white bread in addition; in cold weather the Prisoners may have the water which they drink warmed for them, if they desire it, and all those who work at the Mill may claim a handful of Oatmeal to mix with the water when they leave off work.

PROVISION shall be made for the instruction of Prisoners of both sexes in reading and writing; and this instruction, shall be afforded under such rules and regulations, and to such extent, and to such Prisoners, as to the visiting Justices may seem expedient.

GENERAL REGULATIONS.

THE CELLS shall be unlocked at six o'clock in the Morning, from the first day of April, to the thirtieth day of September, and at sun rise during the remainder of the year.

THE PRISONERS shall be locked up in their Cells at such times as the visiting Justices may deem expedient.

CONVENIENT places for washing shall be provided in each Ward for the Prisoners, who shall be allowed an adequate allowance of soap and towels and combs.

SCALES, Weights, and Measures shall be provided by the Keeper, at the expence of the County, open to the use of any Prisoner.

SUCH ALLOWANCE of fuel shall be ordered by the visiting Justices for the different Wards, as experience shall prove to be requisite.

THE HOURS of beginning and leaving Work, of Meals, and of return to labour shall be notified by the ringing of a Bell, fixed in a proper situation for the purpose.

A WARNING BELL shall be rung every Morning half an hour before the Cells are unlocked, and every Prisoner shall be required to leave his or her Cell as soon as it shall be unlocked.

NO TAP shall be kept in the Prison, nor shall spirituous Liquors of any kind be admitted for the use of any of the Prisoners therein under any pretence whatever unless by a written order of the Surgeon, specifying the quantity and for whose use. No wine, beer, cyder, or other fermented liquors, shall be admitted for the use of any Prisoners, except in such quantities and such manner, and at such times, as shall be allowed by the visiting Justices.

NO GAMING of any kind shall be permitted in any Prison, and the Keeper shall seize and destroy all dice, cards, and other instruments of gaming.

NO MONEY under the name of garnish or any other remuneration, shall be taken from any Prisoner on his or her entrance into the Prison or any other occasion on any pretence whatever.

LEGAL ADVISERS whose attendance shall be required by the Prisoners, shall have free access to such Prisoners, between the hours of unlocking the Cells in the Morning and locking them up in the Evening; but if they shall require to be admitted at other hours, they shall obtain the order of a visiting Justice.

FRIENDS of Prisoners shall be admitted by order of any Magistrate to the visiting Room, there to see such Prisoner in the presence of the Keeper, or other Officer, between the Hours of ten and twelve in the Morning, and two and four in the Afternoon; but no friends shall be permitted to see such Prisoners in private, except by the order of a visiting Justice, or in the case of untried Prisoners of the committing Magistrate. No visitor shall be admitted to see any person under confinement on a Sunday without an Order from a Magistrate.

Mid-nineteenth-century rules and regulations for Little Walsingham House of Correction.

1 APRIL **1713** *The last hanging at Wymondham.* Robert Basset and William Boughton were hanged on a gallows before a large crowd in the Market Place, for the murder of James Pointer on 8 October 1712. George Taylor, the vicar, wrote in the Abbey register of the fate of the executed men's bodies: 'the same day hung in chains on a gibbet on Norwich Common, on the west side of the highway leading to Hethersett from Wymondham . . . where their carcasses now remain in terrorem'. The Town Book records a cost of £7 10s 0d for the building of the gibbet.

2 APRIL **1784** Four men were dropped by the executioner on the scaffold at Norwich Castle Hill on this day, namely Robert Cademy for sheep stealing, John Ferrett for housebreaking, William Newland for forgery and Robert Randall for highway robbery.

3 APRIL **1779** A Saturday execution of five malefactors on Norwich Castle Hill, after sentencing at Thetford Assizes: Thomas Bell for shooting and maiming Lord Walpole's gamekeeper; Thomas Boddy, Zorobabel Partridge, Miles Bridges and John Griffin for several burglaries and highway robbery. 'They all behaved with fortitude and a becoming decency' on the scaffold. During the execution, observed by a crowd of about 20,000, it was noted that many pockets were picked, one man not only losing his watch but all his silver.

4 APRIL **1801** Executed this day at Thetford: John Allen (aged 23) and John Day (aged 26) for burglary at the house of the Revd Isaac Horsley at North Walsham; Richard Grafton for stealing a cow and three heifers; and James Chettleburgh (aged 36) for stealing six sheep at Saxlingham. It was noted that Day was the 'greater of the scoundrels', having confessed to an additional four burglaries and having deserted 13 times from different regiments.

5 APRIL **1875** William Sillis was found guilty of feloniously assaulting Miss Ann Elizabeth Blyth at Great Massingham on 12 October 1874. The sentence passed was 18 years' penal servitude and 20 lashes of the cat.

6 APRIL **1832** News spread that the first outbreak of cholera in Norfolk was discovered at Stow Bridge on the previous day.

7 APRIL **1828** The entertainer Ching Lau Lauro received what was described as 'the worst review in the history of performance in Norwich'. It was such a shame really; you couldn't fault the poor chap for effort, as apparently the culmination of his act was to 'swallow his own head'. What a trooper!

9 APRIL **1803** Henry Ford was executed at Thetford for stealing a silver watch, coat and jacket from Thomas Aylmer of Pentney.

9 APRIL **1744** In the corner of the Hare family chapel in Stow Bardolph church stands what appears to be a fine mahogany wardrobe; open the doors and

The wax effigy of Sarah Hare (before restoration).

you will get a shock, for looking back at you is the life-size wax effigy of Sarah Hare who died on 9 April 1744. For many years the local story told of how she was punished for sewing on a Sunday by contracting blood poisoning: it was even claimed that a piece of sewing was held in her hands to warn others of her tragic end. Sadly this wonderful tale is just a story. The truth is that the 'sewing' she held was in fact a short piece of silk pinned to the front of the effigy, to give the effect of a petticoat, while the truth about the figure is to be found in Sarah's will. '[After] six of the poor men in the parish of Stow or Wimbotsham may put me in the ground they have five shillings a piece for the same . . . I desire to have my face and hands made in wax with a piece of crimson satin thrown like a garment in a picture, hair upon my head and put in a case of mahogany with a glass before.' Over the years her effigy became yet more eerie as mice nibbled at the fabric and the face took on the appearance of Stilton. However, once the rarity of this figure had been realised (it is the only wax funary figure to survive outside Westminister Abbey) it was recently restored. Its red satins are now vivid again, and her eyes are bright and blue. Sarah Hare has truly been resurrected by conservators!

10 APRIL **1813** Charles Harper (aged 26) and Edward Impson (aged 21) were executed on Norwich Castle Hill, Norwich, for a burglary at the house of John Butler of Barney. 'After hanging the usual time their bodies were delivered to their afflicted relatives and by them conveyed home for interment.' On this very same day in 1830 another two were dropped on Norwich Castle Hill by executioner Calcraft for burglaries at Thorpe, namely John Simmons (aged 31) and William Lovett (aged 20). After execution their bodies were laid out in Mill Yard at the castle, and the prisoners marched past.

11 APRIL **1837** James Greenacre was found guilty on this day at the Central Criminal Court of the murder of Hannah Brown, probably with a rolling pin, in the Edgware Road, near London. Greenacre was a Norfolk man, born at North Runcton in 1785. He was a property dealer, and it transpired that he had been involved in the Cato Street Conspiracy. His victim was a Norfolk woman who had been in service of Lord Woodhouse at Kimberley Hall, Greenacre had followed her to London upon learning she was pregnant – a situation that threatened his co-habitation with his new paramour Sarah Gale. After murdering Hannah he attempted to cover his tracks by dismembering her body and distributing it about the town. He was executed on 2 May. The hot pies sold at the execution were rather macabrely named 'Greenacres' – a name which stuck for many years afterwards.

Trial, Execution, & Confession

OF

SAMUEL YARHAM

For the WILFUL MURDER of HARRIET CANDLER, of Great Yarmouth, who was executed on the Castle Hill, on Saturday April 11th, 1846.

SAMUEL YARHAM was placed at the bar at the Norwich Assizes, for the Murder of Mrs. Candler, at Yarmouth, on the 18th of November, 1844. It will be recollected, that Mrs. Candler occupied the lower part of a house at Yarmouth, the upper part being held by an attorney named Catchpole. Yarham's wife was servant to him, and Yarham himself was allowed to persue his business of a shoemaker on the premises. At the time of the murder, Yarham, and three men, named Royal, Mapes, and Hall, were apprehended, and Yarham made a confession, implicating the three men in the murder. They were tried for the offence ; each, however, succeeded in proving an alibi, and acquittal followed. So insensed were the public against Yarham, that he was obliged to quit Yarmouth. Subsequently Yarham made a confession to Mrs. Dick, (the individual who found the money that was stolen,) that he was the party who cut the old lady's threat ; he was, in consequence, apprehended in Gloucestershire, and now appeared to take his trial. In a measure the testimony was substantiated by Mrs. Dick's daughter, who swore that Yarham was the identical individual who was observed, after the stolen property was found, poking in the sand for the treasure. Mr. Dasent made a powerful address to the jury in favour of the prisoner, arguing that the fact of Mrs. Dick having withheld this important evidence so long, was sufficient to throw distrust upon her testimony. The judge having recapitulated the evidence, the jury returned a verdict of Guilty, and the prisoner was sentenced to be hanged. The wretched man, who had listened to the trial with close attention and to the auful sentence of the Learned Judge without evincing any emotion, save a slight and occasional quivering of the lips and eyes, was then removed from the dock. while the shouts of the populace on the "hill" resounded in his ears.

My hour is come, my glass is run, now by the law's decree,
On Saturday next condemn'd to die upon a fatal tree ;
All for a cruel murder as all do understand,
Which has caused great sensation and horror thro' the land.

In vain I sought to cloak my crime, and steadfastly deny'd,
That I had been her murderer, and many schemes I try'd ;
Thinking thereby to save my life, but vain was every plan,
For in the minds of all mankind I stood a guilty man.

When I review my wicked life, I shudder with dismay,
No consolation cheers me—a wretched cast-a-way ;
No ray of hope revives my soul, to look beyond the sky,
While every moment seems to say, "To-morrow you must die.

CONFESSION

On the 19th of November Yarham stated to Mrs. Dick that he was the murderer, three weeks after that he met her in the market, and said, he let them (Mapes, &c.) in at the back door, he told them that she kept her money in her bedroom. While they were there Mrs. Candler came in sooner then they expected, on hearing her come in they put out the light, and sit upon the bed, Royal went in & asked for half-an-ounce of tobacco, and as she was getting it. Hall knocked her down with a pair of pincers, they thought she was dead. Mapes then ran to the Feathers' tap. As he was going along the Market Gates he saw a person turn a light on him, who afterwards appeared to be Layton. He then ran home telling the others to bury the money and give him a signal. When he went home he cut her throat with the lard knife. Royal gave the signal and he opened the window and saw Royal going down the street, a man came up and they both went away together.

THE EXECUTION.

This morning the above unhappy malefactor paid the forfeit of his life to the offended laws of his country. No execution of late years has attracted so large an assemblage of spectators, some thousands being present. About nine o'clock he took some refreshment, and shortly afterwards the sheriff arrived at the castle, and immediately proceeded to the condemned cell. The usual melancholy preparations having been completed, Yarham was brought to the room where he was to be pinioned. He appeared quite calm & collected, and walked with a firm step. The melancholy procession then proceeded towards the scaffold, which he mounted without any assistance, and in less than a minute the drop fell, and the wretched culprit was launched into eternity.

The sacred laws of GOD and man I spurned with disdain,
Left no dishonest means untried, my purposes to gain ;
But now my crimes have found me out, the blood my hands have
Now cries aloud for vengeance on my devoted head,   (shed,

O could I for one moment a list'ning world address,
If in this world or that to come, the hope for happiness ;
The ranks of factious traitors, as from destruction run,
Flee from those hellish counsels, which thousands has undone

For had I been by timely wise, and kept the honest way,
I might have been a prosperous and happy man this day ;
But mark the sad alternative——I die by law's decree,
A wretched malefactor upon a fatal tree.

Walker and Co. Printers, Church Street, St. Miles, Norwich.

12 APRIL **1834** William Thirkettle (aged 27) was executed on Norwich Castle Hill for the attempted murder of his wife. Standing beside him for this 'treble on the trap' were William Pye (aged 31) and Gilpin Reynolds (aged 24), who paid the ultimate penalty for being found guilty of arson.

13 APRIL **1822** Noah Peak and George Fortis were executed on Norwich Castle Hill for setting fire to three haystacks on 25 February. Both men had been soldiers: Peak was at the battles of Busaco, Albuhera and Waterloo; Fortis was also present at Waterloo. The report of the execution concluded: 'It is not three years since Peak came to Norwich and conveyed home for burial the body of Edward Fisher, his fellow parishioner, who was executed on the Hill in August 1819 for stabbing William Harrison.'

14 APRIL **1898** *The Sprowston Murder.* George Watt, having been separated from his wife for a short while, attempted reconciliation by writing her a letter. He then went round to 25 Denmark Terrace to see his wife, Sophia, in person. When he arrived by the back gate she was putting her linen line out. Her little daughter, who was also in the garden, ran indoors, to which Sophia was heard to say 'I expect she is afraid of you'. He answered something to the effect that he wouldn't hurt her. As Sophia walked a little way into the garden Watt followed her. He seemed as if he wanted to be reconciled, but she replied 'I won't have anything more to do with you. I have heard your promises so often.' She walked up the garden and took up a mat she had hung out to dry, knocked the mat and hung it to dry again. He had been standing still; she then made a movement as if to pass him. When she was near he raised his hand,

Sophia and George Watt. *(Norfolk Constabulary Archives)*

which contained a revolver he had recently bought from John Henry Emms, the gunmaker of Orford Hill. Pointing the weapon at her head he shot, and Sophia fell. He shot again and again, and then when she hit the ground he beat her about the head with the weapon. Neighbour George Henry Drake cried 'Murder!' and then chased Watt up the road. Watt threatened Drake outside the Norfolk and Norwich Arms with the pistol; Drake backed off, and Watt made his escape through the pub and out of its back entrance. Soon in the hands of the police, Watt was tried at the Assizes, and eventually confessed his crime, with the resolution 'I shall die like a man.' He has the dubious distinction of being the first man executed at Norwich Prison on Plumstead Road. The execution was carried out in the Coach House by father and son team James and Thomas Billington. Watt was launched to eternity 'As the words fell from the Chaplain's lips "Good Lord deliver us"' on 12 July 1898.

1830 One of the last public flagellations in Norfolk was carried out on this day when William King was whipped in Norwich Market as a punishment for stealing a pewter pot.

15 APRIL

Whipping at the cart's tail. *(Johnson Collection)*

16 APRIL **1840** Children who are sickly are taken to a woman in St Lawrence, Norwich, for the purpose of being cut for a supposed disease called spinnage.

17 APRIL **1813** Mary Turrell, apprehended on suspicion of being the mother of a newly born child, whose dead body was found in Vipond's Pond at Harleston, committed suicide by poisoning. The coroner's jury returned a verdict of *felo de se*, and on the same evening at about seven o'clock she was buried in the high road with a stake driven through her body in the presence of a vast concourse of people.

18 APRIL **1829** Executed on Norwich Castle Hill this day, John Wood (aged 41) and Thomas Butler (aged 29) for sheep stealing and Richard Everett for horse stealing. They were obviously popular chaps with the ladies, and in the crowd of several thousand women outnumbered men two to one. Also on this day in 1835 James Clarke, aged 20, was executed on the Castle Hill for setting fire to a wheat stack at Buxton. An old man in the crowd named Wyer proclaimed he would take the young man's place for 5*s*. When this was not allowed the old man went home and hanged himself.

19 APRIL **1779** The Revd James Hackman (aged 27), Rector of Wiveton for a mere 50 days, was executed at Tyburn, London. A former soldier, he went to London in pursuit of a hopeless infatuation. He was entranced by a London staymaker's daughter named Martha Reay, who also just happened to be the mistress of the fourth Earl of Sandwich and mother of his children. Hackman tracked her to the Piazza, Covent Garden, where as she was leaving the theatre he shot her in the head in a fit of frustration and jealousy. Turning the pistol on himself he failed to commit suicide, was arrested, tried and executed 12 days later.

20 APRIL **1843** On or about this date was apprehended at Surlingham one James Fisk, a notorious housebreaker. Found sewn up in his waistband was found a copy of the Lord's Prayer written backwards, by which charm he fancied he was 'given protection against the power of human law'.

21 APRIL **1887** James Rivett (aged 71) was brought before the Norfolk Assizes for the wilful murder of of Henry Baker, an inmate of Kenninghall Workhouse who was employed as a nurse in the old men's sick ward on 12 February. Rivett was a quarrelsome man prone to bouts of sullen behaviour and paranoia. The witness stated that on the night of the murder Rivett paced his room (this was nothing new), then, appearing near the witness, wished to shake hands with him for no apparent reason. Leaving the room, the witness heard a noise and concluded it was one of the old men in the sick room tumbling out of bed. The alarm was raised by one of the poor old men in the ward and Baker was found to be on the floor, repeatedly stabbed, with one cut severing the jugular vein. Rivett was revealed, knife still in hand, when a light was put on in another room. He exclaimed: 'I have been fighting with

a man all night. Where he is I don't know. I am a murdered man. I am a murdered man.' Following a careful trial where Rivett's mental stability and culpability were considered at length, the jury found him responsible for his actions and a death sentence was passed – but this was later commuted to imprisonment.

1834 Final preparations are carried out at Norwich Castle Gaol for 54 convicts who had been sentenced to transportation at the County Assizes and Session for assorted crimes. Over the ensuing days they were taken aboard the *Sarah* (commanded by Captain Moore), lying in the river by Norwich. On the 30th 'the hatchways were closed at twenty minutes after two in the morning, and this London trader sailed immediately for Lowestoft, which harbour was reached about 11 o'clock. In three hours the vessel was out of sight and on her way to Portsmouth', and her ultimate destination of the penal colonies of Australia.

22 APRIL

A FULL ACCOUNT OF THE

HORRID MURDER

Committed by James Flood, on the body of Jane Field, in Common Pump Street, near the Castle Ditches, Norwich, on the night of Tuesday the 22nd of April, 1851.

An Inquest was held at the Eastern Counties Railway Tavern, St. Peter per Mountergate, before Mr. Mendham, on the body of a young woman named Jane Field, who resided in Pump Street.

William Skelt, watchman, deposed that he was on duty about one on Wednesday morning, near the corner of Rose Lane King Street, when he heard a cry of murder in Pump Street. On hastening towards the spot, he saw the deceased, Jane Field, running, and a man named Flood, running after her. Witness saw Flood knock her down between the pump and Mr. Lincoln's, the pipe maker. Lefevre, another watchman, was with him, and Flood was taken into custody. The deceased lay motionless and senseless. Flood was handcuffed, and taken to the station house. J. B. Lefevre confirmed Skelt's evidence.

Jane Smith, a single woman, living in Pump Street, said that she had known the deceased eight or nine years, and resided in the same house with her. James Flood lived with deceased. They were frequently quarreling. Saw the deceased and Flood together several times on Tuesday; they appeared then on good terms. About half-past eleven that night deceased came in rather tipsy. When she went out she said she was going after her sweetheart. About half-past twelve Flood came in and lighted his pipe. He was very tipsy. He went upstairs to go into the deceased's room, but the door was fast. He appeared very angry, and asked if the deceased was in bed. Witness said that she was gone after him, upon which he threatened with an oath to do her some bodily injury. About an hour afterwards witness heard the deceased shrieking "Murder!" in the street, and saw the watchman take Flood into custody. Deceased was covered with blood and insensible. There was a cut on her forehead, about an inch and half long. She threw up a quantity of blood. In about half an hour Mr. Day, the surgeon came. He put his finger on the wound on the forehead, and deceased held up her hand and said "I am dying." Witness remained with the deceased until she died, which was about ten minutes past seven on Thursday night. When deceased had her senses, she told witness that Flood had ill-used her and knocked her down in London-street.

Caroline Collins, a single woman, residing in Pump street, stated that about a quarter before one on Wednesday morning she was coming home from the Shirehall Tavern, on the Ditches, when she saw deceased and Flood together near her house. Heard Flood twice threaten to kill her, and saw him knock her down. After she was down Flood kicked her on the head.

The Jury directed a post-mortem examination and the inquest was then adjourned till eight o'clock, at which time they again met, and after a patient investigation they returned a verdict of WILFUL MURDER! A warrant was ordered for Flood's committal, who now awaits his trial at the next Assizes.

(Johnson Collection)

23 APRIL, **1836** In a prosecution arising from the famous 'Burnham Poisoners' trial of Billings and Frary in August 1835, Peter Taylor, the husband of the poisoned Mary, was found guilty in the April Assizes of 1836 of being an accessory before the fact of the murder. Protesting his innocence to the last, he was hanged on this day upon Norwich Castle Hill before a large crowd.

24 APRIL, **1851** Samuel Woodhouse of Plumstead and William Pyle of Holt were buried alive in a well 115ft deep at Docking, after the falling in of 36ft of soil. 'Some of the inhabitants proposed to fill up the well and let them remain in it, stating that the same thing had been done at Tittleshall, where an inquest was held at the mouth of the well and the body or bodies remain there to this day.' The bodies were recovered in mid-May: 'though the bodies had been buried exactly three weeks on their being brought to the surface and moved about, blood flowed freely from both of them'.

25 APRIL, 1813 Died this day in his 67th year James Bullard, many years master of the Bethel Hospital for Lunatics, Norwich (the first 'bedlam' outside London). His death resulted from a wound in the stomach inflicted with a scythe by a patient named Jonathan Morley, who was engaged in mowing the lawn in the inner court. The coroner's jury returned a verdict of wilful murder, but at the Assizes it was decided Morley was insane at the time he committed the act, and he was ordered to be kept in custody. In December 1816 the Secretary of State ordered Morley's removal to the new criminal lunatic asylum in St George's Fields, London, where he died.

26 APRIL, **1821** A smuggling boat was captured at Great Yarmouth between the Nelson Monument and the old jetty by boats of the Revenue cutter *Ranger* under the command of Captain Sayer. The smugglers had on board about 400 tubs of Geneva and a quantity of dry goods. Her crew, however, had escaped – they dived overboard and swam ashore.

27 APRIL, **1839** Charles Daines, 'the Hempnall Poisoner', was executed on Castle Hill for the attempted murder of his wife, Elizabeth, daughter and neighbour on 11 March. He had already stood trial for the murder of his infant daughter and had been acquitted, but immediately afterwards was charged with the attempted poisoning of his wife with arsenic. Found guilty, he was sentenced to death. He appeared to die an exceedingly hard death. After the trap had dropped on the gallows 'He clasped his hands, and raised his arms several times towards his breast, as if in the act of prayer, unquestionably showing that consciousness had not left him'. His remains were buried in St Michael-at-Thorn churchyard.

28 APRIL, **1900** Thetford Petty Sessions heard the case of James Good, an inmate of Thetford Union Workhouse, who was charged with maliciously wounding Thomas Denney with a table knife. Referred to the Quarter Sessions on 9 May, he was sentenced to three months' imprisonment.

HE LIFE, TRIAL, CONFESSION, & EXECUTION OF

CHARLES DAINES, AGED FIFTY,

Vho was Executed on Saturday, April 27th, 1839, for poisoning LIZABETH DAINES, his Daughter, 3 years old, and ELIZABETH ILLS, his Neighbour, at HEMPNALL.

CHARLES DAINES, was a Carpenter, and resided at Hempnall, in Norfolk, was married, and had three children; he was considered a udy industrious man, and appeared affectionate to his children, for which several persons subscribed for counsel to defend him on his trial, he was respected previous to his imbibing those horrid ideas, the perpetration of which has brought him to his untimely end.

On the evidence which was given on Thursday, (the first day of the trial) Mary Alexander deposed that Mrs. Daines the wife of the Pri ner came to her house very ill on the 11th of March, after sending for her husband, I found her very sick outside the door, she vomited very ch, I led her home, Elizabeth Mills was sitting in a chair very sick and ill: there was on the table some sop in a basin, and tea in a cup, ere was a tea kettle on the fire place. When the Prisoner came home he asked what was the matter, he said is Elizabeth ill? I said yes, he ked me what they had been taking; I answered some tea; he said surely there is nothing in the water; he reached hold of the kettle and nt out with it; on his return he said he had emptied the kettle and rinsed it out and filled it with fresh water; he pointed to the sop and ked ff that was any thing they had been taking of, and said he would take that and throw it away; I answered we had sent for Mr Utting, d I thought it ought to be there when Mr. Utting came; The Prisoner went to the pantry and brought out some powder in a broken basin, said it was some powder he had bought to kill mice; he said he did not know how it should come into the kettle, except the mice had en in the broken basin and then into the pint pot with which he had filled the kettle; the women (Fryer and Rackham) said, a Doctor ght to be sent for; he said he thought it better to get some medicine quicker than he could get a Doctor; Prisoner went for some, it was imony wine and castor oil.—The Child died about four o'clock.

John Daines aged 18, son to the prisoner stated, he came home about nine o'clock on Sunday Evening, the 10th March, my mother was stairs, not in bed, my father in bed; when I came in, the two children, my father and mother were the only persons in the house; I locked e door after me; a pail of water stood in the back house; I drank out of it with a pint mug; I went to bed; I got up about six o'clock xt morning; my father was up; my mother came down as I was fit to go out; my father went out before me; before I went out I drank me more water from the same pail, with the same mug; I went to work with my father; the kettle produced is the same; when I took the ug from off the stool, several things were on it; the kettle usually had the lid on.

Sarah Friar stated, I heard Prisoner say he never had any Poison in his house until he got two-pennyworth of Figs, to destroy the mice, he d he asked for fig powder or arsenic; he said the person who served him said she dare not sell arsenic without a witness; Prisoner said he uld not have any, as he must have a witness.

J. Utting. Surgeon, Long Stratton, was sent for to Hempnall; I found the little girl, the son, and Mrs. Mills very ill; I went to Mrs. aires, she had symptoms of poison (arsenic) in her stomach; I took possession of the sop and tea.

Mr. Firth, Surgeon, Norwich, analysed the stomachs of the victims, together with the sop and tea, he found them to contain arsenic; he so analysed the powder in the basin which was nux vomica and arsenic; he washed the kettle three times and found arsenic each time.

The Judge proceeded to comment on the evidence, leaving the Jury to decide if the cause of their deaths arose from poison and whether ministered by the Prisoner, if so, they would find him guilty, and if in case of any doubt, they would acquit him.—The Jury retired for half a hour, and on returning, acquitted the prisoner!

On the following morning he was again placed at the Bar on a charge with having attempted to poison his wife. Mr. Evans stated the case r the prosecution, who said he was the last person to complain of the verdict of the Jury on the former trial. He could not then call the e before them, but in this instance where the injury was personal to the wife she would be made an evidence. Another circumstance was, at, unfortunately, the prisoner during the last two years had formed a criminal connexion with a woman named Lloyd who proved the isoner said to her. his wife was an ailing person, and he wished her to keep single that he might marry her if his wife died.

Hannah Daines the wife of the prisoner was sworn. I drank tea on the 10th March, I used a copper tea-kettle; my husband drank tea ith me; I felt no bad effects; I put the kettle in the back house, against the boiler, under the shoe shelf; the lid of the kettle was on. My usband got up rather before six next morning; I got up soon after six, and came down stairs; my husband was just leaving the house as I me down; my son left almost directly after; I found the fire lighted, my husband usually lights the fire when he gets up first; the kettle as filled and on the fire; my husband usually fills it if he gets up first; no one was in the house till I got my children up; I dressed them d gave them their breakfast, it consisted of sop made with some water from the kettle, I then made tea for myself, I drank one cup, about minutes after I felt bad in the stomach, there was a sort of heat in my throat; the children kept throwing up very much; I sent for Mrs. ills, she came directly, she took a cup of tea, she seemed struck very bad; I went to Mrs. Alexander and she sent for my husband; I know n Lloyd, she is a widow, my husband has been acquainted with her about a year and a half; I have had words with my husband about her cause he did not behave so kind to me as he used to do.

The evidence of all the witnesses were similar to those on the Thursday, and the case for the prosecution being closed, his Lordship summed p the evidence. The Jury retired, and after an absence of an hour returned a verdict of GUILTY! The learned Judge in a most impressive anner proceeded to pass on the prisoner the awful sentence of the law, earnestly imploring him to repent of his crime and to make his peace ith God.—The prisoner almost immediately after being taken to his cell, made an entire CONFESSION of his guilt to the Chaplain of the aol. He also acknowledged he had made the attempt on two former occasions—one by putting a small quantity of arsenic on some fried otatoes, and the other by mixing a portion in some peasoup. After his condemnation he became quite resigned to his fate, acknowledging e justice of his sentence, and endeavoured with the assistance of the Chaplain to prepare himself for the awful change.

On the morning of EXECUTION, the throngs of persons from the villages for miles round kept entering into the city till the hour approach d, and up till 12 o'clock numbers were seen thronging up every entrance to the Castle hill. At the usual time the mournful procession ommenced moving from the Castle to the foot of the Scaffold, which after a few minutes the wretched man ascended, he appeared resigned, e executioner having adjusted the rope, the necessary preparations being completed, the bolt was drawn and he was launched into eternity

(Norfolk Local Studies Library)

29 APRIL **1905** Sarah Bower of Row 28 was summoned before the Great Yarmouth Magistrates for keeping a disorderly house, 'the worst house in Yarmouth'. PC Herring said that the defendant had no occupation; he and PC Batley had watched the house and he described what they had seen. (The sensitive audiences of newspapers at the time were not exposed to the coming and goings of a bawdy house in print.) The chief constable said the prisoner had been convicted of a similar offence the previous November when she was sent to gaol for a month. On coming out of gaol she recommenced the same practices. DI Moore said he had kept the defendant's house under observation since Christmas and he considered it 'the worst house in Yarmouth, girls having been decoyed there'. Sarah Bower was found guilty and sentenced to four months' hard labour.

30 APRIL **1881** The little village of Worstead comes to terms with the previous day's actions of Charles Monsey, a Superannuation Excise Officer who lived in the village with his wife. Flying into a fit of anger, he had grabbed a hatchet and cleaved her about the head. Law officials and doctors decided he was quite insane, and he was detained at Her Majesty's pleasure as a 'criminal lunatic'.

APRIL **1751** Late in this month a horrible and tragic murder was committed on South Lynn Common. William Chaplain and Mary Gafferson had been in a tempestuous relationship for almost a year. Losing her love for Chaplain as her emotions grew for another suitor, Mary became coquettish and made no effort to please Chaplain when she didn't feel like it. Chaplain had suspicions and they walked where they had first met, on South Lynn Common. Questions became more heated, challenges more direct. Cursing and taunting each other, their rages erupted and Chaplain struck Mary. She fell to the ground and he clubbed her to death. As the red haze before his eyes cleared he stumbled off across the common into a night watch patrol. It was obvious from his demeanour that something was afoot, and Mary's body was soon found. Standing trial for his crime, Chaplain was found guilty and executed at Norwich. His body was brought back to the scene of the crime and gibbeted as a warning to others.

MAY

Engraving of Great Yarmouth Suspension Bridge shortly after its collapse
on 2 May 1844.

1 MAY   **1876**   Henry Webster was executed by public executioner William Marwood inside Norwich Castle for the murder of his wife.

2 MAY   **1844**   *Great Yarmouth Suspension Bridge disaster.* On 2 May 1844 Yarmouth was abuzz with excitement following the arrival of Cooke's Circus to the town. A publicity stunt was advertised: Nelson the clown would sail down the River Bure in a washtub towed by four geese. The best place from which to view this spectacle was generally agreed to be the suspension bridge. Hundreds turned out, cramming themselves on to the bridge. When Nelson hove into view the crowd rushed to the side he was approaching from, unbalanced the bridge and it collapsed, plunging everyone on it, the majority of whom were children, into the river. All available boats rushed to the scene and many spectators were saved, but tragically 130 men, women and children perished in the river that day.

Great Yarmouth Suspension Bridge disaster, 2 May 1844.

2 MAY   **1804**   The 48ft high gibbet on which the body of Payne the pirate was hung in chains, about 23 years previously (1781), upon Yarmouth North Denes was taken down by order of the corporation. Payne had been executed in London; his body, already bound, tarred and encased in a metal gibbet cage, was conveyed to Yarmouth in a wooden box by wagon. 'A ludicrous circumstance happened the night it [the gibbet frame] was erected. The different tackling being all adjusted before putting down the gibbet the day before Payne was hanged, some daring licencious bloods hoisted up a

young ass by the hind legs to the amusement of the spectators surprised to find the gibbet so occupied the following morning.' In consequence the tackling had become so entangled that it took a young sailor to climb the gibbet and untangle the mess before the body of the prisoner could be suspended.

1908 *Lynn Body Mystery.*
A month earlier, a body, identified as that of 18-year-old John 'Jack' Stork, a King's Lynn porter, was recovered from the River Orwell about 15 miles from the town by PC Medlock. At the inquest the body was positively identified by his sister, Mrs Hall, who had put out bills enquiring as to his whereabouts. Dr Hills of Upwell voiced his opinion that the body recovered from the river did not appear to have been in the water three days, let alone the 25 days John had been missing. There was nothing to say that John had not wandered or been elsewhere

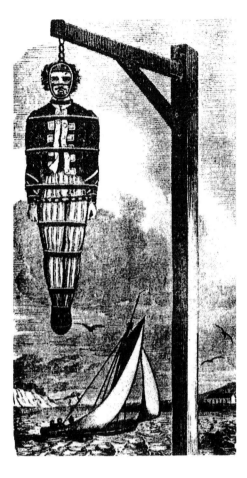

Another notorious pirate, Captain Kidd, swinging from his gibbet.

3 MAY

before he finally ended up in the water. Positive identification by Mrs Hall was accepted by the coroner, and a verdict of death by drowning was passed. John was buried the following week by his family. On this day another man's body was recovered from the mud by the River Ouse at Wiggenhall St Mary's. Police Constable Capman who examined the body found money and papers which left no doubt that *this* was the body of John Stork. . . .

1851   A pauper named John Rowland, who had had a remarkable career, died at Lynn Workhouse. He was educated at Eton and was afterwards a Fellow of King's College, Cambridge. Ordained deacon and priest by Bishop Horsley, he officiated at St James's, Westminster. Subsequently he threw off his gown – or it was taken from him – and he became a blacksmith and coach-spring maker on Norfolk Street, King's Lynn. Apprehended, tried and found guilty for stealing iron, he was transported. Rowland eventually returned to Lynn and lived out his last years there in the workhouse dying at the ripe old age of 78.

4 MAY

5 MAY **Norfolk Bridewells and Gaols visited by Prison Reformer John Howard**

Aylsham Bridewell: Following his visit in 1779, when four prisoners were held in its walls, Howard reported 'In the floor of the work or day room is a trap door into a dungeon, which is 9½ ft by 6 ft. Above stairs are three rooms, not secure. No fire-place: no straw: court not secure: prisoners only in it on Sunday: no water: no sewer: no implements for work: no allowance but two pennyworth of bread a day to vagrants.'

6 MAY **1805** A 'press gang' visited Great Yarmouth on this day. Impressment parties stopped every person they met without discrimination or respect for appearances. No less than 300 persons were impressed. Some were confined to the place where the gang rendezvoused, while others were marched to the barracks or conveyed to the boats lying in readiness at the jetty. All were carried during the night on to the *Monmouth*. Next morning a regulation took place and only 50 were detained.

A thump-up with the Press Gang.

7 MAY **1842** Following an abortive approach to Norwich Magistrates the previous day to obtain permission to sell his wife, Samuel Wilkinson still went ahead, saying, 'I'll take the risk.' Near the Prussia Gardens in the city he sold his wife to Samuel Springle for a guinea, and received a sovereign on account.

1845 Walter Morgan, one of the two founder brothers of the famous local brewery Morgans of King Street, was inspecting his vats of beer when, overcome by fumes of carbonic acid arising from the fermenting beer, he toppled over into one of the vats and drowned in his own beer.

1674 John Quantell was executed in the ditches of Norwich Castle for felony and burglary.

1900 After the shocking death of a Norwich publican, an inquest was held at Salhouse railway station before Mr H.R. Culley, County Coroner. The body of Peter Ront, landlord of the Coachmakers Arms on Bethel Street, Norwich, was found by the railway lines. He was believed to have been put in a stupor by the contents of the bottle found beside him. The coroner recorded: 'Deceased met with his death by injuries accidentally received having fallen out of a train.'

Norfolk beliefs and omens that warn of the approach of the Angel of Death.

It is unlucky to fit on a dead person's shroud, or get into a newly made coffin for jest.

If a bumble-bee flies into the house and dies, it is a sign some member of the family will be brought home sick.

A creaking door or furniture, or the furniture cracking foretells sickness in the house.

A bunch of may or whitethorn brought into the house, brings with it misfortune and death.

1874 Adverts and handbills were circulated in Great Yarmouth for R. Ceiley's Worm Powders; he claimed to be a medical botanist on Church Plain. Ceiley describes the symptoms of worms in children thus: 'grinding of teeth, picking the nose, irritability, paleness, loss of flesh, flabbiness, sallowness of complexion, fits and stoppages'. He quoted a number of testimonials in his newspaper advertisements, including that of one Peter

Wiseman of Lower Road, Great Yarmouth: 'Sir – I am happy to say your valuable Worm Medicine has expelled a tape worm from me over 200ft long.' Ceiley stated that he could be consulted at his own residence from 10 in the morning to 8 in the evening for cases of bad legs, sore breasts, scrofula and all manner of skin diseases. Worm powders were sold at 7½d, 10½d and 1s 1½d a packet.

13 MAY **1802** Mrs Beaton of St John Maddermarket, Norwich, died on this day aged 85. 'She was a native of Wales and commonly called in her locale "The Freemason" from the circumstance of her having contrived to conceal herself one evening in the wainscoting of the lodge-room where she learnt that secret, the knowledge of which thousands of her sex in vain attempted to arrive at.' She was a very singular old woman, and kept what she saw secret until her dying day.

One of the secret ceremonies of the Freemasons, *c.* 1750.

14 MAY **1829** The body of Lorina Gooderham, aged 46, was found murdered by stabbing, lying in the road a short distance from Diss on Brome Lane, adjoining the road leading to Lopham. Despite exhaustive enquiries and wide circulation of handbills and broadsheets, her murderer was never brought to justice.

Diss: PRINTED BY E. E. ABBOTT.

A TRUE AND PARTICULAR ACCOUNT

OF A MOST

Cruel and Bloody Murder,

COMMITTED

AT DISS, IN NORFOLK.

" And it was so, that all that saw it said, There was no such deed done nor seen—unto this day: consider of it, take advice, and speak your minds."—Judges xix. 30.

LORINA GOODERHAM, the subject of this melancholy memoir, was forty-six years of age, and was the wife of James Gooderham, whose age is about thirty, to whom she had been married about six years; her maiden name was Bryant, and was a native of Diss. She was twice married, and had three children by the first husband, and one by the present, a girl, now about five years old. From some domestic difference, they had been separated for the last eighteen months, she residing at Diss, and he in London, where he was employed as a private Watchman, and made her a weekly allowance which was regularly paid. On the morning of Thursday, May the 14th, 1829, a considerable alarm was excited in the town of Diss, a parish remarkable for the strictness of its police, and the peaceable behaviour of the inhabitants, by the report of a Woman being found cruelly Murdered, at a very little distance from the town, in a lane called Brome Lane, adjoining the road leading to Lopham. This lane being much resorted to, as it afforded a very pleasant walk, and led round to Shelfanger lane, was a very public one. A young woman passing through this lane about a quarter past six o'clock on the morning in question, saw a woman lying in the road, in a most unusual posture; she was afraid to approach, till a man coming in the opposite direction emboldened her to a nearer view of the object; she then turned back, and soon communicated to several of the nearest neighbours what she had seen: many persons now came to the spot, whose horror may be well conceived, when they beheld the murdered woman dead and cold. She appeared as if first struck with a violent blow on her head, and then, while clenched to the ground, her face, throat, breast, and body were barbarously stabbed in a most brutal manner, supposed to have been inflicted with a knife, or small dirk. No attempt was made by the inhuman wretch to conceal the mangled body, as it appears she was murdered on the very spot where first she fell, and on which she was found, lying near the bank extended on her back, with her head a little reclining, and her face and neck covered with blood. Her leghorn bonnet, crushed and bloody, lay near her head; her cap, a set of curls, and a pocket were torn off, and a silk handkerchief was round her neck.

The alarm being spread through the town, the proper authorities took possession of the body, and the attendance of the county Coroner was immediately required. A meeting of the gentlemen of Diss was held in the forenoon, at the Assembly Room; a worthy and reverend Magistrate was in the chair, and the several persons who had last seen the deceased were in attendance, as well as those who had discovered her lying dead in the morning, with all the medical gentlemen who had previously inspected the body; in examining which it appeared that she had received more injuries than were at first apprehended. So determined had been the assassin in the work of her destruction, that he had attacked her in a manner which indicated such diabolical malice, that it seemed as if had she been possessed of

"As many lives as hairs, their great revenge,
Had stomach for them all."

A severe wound was inflicted near the right ear, which had divided the bloodvessel; there was a deep gash in her neck, and also a deep cut in the breast; but the most frightful wound was one about four inches long, on the right side of the body, injuring the intestines in several places, and through this awful

gash a considerable part of her bowels gushed out. The handkerchief and ribbon of her hat were tied round her neck as if for the purpose of strangling her, but no marks of strangulation were visible Still, from all appearance, her struggles had been severe, and her death horrible, beyond conception. A woman living within 200 yards of the spot heard a peculiar kind of noise at the moment the church clock was striking 12, which she thinks must be the groans of the poor creature.

At the investigation, the few persons who had seen her last, said, that she had been seen walking that way several times in the afternoon, appearantly expecting to meet some person. She left the house in which she lodged about a quarter before nine on Wednesday evening, it is believed without any money in her pockets, and was afterwards seen by a woman and two children walking with a man, whom they knew not, rather respectably dressed. The woman, in whose house Gooderham lodged, said she had no suspicion of any person or persons on whom to ground a conjecture of being concerned in a transaction so truly horrible; and that the deceased was not in the practice of being absent from her home late in the evening, nor ever before to have been absent all night.

The body was ordered to be removed to the Bowling-green room, at the Cherry Tree Inn, there to await the inquisition of the Coroner, which took place the same evening, before E. Press, esq. one of the coroner's of the county, and a Jury of very respectable inhabitants of the town: but after sitting for several hours, no new light was thrown on the subject, the inquest was adjourned without coming to any conclusion.

A reward of Fifty Pounds has been offered by public authority for the apprehension of the murderer or murderers, but hitherto with out effect. On Sunday evening, the husband of the deceased having arrived from London, the funeral took place at eight o'clock, and the remains of the unfortunate victim of revenge and cruelty were interred on the south bank of the church yard, at Diss. From the general excitement which this transaction occasioned among all ranks of people, a great number of persons attended to witness the last solemnities; and it was computed that more than a thousand persons were assembled on the occasion, many of them from the adjacent villages, all eager to collect information. But this most extraordinary occurrence remains involved in mystery, which time seldom fails sooner or later to bring to light;

"For murder, though it hath no tongue, will speak
With most miraculous organs."

And let the murderer or perpetrators of this horrid deed, whoever they may have been, not deceive themselves in a fancied security, for there is an eye to which the most secret and mysterious transactions are clearly discovered, and who in good time, "discovereth deep things out of darkness, and bringeth to light the shadow of death." For there is no place so secret where the perpetrators can hide themselves from him: and that he will infallibly "bring to light the hidden things of darkness, and make manifest the counsels of the heart."

The Coroner's Inquest was resumed on Wednesday morning, May 20th, at 10 o'clock, when a vast number of witnesses were examined, but after sitting till past 11 that night, without coming to any satisfactory evidence, the Jury again adjourned till next morning.

THE MURDERED WOMAN'S LAMENTATION.

Come all ye thoughtless, gay and fair, a warning take by me,
And in the paths of virtue tread, let quickly you shall see,
That in a dreary dismal lane, my fate was soon to come,
For to be murdered by some one, was my poor wretched doom.

'Twas near Diss town as you will find, on Thursday morning last,
That I was found all streich'd along, by one who quickly pass'd,
But she return'd with great amaze, and found that I was dead,
And with her fright at seeing me, came back in hasty dread.

She to a neighbour quickly told, a tale of piteous woe,
That by some bloody murderer's hand, I'd met a dreadful foe,
The news was shortly spread about, and many people ran,
For to find out the worse than brute, who call'd himself a man.

'Twas over night when dress'd so neat, and walking up and down,
He did betray me from my seat, my cottage in the town;
Then to the sorrow of my friends, leave me as many more,
With stabs and cuts he gain'd his ends, and left me in my gore.

Then plunderd me of all my cash, and covered me with shame,
That all the people did him lash with a disgraceful name,
Oh, he that was my murderer, was quickly out of sight,
And to some silent spot did stir, while it was still moonlight.

What act his feelings now to hear, how many people came,
To church together far and near, to see my lasting home.
Yes, many hundreds for me sigh'd, and shed a piteous tear,
For of my life I was depriv'd, and carried on a bier.

Plung'd in sorrow and in grief, the young and old did say,
Oh if they could but give relief and see the glorious day,
That he or th-y to justice brought, to answer for their crime,
For having kill'd me in a spot, I walked in many time.

For taking of my life away, while I was unprepared,
And hastening me to that great day, of which I've often heard,
A friendly hint I leave with all, who follow me behind,
That they be careful great and small, what customers they find.

For in an evil treacherous hour, I in my blood was found,
All covered o'er with dust and gore, and lying on the ground,
Depriv'd of strength in vain I cried against my murderer's hand,
Who grasp'd me tight with all his might, as I lay on the land.

Be careful when you meet a friend, that he don't prove a foe
To you, to gain his brutal end, and leave you for to rue
The unlucky hour you ever spent, with such a monster kind,
And all your friends in sorrow bent, will have upon their mind.

Farewell ye thoughtless gay and fair, again I say to all,
Think of me much and pray beware, no one prove your downfall.
I once was fresh and fair and gay, and call'd by some Love,
But now I'm in my bed of clay, say what you will of me.

My husband left me in this town, bereft of all my friends,
And now I'm murdered by some one, who gain'd their brutal ends.
I've left my little babe behind, for you to grant relief,
And pray that God may bless you all, who drive away her grief

15 MAY   **1902**   A reported love tragedy on Newmarket Road, Norwich. Arthur Crowfoot, a young man aged 20 who had been staying for some time at Mrs Harriet Watson's lodging house, 8 Eagle Walk, Newmarket Road, was found lying dead in his bedroom with his throat cut. An inquest was held at The Eagle pub where it was revealed that Crowfoot had become much enamoured with a Miss Ethel Bridges, to whom he had been engaged since the previous January. Paltry disagreements saw their love waning, and finally at The Griffin she said she had had enough and wanted to leave him. Fatally depressed, Crowfoot first attempted to take his own life by throwing himself across the path of a tram near Brunswick Road. This did nothing more than frighten the wits out of William Morse, the poor driver, who pulled the tram to a halt before the cow catcher on the front of the tram touched him. Not to be deterred, Crowfoot returned to his lodgings on the Wednesday night with a brand new cut-throat razor and took its name literally. Mrs Watson was asked what aroused her suspicions about the events in her lodger's room. After confirming that she heard Crowfoot come in, she heard a noise, 'a gurgling noise from his throat'; she then woke her husband and declared, incredibly perceptively, 'I believe Mr Crowfoot has done something to himself.'

16 MAY   **1905**   Special Sessions at Holt. Charles 'Shirts' Rudd (see also 6 January 1896) and John 'Jambo' Warner, labourers of Edgefield, were charged by Inspector Lewis of Holt with unlawfully and maliciously wounding F.W. Moore the Baconsthorpe constable. Appearing in court with his head bandaged, he was allowed to give evidence seated. Moore stated that he was on the highway at Edgefield at 8.15 p.m. when he saw the defendants coming from the direction of Barningham, one on each side of the road looking in the hedges. He challenged Rudd, saying that he had unlawfully obtained eggs in his possession, and proceeded to search him. Rudd threatened to knock his brains out, and punched the Constable in the mouth. Both falling to the ground in the grapple, the constable attempted to cuff Rudd. Warner then joined the melée; the Constable's helmet already having been knocked off, Warner thumped Moore on the head. Trying to stand, Moore was knocked to the ground and rendered unconscious by Rudd. Coming round, he saw Rudd standing over him with a large stick in his hand, saying: 'I have a good mind to finish you now. I shall get six years for it.' He then called to Warner: 'You're not afraid, are you Jack?' He replied: 'It would take more than that to frighten me.' Rudd then went away, and when near Warner said: 'Let's go back and finish the b- off.' Moore tried to get up but the rogues kept walking. PC Moore eventually managed to get to Chapman's farm, was taken to Holt and was treated by Dr Hales. Appearing at the Norfolk Assizes, Rudd and Warner were sent down . . . again.

17 MAY   **1595**   Norwich Mayor's Book records on this day: 'It is ordered that Thomas Barney, prisoner in the Guildhall shall go and travel with Barnaby Langdon the whipper in every parish within the city with the basket to gather and collect the devotion and relief of the inhabitants to be given and distributed amongst the pore prisoners of the same gaol.'

1810   Accounts of this time record that a young woman of Dereham, being strongly attracted to a soldier in the 24th Foot, resolved to follow him to the wars. Dressing herself in men's attire, she enlisted by mistake in the 54th Regiment of Foot, who were recruiting in Norwich. Her sex was soon discovered and her intentions frustrated. She is immortalised in *Beat the Drum Again*, the spirited Norfolk ballad about a female soldier.

18 MAY

1536   *Anne Boleyn beheaded.*

19 MAY

Married in secret to King Henry VIII in January 1533, Anne Boleyn (right), daughter of Sir Thomas Boleyn of Blicking Hall in Norfolk, was Henry's second wife. To marry her he had to divorce Catherine of Aragon, thus breaking with the Roman Catholic Church, which provided the official reason for the Reformation in England. Providing Henry with a fine daughter who grew up to become Elizabeth I, Anne fell out of favour with Henry for not giving him a male heir. On trumped up charges of adultery and witchcraft she was beheaded, kneeling upright, with one cut by a French swordsman on Tower Green at the Tower of London, the only person to have been executed so since Norman times. Anne was buried upright in an arrow chest under the altar of St Peter ad Vincula chapel within the walls of the Tower. Folklore claims that bodies were switched and her body was smuggled out of London and back to Norfolk, to be buried in secret in the ancient Boleyn family church at Salle. It is also claimed that a ghostly carriage careers around the Aylsham area up to Blickling on the anniversary of her execution. In it sits the spectral Anne, her neck a raw stump, while her hands hold her head firmly on her lap.

20 MAY **1816** A riot took place at Downham Market. The magistrates assembled at the Crown Inn were publicly insulted, and so much disorder ensued that the Upwell yeomanry cavalry were called out and the riot act was read, after which the crowd gradually dispersed. A demand had been made for wages of 2s per day to be paid every Monday and Thursday. When the farmers refused to comply another disturbance took place on the 24th; two women and a number of men were arrested and committed to Norwich Castle. Charged at the Assizes before Lord Chief Justice Gibbs, 16 were found guilty and sentenced to death. Sentence was only carried out on two – Daniel Harwood and Thomas Thody on 31 August. 'The recollection of his wife and children and the horror of immediate death overcame Thody's fortitude. He was nearly sinking down under the agony of grief and terror, which he expressed by convulsive shrieks and was obliged to be supported by several men until he was silenced by the drop of the gallows trap.'

21 MAY **1853** For a few days around the 21st there were no prisoners in Lynn Gaol. To celebrate this unique circumstance the prison doors were thrown open, and the mayor entertained the whole borough police force and officials to a dinner served within the building.

22 MAY **1882** William George Abigail (aged 19) was executed inside Norwich Castle for the murder of his betrothed, Miss Jane Plunkett. Having lost her position as a servant through her connection with Abigail she was living with him as his wife at Mill Hill, New Catton. Early in the morning of 25 April Abigail shot her in the head and the left breast as she was lying asleep in bed, and decamped immediately. No one appears to have reacted to the shot in the house, others living there only investigating when she did not come down for breakfast. For some reason Abigail hung around the city and was arrested on Dove Street in the evening. Maintaining 'a most callous demeanour to the last' he was finally executed after due trial by public executioner William Marwood.

23 MAY **1837** Convicts Smith and Middleton returned to Norwich Prison on their recapture at Dereham after two days on the run, having escaped from Norwich City Gaol. One had lowered himself on a rope of blankets while the other leapt down a depth of 25ft.

24 MAY **1878** John Pilgrim, a weaver of St Augustines, Norwich, was summoned to Norwich Shirehall, charged with sending a quantity of tobacco into the Norwich Castle Prison contrary to the rules and regulations made and provided for the prison. One of the warders at the castle said that the defendant had brought in a parcel for his son, who was then in custody, and left it lying on a bench in the lodge. The package was opened and found to contain a sausage roll of huge dimensions. Inside the roll and lying neatly embedded among the sausages was a quantity of tobacco leaf of 'unsavory odour'. There could be no doubt that the introduction of tobacco, whether

Nelson's Monument,
Great Yarmouth,
scene of a daring
escapade and horrible
death on 26 May
1863.

for chewing or smoking, was in contravention of prison rules. Mr Miller, the tobacconist of London Street, was called in by the defence who ingeniously enquired if it really was tobacco. Miller said that if it was tobacco it was of 'dubious sort and quality'. However, the case really was against Mr Pilgrim; he was found guilty and fined 1s plus costs.

25 MAY **1887** Inquest into the 'Shocking affair at Witton' concerning the death of Joseph Turner reported today. Giving evidence at the inquest, one of his servants, Eliza Bell of East Ruston, declared: 'he had been in a very strange manner of late'. Her mistress had called 'Oh, come here, what has your master done?' Bell ran into the sitting room at once. When she got there she saw her master standing before a looking glass in the adjoining store room where he was cutting his throat with a carving knife 'sawing at it as it appeared to her'. A verdict of suicide was confirmed by the coroner.

26 MAY **1863** Negro vocalists Charles Marsh and Henry Wharton tried to climb the Nelson monument at Great Yarmouth. Wharton succeeded, but tragically Marsh slipped and fell 144ft to the ground below, where he was killed instantly.

27 MAY **Norfolk Old Dame's Leechcraft**
Whooping cough can be cured by placing a live flat fish on the breast of the patient and letting it remain there until it dies.
For colds, smear one's nose with tallow for a cold in the head. The tallow plaster for the chest must be cut in the form of a heart in brown paper.

28 MAY **1832** The Revd Arthur Ireson of South Lynn murdered by a pistol shot fired by his son Thomas, a young man adjudged to be of unsound mind. The deceased was rector of East Bradenham and perpetual curate of Shouldham, Shouldham Thorpe and Tottenhill. At Lynn Quarter Sessions on 9 July Thomas faced the charges of murder of his father. The jury found he was insane at the time the crime was committed and he was ordered to be detained in custody. He remained at Lynn Gaol until 3 September when he was removed to 'the lunatic asylum in St Lawrence, Norwich'.

29 MAY **1825** At Great Yarmouth Quarter Sessions the case of the Neal family was heard. Mary Neal, who lived in Row 133 along with her children Susan and William, stood charged with the attempted murder of local cordwainer William Halls (or Hales) and his family by poisoning. Young William, who was apprenticed to Mr Halls, eventually confessed he put arsenic into the boiler where the Halls family dinner was being cooked, and the Neals were sentenced to death. This was the last time the Yarmouth Quarter Sessions ever passed the ultimate penalty; as it transpired the sentence was not carried out, and their punishment was commuted to transportation to Australia.

1900 Report of the inquest held at the Town Hall into the Yarmouth River
Mystery. Mary Anne Carrier, a married woman, disappeared two weeks
previously from her lodgings in Quay Mill Walk. Her estranged husband
said he had seen her on 10 May but they had lived apart for about nine
months after he told her to clear out 'in consequence of her conduct'.
Mrs Carrier 'was accustomed to go out alone at nights
and had sometimes been the worse for drink'. On
the night of her disappearance she had had
a lot of drink and attempted to bring back a
male acquaintance to her lodgings, but her
landlady objected and a series of altercations
followed with the deceased woman walking
out, then returning fired up again. On her
final visit Mrs Carrier exclaimed she would
throw herself in the river. Leaving her
hat, handkerchief and jacket in a boat in
Houghton's Yard she did just that. Her
body was recovered floating upstream
near Breydon Bridge by William Rowe,
a labourer, and taken to Houghton's Yard.
PC Burgess was summoned and he arranged
removal to the mortuary. The verdict of the
jury was suicide, but it was pointed out that
there was insufficient evidence to determine
the deceased's state of mind at the time. The
newspapers drew their conclusions, titling this
story 'A Sad Story of a Wife's Shame'.

1889 Eliza Ann Noble, married woman of Chapel Street, Lakenham, a very
respectable looking lady, attempted to jump into the river Wensum near Pull's
Ferry, to commit suicide. PC Potter of the GER force was on duty at Thorpe
Police station when he was called to the river. When he was about 12 yards
away from Mrs Noble she got under the railings that separate the pathway
from the river, and made a jump towards the water. Two young men rushed

up and prevented her from going in. The officer asked her what she meant by this and she said she was very unhappy in her mind and meant to drown herself. Her husband had been beating her 'on account of a soldier'. Although she had been drinking she had the sense to know what she was doing. Giving evidence at the Guildhall, Mrs Noble wept piteously; she claimed she didn't remember giving the statement recorded, and claimed it was untrue. She pleaded that she had five little children and that if the bench would let her off she would never touch a drop of drink again. She had never offended before and if she was sent to prison 'it would be the death of her'. The bench, taking into consideration her promises, demeanour and children, dismissed the case.

Norwich City Police, c. 1885. (Norfolk Constabulary Archive)

June

Ned Denny, 'The Norfolk Samson', pulling the Fakenham Mail Coach. *(Simon Pegg)*

One of the strangest duels ever contested was between Ned Denny, and Seth Blowers, 'The Suffolk Giant', fought on a hot summer's day in 1795. Denny was to pull the mail coach containing his backer, Sir Harry Vernon, and nine others, while Blowers was to be the human mount of his backer, Lord Beauchamp. Having set off from the Crown Inn at Fakenham, and only ten yards away from their destinaton, the Royal George Inn at Walsingham, the coach sped past Blowers, but under its own momentum – Denny was dead in the harness. Staggering across the finish line Blowers collapsed.
He died three days later.

1 JUNE **1833** The first of a series of remarkable accounts of ghostly visitations at Syderstone Parsonage, the residence of the Revd Mr Steward, was published on this day.

2 JUNE **1880** Obediah Cook was brought up before Swaffham Petty Sessions charged with the attempted murder of his wife, Susannah. A man known for his drunken temper, he had returned home in a bad state and had started messing around with his gunpowder. Fearing for the children she protested but 'he put her out of the house'. After a number of attempts to get back in at about 3 a.m., Cook shot his wife from a ground-floor window as she approached the door. Luckily Mrs Cook was only wounded. Admittedly the majority of her wounds were from glass fragments but Cook's defence of claiming he did not shoot at her but threw a rabbit waiting for the stew pot at the window beggared belief. The magistrates referred the case to the Assizes.

3 JUNE **Norfolk Old Dame's Leechcraft**

Hands of the gallows' dead. Great store was put on the mystical charms of the hands of those executed on the gallows, especially in the cure of afflictions of the neck and throat and wens. It was known for women to attempt to get below the gallows or bribe the hangman on Norwich Castle Hill to get a really fresh brush from the hand of the executed before he had gone cold. Wayside gibbets also attracted those seeking the 'healing hands', the efficacy in this case extending yet further to remove barrenness in women unable to conceive.

'Cure' from the hand of the gallows' dead.

1900   Report of the inquest at Havelock Tavern, Great Yarmouth, into the death of Frances Ellen Iles, a masseuse and nurse. Her father gave evidence that he had noticed a strangeness about her for about a fortnight, 'something strange in her eyes' but he thought better of asking her about it. Dr Wyllyn, with whom she worked, asked if she had a headache, and she said she was not at all well. Having arranged to go home to pick up the needed equipment for a house call, and then meet the doctor again, Frances didn't turn up. Dr Wyllyn was called to her side and was informed she had taken laudanum. Her stomach was pumped, but all was lost. Under her pillow was a 3oz blue poison bottle which had contained laudanum, and was quite empty. The doctor suggested that if she was ill and could not sleep she could have taken twenty to thirty drops to rest in safety. The jury considered suicide or error in dosage when trying to sleep, and decided death by misadventure was the best verdict.

4 June

1940   Place of many a grim and tragic tale is the Norwich mortuary on King Street (below) in about 1940. Deputy Chief Constable Herbert Balls watches the Coroner's Officer (Police Constable assigned to assist the Coroner) PC Bill Hoskins (left) and police Surgeon Dr Lincoln Hurn conducting an examination of a body prior to full autopsy. Up to the early twentieth century it was quite common practice to hold Coroner's Inquests into deaths which occurred in the city, particularly drownings, in the Waterman public house on King Street. This pub was situated opposite the City Mortuary, thus bodies could be identified and observed by the jury 'on the slab' and the main inquiry itself conducted just across the road in the pub. I think I would need a stiff drink afterwards too!

5 June

6 JUNE 1566   According to the Norwich Sessions Guild Book, Richard Ingham, a man suspected of felony was subjected to Peine Fort et Dure or pressing because he refused to plead guilt or innocence to the crime that he was accused of. Old English courts were in a quandary if suspects refused to plead. If a prisoner pleaded guilty the law stepped in, confiscated his estates and meted out punishment – frequently the death penalty. If he pleaded innocence a trial would ensue; if found guilty the convict would be punished and again all possessions were forfeited to the crown. Defendants might decide to remain mute and under old laws would stay unconvicted, as it was not until 1827 that silence by a defendant was construed as a 'not guilty' plea. Before that time their goods could not be touched, and although the accused could be incarcerated families of the accused enjoyed a degree of protection. This was a powerful incentive for many not to plead – so pressing became the law's equally persuasive method of forcing a plea. The victim would be spread-eagled on the floor of a cell, minimal sustenance given, and over the course of three days weights were piled up, leaving the prisoner with the agonising choice of plead or die. The 1566 register of St John's Church on Timberhill records simply: 'He that was prest to deathe was buried the XV daie of June Anno predict.'

Pressing for a plea in the eighteenth century.

7 JUNE   **Old Punishments – The Drunkard's Cloak or Spanish Mantle**
Folk drinking to excess and becoming unruly is nothing new. In the seventeenth and eighteenth centuries the judiciary employed a simple punishment for 'lager-louts'. Removing the base of a barrel and cutting holes for head and arms to poke through created 'the Drunkard's Cloak', which the culprit was made to wear. A metal collar was locked around the offender's neck, and by this he was led by a beadle or law official around the town.

1929 *Reported double tragedy at Cringleford.* In the corner of a field at Hillside **8 JUNE** Farm, by the main road to Hethersett, a grim discovery was made. Under the shelter of a hedge the bodies of two young men were discovered. First thought to be asleep, on closer inspection they were both seen to be suffering from gunshot wounds. Identification was instant: one of the boys was Frederick Durrant, and the woman who discovered the bodies was his aunt! Beside young Frederick was his close friend and workmate Frederick Turner. Both the men were well liked, and steady workers in the employ of Mr Ernest Morse of Eaton, the well-known farmer and nurseryman. The evidence pointed to a tragic story. Both young men had gone out shooting rabbits, and in a terrible accident Turner had shot Durrant. In sudden remorse Turner had pulled his cap down and turned the weapon on himself.

1843 An advertisement appeared in the *Norfolk Chronicle* on this day: **9 JUNE** 'Wymondham House of Correction – Female Turnkey Wanted Immediately, to assist the Matron in the duties of the prison. She must not be less than 35 years of age, be able to read and write and produce unexceptional testimonials of her ability for the situation. A widow without incumberance will be preferred. Application to be made to Mrs Johnson, the matron of the prison.'

1881 An 'incorrigible youth' named William Tuffs (aged 10) of Surrey Street **10 JUNE** was summoned before the court at Norwich Guildhall for stealing *2s 6d*. It transpired that the boy had fallen in with 'a bad crowd' and had got up to much mischief, including stealing important glass slides from Dr Roche. He was found guilty, and after due consideration the lad was sent to Ardwicke Green Industrial School until he reached the age of 16.

1895 Frederick Miles, a 27-year-old Norwich labourer, was indicted for the **11 JUNE** murder of his wife Mildred at St John Timberhill on 1 June. Although found guilty, he pleaded extreme provocation, and unusual mercy was shown in his sentence of nine months' imprisonment.

1827 *A serious riot at Norwich.* A party of Wymondham weavers who had **12 JUNE** damaged looms and destroyed silk to the value of £1,000 at Ashwellthorpe had been conveyed to Norwich Castle in hackney coaches, escorted by a detachment of 12th Lancers, to await examination. Norwich weavers who had barricaded the Golden Ball Lane entrance to Castle Meadow with a wagon and had placed a similar obstruction near Castle Bridge received the military with a volley of stones. The witnesses were conveyed via Timberhill to Orford Hill, and while a large body of special constables displaced the wagon at the bridge a second lieutenant came from the barracks and charged the mob at full gallop, dispersing them in all directions. An attempt to rally the mob was frustrated by a second charge. The militia staff were under arms on Castle Hill, and the streets were patrolled by Norwich Light Horse Volunteers. David Secker, Henry Rix and William Thurston were charged with the capital

MAD DOGS.

Notice is hereby given,

In consequence of many DOGS being still at large in the Streets of this City without sufficient muzzles, notwithstanding the public Notice which has already been given to the contrary, that all such Dogs will be seized and detained, and such as are not owned within twenty-four hours will be destroyed; and by way of encouragement a Reward of

HALF A CROWN

will be paid to al. Constables bringing such Dogs to the OLD GAOL.

By order of the Mayor.

W. DAY,
Swordbearer.

Guild-Hall, Norwich,
June 12th, 1830.

(Norfolk Local Studies Library)

offence of riotous assembly. They would almost certainly have been hanged but their counsel, Mr Cooper, found an error in the wording of the Riot Act read at the time of the disturbance. The learned judge pronounced the objection valid, and expressed the hope 'the prisoners would go home sensible of the blessings of Providence in having shielded them that day and saved them from an ignominious death'. The Ashwellthorpe rioters were bound over in the sum of £50 each.

1888 Robert Large, notorious poacher and gaol-breaker, was before the
Swainsthorpe Bench charged with assaulting PC Balls while in the execution
of his duty at Little Melton. Large left the Barford Cock in the company of
two others, and they all set off in the direction of Little Melton. Constable
Balls watched them search the hedgerows all the way up to Melton
Hall. When he lost sight of them the constable, by a cunning process of
elimination, concluded he would find them in the village pub – the Rose &
Crown. Just as they were coming out Constable Balls arrived and told Large
he suspected him of having game eggs about him, to which Large replied
'I've got no eggs and I don't allow any — man to touch me.' Taking Large
by the collar Balls commenced to search him. Large called to his reprobate
friends to come to his assistance; a man named Johnson struck the constable
with a stick, while Large punched Balls in the face, breaking one of his teeth
and cutting his lip. Large slipped free and ran off. In court Large pleaded: 'I
am charged with my name this time, gentlemen, and not with this case. .
. . I don't know what they kiss that book for gentlemen and then tell such
barefaced lies. . . . This is a mixed up affair and they would hang me if they
could.' The bench retired, but after deliberation said that Large might well
complain that he had a bad name seeing the list of previous convictions
against him. Large was sentenced to one month's imprisonment with hard
labour; if the costs of 19s 6d were not paid he was to remain in prison for
an additional fourteen days. It was hoped that being a young man he would
reform.

1931 *West Runton beach tragedy*. It seemed like a normal morning in the
Payne household. After tea with his wife Mabel in bed Jeremiah Payne
went to his allotment before breakfast, leaving Mabel to do some ironing
and their little daughter Alice in bed. When he returned home for
breakfast just before 7 a.m. both wife and child were nowhere to be found
and an ominous letter was left in the sitting room. Dashing out of the
house in search of his wife, Jeremiah went down to the beach, to find his
wife and child lying on the beach partly in the water. He and a neighbour
ran to the mother and child who had 'water dashing over them. Mother
had her right arm around the body of the child.' They pulled both out of
the water and a doctor and the police were sent for. Although artificial
respiration was given the little girl could not be revived. Mrs Payne was
constantly asking after her daughter and repeatedly said she was cold.
She was taken to hospital, where she recovered and was charged with
murder of her daughter and attempted suicide. After being cautioned Mrs
Payne stated: 'I don't remember anything about it. I remember someone
calling out, "What are you doing here?" and that is all I can remember
that morning.' During her trial at the Assizes strong medical evidence
was presented by doctors that she was of unsound mind. The jury found
the prisoner guilty, but insane, and the judge ordered her to be detained
'during His Majesty's pleasure'.

17 June   **1819**   At dawn on this date a small group of officials including a surgeon gathered in St Julian's churchyard, Norwich. Their purpose was to open the grave of an unnamed woman who had been buried within forty-eight hours of her death from smallpox. Noises were said to be heard emanating from her grave, and it was opened on the suspicion she had been buried alive. She was dead when exhumed, but was she dead when buried? Their findings were 'inconclusive'.

18 June   **1801**   The body of William Suffolk, who was executed in March 1797 for the murder of Mary Beck of North Walsham, was taken down by authority of the magistrates and interred on the spot near the scene of the crime where the gibbet had been erected.

THE

LAST DYING

Speech and Confeſſion,

OF

William Suffolk,

Who was executed this Day on the CASTLE-HILL, Norwich: For the moſt cruel and barberous Murder of MARY BECK, (who is to be hung in Chains near where the Murder was done.)

I WILLIAM SUFFOLK am in the forty-ſix year of my age, was born in the pariſh of Sweael, in the County of Norfolk, of poor but honeſt parents, following the employ of huſbandry, till this unhappy thing took place. Accordingly I became acquainted with Mary Beck, and having gone up and down the graſs countries for ſome years we cohabited together as man and wife; ſhe living near to me, we ſecretly carried on the wicked correſpondence together as we had done before, during which time ſhe fell with child by me, tho' unknown to the public; after this we went into the graſs countries again, where ſhe was delivered of her infant child, which I confeſs as a dying man, that ſhe and I was both confederate in the murder of the infant, tho' unknown to the world; therefore as a dying man I confeſs the juſtice of my ſentence being guilty of the murder.

She having ſold three buſhels of wheat, upon the return, I requeſted the money which ſhe refuſed to give me, telling me it was not her pronerty to give, for the owed it to her brother: I then aſk her why ſhe yield'd to me the night paſt, ſhe ſaid ſhe would not yield to me no more, nor be no more in my company. I then ſtroke her a blow with a cudgel I had in my hand, upon which ſhe fell to the ground; I than repeated the blows three times, and left her for dead for what I know: I then took and dragged her croſs the horſe-road, and left her head in the cart-rutt, ſuppoſing the people would think ſhe was kill'd by accident; but herein ſin and the devil deceived me, for no ſooner had I done it than I was forc'd to confeſs of the murder: But being harden'd in ſin I told the Juſtice if I got acquitted of this, I had two more to murder, and that was my Wife and the Brother of the deceaſed; but here I hope they will freely forgive me. My Mother has been dead a long time, but I have a poor aged Father now alive, a Wife and four poor little children, herein I

earneſtly beg that all good people would not caſt any reflection on them for my conduct. I die in peace with all mankind.   Witneſs my Hand

William Suffolk.

The awfull reflection on the horrid crime of murder, firſt murder committed with premeditated deſign is in general the laſt ſtage of a long courſe of wickedneſs, during which the villain is hardened by conſtant; practices, to ſuch a degree as to ſtop at nothing to obtain his purpoſes what ever they are, men of this diſcription tho' they perhaps may commit murder, but once in their lives, it is not from a ſence of its wickedneſs, for they are always capable of it, but from a dread of its conſequences, ſo certain is the truth of the old ſaying murder cannot be hid, that, they know that by committing this laſt and worſt of crimes, that they would ſum up their wickedneſs, and fill the meaſure of their iniquities: Secondly murder is frequantly the reſult of a ſuden impulſe of paſſion, proceeding from provecation, murder committed under ſuch circumſtances is in generally conſidered as leſs wicked, and people are apt to think the murderer rather unfortunate than guilty; eſpecialy it his former conduct of life has been without reproach, men that have ſo little guard over their paſſions, ſhould for the aſſiſting grace of God; otherwiſe they may ſome time commit a ſin of the moſt henious kind, the puniſhment of which is certain and ſevere. To conclude murder is the greateſt of crimes, as it render the perpetrator of it the abhorrence of his fellow creature, brings him unpitied to a ſhameful death, and above all draws down upon his guilty head the heavy diſpleaſure of Almighty God. Let us pray therefore leaſt we fall into temptation, either from diſhoneſty or paſſion, that may lead us to ſo dreadful a ſin.

1840 John Randalsome killed his wife in a fit of anger with a hedge stake at Thwaite. After hitting her about the head he threw her in a fish pond. Indicted at the Assizes on 3 August he was found guilty of the crime, and was executed on Norwich Castle Hill on 22 August.

1851 One of the strangest cases of murder in the history of Norwich was committed on or about this date. William Sheward was a shiftless, hard-drinking man who eked out a precarious existence as a tailor on Tabernacle Street. His wife, a woman considerably older than himself, was a querulous, nagging woman whom he stabbed to death with a pair of tailoring shears in a fit of rage. Nobody was surprised when he announced she had left him, and nobody appeared to connect her departure with the mysterious dismembered body parts which appeared distributed around the city and its outlying villages over the ensuing week or so. Her long hair was cut into small pieces that Sheward cast to the wind as he walked along; her head was never found. In 1862 he married again and worked as a pawnbroker on King Street. After

William Sheward going about his grisly business.

the failure of that business he did better as landlord of the Key and Castle Inn at St Martin at Oak. Eighteen years after the murder, while staying with his sister in Walworth for New Year his conscience pricked him and, probably stiffened by alchoholic indulgence, he walked into Walworth police station and confessed his crime. He tried to retract when sobered up but he had gone too far, and he was convicted and sentenced to death. He was one of the few criminals ever to be executed on the roof of the Norwich City Gaol outside St Giles Gates; this took place on 20 April 1869.

21 JUNE **Norfolk Old Dame's Leechcraft**
Warts or 'writs' are often got rid of by charms, which include the following. Rub them with a copper coin. Write the exact number of warts that afflict you on a piece of paper and bury it. Steal a piece of raw beef, rub it on the warts, then bury it – and as the meat decays the warts disappear. Take a 'dodderman' (snail), rub it over the warts and then impale it on a thorn bush. Gather an unripe sloe, rub it on the warts and throw it over the left shoulder. Make the sign of the cross on each wart with a needle or pin, and throw it away.

22 JUNE **1895** Discovered on this day, two bodies in Steam Mill dyke at Caister. The story emerged that George Stanford had drowned his fiancée Edith Mary Argyle, and then committed suicide by drowning himself.

23 JUNE **1846** PC William Callow of the Norwich Police died on this day, the first Norfolk police constable to die from injuries sustained in the course of his duty since the formation of the 'new police' in the county in 1836. Constable Callow's duty along with a number of fellow officers was to escort a large number of refractory paupers from the workhouse at St Andrew's Hill to the city gaol at St Giles Street. A jeering crowd of some 2,000 persons had assembled along the route, and large stones, bottles and sticks were thrown incessantly by the mob. A number of police officers were injured. The mob did not disperse, and when the policemen left the prison they were met once again by volleys of stones, and a full scale riot ensued. Under considerable pressure Inspector Peck gave the order 'right about face – quick march – go in for them.' Innocent people became embroiled in the mob, while people were trampled and shrieks of 'murder' were heard and another volley of stones followed. Several people sustained severe injuries, including Constables Barnard (spinal injuries), Day and Harman (head wounds) and Constable Callow, who died seven days later from his head wounds.

24 JUNE **1854** A case was reported on this day of the young daughter of a man named Sykes who was working on the New Estuary at King's Lynn. She was playing on her own on a gate at the further end of the estuary when her prolonged lack of movement drew concern. When folks arrived to see if all was well they were horrified to find the girl blue in the face and quite dead. The cause was clear. While playing on the gate she had become entangled in her own pinafore, and had strangled to death wrestling to extricate herself or summon assistance.

Norfolk Old Dame's Leechcraft

Epilepsy is cured, in the case of an unmarried woman by begging from nine bachelors as many silver coins – generally threepenny bits. These are made into a ring and worn by the sufferer on the fourth finger of the left hand. To cure a man, 'maidens must supply the needful'. A ring made of a half-crown from the communion offertory is also worn for the same purpose. The blood of a live mole dropped on a lump of sugar was believed to be a good treatment for fits.

1776   *An eighteenth-century advert for viagra?* 'Dr Becket's Sovereign Restorative Remedy, or cordial drops, which affords immediate powers, and gives vigour and abilities to either sex languishing under Debility, or relaxed causes which destroy the generative faculties. This excellent remedy, so high approved by the Most Eminent of the faculty, and recommended for their real virtue and excellence, they need no other econiums. So Sovereign a friend to nature are these Restorative or cordial drops, that they remove barrenness and produce fertility and conjugal felicity. Even old age and persons who have injured their constitutions by that unworthy practice self pollution are restored amazingly by taking them.' Restorative was sold in guinea and half-guinea bottles through agents in Norwich and by mail order.

1834   Died this date in Great Yarmouth at the great age of 92 Mrs Hannah Diboll, 'the celebrated twisterer'.

1853   The new cult of 'table-turning' or spiritualism was introduced in Norwich for the first time at a séance given at St Andrew's Hall by a Mr King.

1835   With the announcement that allowances to 'surplus poor' were to paid in kind instead of money, the labourers of Great Bircham and Bircham Tofts rioted upon the ground that the labourers had been imported from other villages. The houses of Mr Ketton and Mr Hebgin were attacked, and the mob did not disperse until the local Yeomanry arrived and quelled the riot. Ring leaders were hunted down, and sentences were meted out at the next Quarter Sessions at Walsingham.

Norfolk Old Dame's Leechcraft

Cramp is prevented by wearing a ring made out of gold coffin handles, or by placing one's boots or shoes by the bedside in the form of a cross tau, or by keeping a basin of spring water under the bed.

JUNE

(Norfolk Constabulary Archives)

Butter wouldn't melt? Henry Thomas Piper, alias Henry Thomas Scupps, a young lad of 16 who came to Norfolk from Stratford in search of work but turned to crime obtaining 9 convictions on 7 separate occasions between July 1888 and June 1893. Given a stern warning and 12 strokes of the birch for setting fire to two stacks of corn (despite his age, just over 50 years before he could have been hanged for this crime.) As he continued to offend his sentences got worse; 25 October 1889 stealing clothing, 10 days, 29 January 1890 stealing lead pipe, 28 days, 22 December 1890 refractory conduct in the workhouse and assault on workhouse inmate, 14 days, 11 January 1892 stealing lead, one month penal servitude, 11 May 1892 stealing books and a ham 10 months with hard labour and 5 June 1893 stealing purse and money, 12 months with hard labour. All of this before he was 21 years of age.

COUNTY OF NORFOLK.

PORTRAIT AND DESCRIPTION OF HABITUAL DRUNKARD.

Name	... WILLIAM CORBOULD.
Residence	... Wymondham
Place of business or where employed	... Wymondham
Age ...	... 50 years
Height ...	... 5 feet 6 ins.
Build ...	... Medium
Complexion ...	... Dark
Hair ...	... Dark
Eyes ...	... Brown
Whiskers ...	... Nil
Moustache ...	... Brown
Shape of Nose	... Broad
Shape of Face	... Round
Peculiarities or Marks ...	... Nil
Profession or occupation	...Labourer

Date and nature of conviction	...	3rd February, 1903—Drunk and Disorderly
Court at which convicted	...	Wymondham

N.B.—Should any known Habitual Drunkard attempt to purchase or obtain any intoxicating liquor at any premises licensed for the sale of intoxicating liquor by retail or at the premises of any registered Club it is requested that the licensed person or the person refusing to supply the liquor will, as soon as practicable, give information of such attempt to the Police of the District, in order that the law may be enforced.

(Norfolk Constabulary Archives)

JULY

Staff and Warders of Norwich Prison, *c.* 1905. *(Norfolk Constabulary Archives)*

1 JULY **1878** *Three cases of drowning at Norwich.* The inquest was held at the Cinder Ovens pub on King Street on the body of William King (aged 17), a solicitor's clerk who had bunked off Sunday school with Tom Harrod and hired one of Wright's rowing-boats, taking it to Bramerton. On the way back King stood up and put his coat on, overbalanced, and fell into the river. Despite other boats coming to the aid of the boys, poor Billy King sank struggling to the bottom and drowned. At the same inquest enquiry was made into the death of James Thomas Harris, a shoe manufacturer of Masons Yard, Ber Street, who was found in the river between the railway bridge and Trowse Hythe that very morning. He was known to be in low spirits and had lost money in a speculation. The jury were kind with the verdict 'Found drowned in the river without any marks of violence, but how he came to his death there was no evidence to show.' In the evening the deputy coroner held an inquest at the Gate House pub on Dereham Road concerning the death of Joseph Stebbings of Cross Street. The poor man had a paralysed arm and was in very low spirits. His brother stated that the family was convinced Joseph was 'in a deranged condition when he committed this sad act'. The jury decided 'that deceased committed suicide while of unsound mind'.

2 JULY **1788** Count Boruwlaski, the Polish dwarf, who stood just 3 ft 3 in high, exhibited himself in Norwich, and 'a liberal subscription was made' for him. Records state he was still alive and well in Durham in the 1820s, and although in his 80s was in 'excellent health and spirits, with perfect use of his limbs and faculties'.

3 JULY **1908** A most lamentable fatality occurred during some shunting operations at Trowse station of the GER before breakfast this day. The victim was an old man named John Walker, better known as 'Goodson', a point cleaner on the railway. At 7.25 a.m. while he was at his work a train caught Walker by his clothes and dragged him under the engine, 'cutting him to ribbons' and killing him instantly. The newspaper article concluded: 'A sad feature of this case was he was on the point of being pensioned off.'

4 JULY **1924** A report in the *EDP* today headed 'Murder and Suicide at Attleborough'. At Besthorpe, near Attleborough, neighbours were disturbed by a commotion. Forcing an entry to the house of Mr and Mrs Snelling, they found Mrs Snelling on the bed with her throat cut to such effect that her head was almost severed from her trunk. With Albert Snelling threatening to cut his own throat a local constable was summoned. On their return the neighbours found Mr Snelling had carried out his threat, but bloody evidence showed that he had paced up and down the room as he delivered the fatal cuts to himself.

5 JULY **1890** *Cheers!* The proceedings of the petty sessions held at Docking tell of William Osborne, charged on remand with manslaughter of William Wadlow by putting snuff in whisky and inducing him to drink it. The Bench informed

FULL ACCOUNT OF THE

Horrid Murder.

On Friday July 4th. Committed on the Body of J. AYTON, Steward to the Earl of Leicester, Holkham, by Geo. GROOM, Aged 32. Norfolk.

Norfolk has gained, and is likely to retain. an unenviable notoriety for crime of the deepest dye. The news of a cold-blooded murder, perpetrated at midday near the seat of the Earl of Leicester, has spread consternation throughout the north-western division of the country. From inquiries made on the spot we learn that the murdered man named John Ayton, 33 years of age, was employed by the Earl of Leicester as superintendent of extensive brick and tile works at Burnham Overy a distance of about a mile and a half from Holkham-hall. It was the usual custom of Ayton to go every alternate Friday, between 11 and twelve o'clock in the morning with a donkey and a cart to Holkham-hall. in order to receive money with which to pay the workpeople and other charges. On returning from the hall, Ayton had to proceed in a direct line through the park to the brickworks passing a small plantation, which enclosed a sandpit, at a short distance from the road side, and about a quarter of a mile from the park gate. The place is quite secluded, and well suited for a deed of blood. Lately a man named George Groom, 32 years of age, residing at Wells, which is about two miles from Holkham-hall, was employed at the brickworks: but being discharged, it is supposed that he entertained a revengeful feeling towards Ayton, though he was still employed as a farm labourer on the Holkham estate Groom was well aware of Ayton's custom of going to the hall to receive money, and also of the direction in which he returned, We learn, that on Friday last Ayton went as usual to the hall, arriving there between 12 and 1 o'clock, he received from Mr, Shellabear, the chief clerk to Mr. Keary, steward to the Earl of Leicester, the sum of £25 5s. 6d. consisting of sovereigns, half sovereigns, some silver and a 5l note of the bank of Messrs. Gurney. After receiving the money he proceeded along his usual route towards the brickworks, but did not arrive, as expected, to pay the men. after the time he should have arrived, a lad named Savory who was on a visit to his friends in the neighbourhood, and who had occasion to pass through the sandpit before mentioned to the farm of Mr.

Doggett. his uncle. saw as he supposed, a man asleep in the pit, and he incidentally mentioned this to four men in his uncle's service who were working in an adjoining field. These men then remembered that between half-past 1 and a quarter to 2 o'clock, they heard the report of firearms, and that they made some remarks to each other on the subject, but they thought nothing more of it. They requested the lad to go back in order to ascertain whether the man he had seen was really asleep or not, but the lad refused to do so not imagining he had seen a dead body At 5 o'clock in the evening one of the labourers saw Ayton's donkey and cart on the road leading from the plantation, and nobody driving. Thinking this very singular, and remembering what the lad had said, he went into the sandpit, and there saw Ayton lying on his side quite dead, and a small clot of blood on the sand There was a wound on the lower part of the back of the head. Dr. Young, of Wells who afterwards examined the body, found that at this wound there was a perforation into which he could introduce his finger at the back part of the head. Dr. Young, of Wells who was driving in his carriage with his three daughters, a labouring man named Joseph Kemp. and a shepherd saw him at different places not far from the spot where the body was found. In fact, he appears to have been watching for the victim. About 1 o'clock Dr. Young was passing the sandpit in his carriage, and he distinctly saw Groom who made an obeisance to him loitering at the entrance of the pit. Dr. Young remarked to his eldest daughter, " That is a Wells man.", having knowing him for some time and attended to his family. The shepherd had seen him running near the plantation, and stooping, as if he wished to avoid being seen. After the time when the shots were heard the shepherd saw him again near the sandpit, and he brushed past the shepherd, with his head hanging down, George Lumley a constable of Wells went to Groom's house found him there at his tea and took him into custody without saying anything to him till they reached the constable's house. On being searched a 5l. note of the bank of Messrs Gurney was found in his possession. When the prisoner was asked how the note came into his possession he said that he had found it about a fortnight before. A watch which belonged to the murdered man also was found on Groom's person. Thus a variety of circumstances tended to prove that Groom was the murderer. On the same evening he was taken before the Rev, R Collyer, examined, and reminded to Walsingham prison. Dr. Young evidence was given afterward he was fully committed for trial at the ensuing assizes.

W. Broadhurst Printer Norwich.

Henry Groom poster, 1851. Groom murdered Ayton at Burnham Thorpe on 4 July and was indicted on 28 July. He was executed on 16 August.

Mr Wilkin, who defended, that the authorities did not consider it necessary to proceed further with the charge of manslaughter, but Osborne was to be charged with misdemeanour and was bailed to appear at the next Assizes.

6 JULY **1887** Brought before the court at Norwich Guildhall, William Winter (aged 35) of St Saviour's Lane was charged with being drunk and disorderly and of assaulting PC Brown at Stump Cross the preceding Monday evening.

Police tackling some of the 'riff-raff type'.

The prisoner, who was defended, appeared adorned with two black eyes. PC Brown had told Winter on several occasions to leave but he had refused to do so. The policeman arrested him, and in response to this Winter struck the constable on the chest, seized him by the waist and threw him to the ground. Maintaining hold of his prisoner, Brown rose again but was lifted off his feet and dashed to the ground again with much force and kicked repeatedly. The whistle he drew to summon assistance was torn from his grasp and thrown into the gathering crowd 'of the riff-raff type'. Undaunted by the crowd, PC Brown with the assistance of two others was able to cuff Winter. Two more constables were soon on the scene and truncheons were drawn to keep the crowd from rescuing the prisoner, who was causing as much trouble as he could in his cuffed state.

In the sober setting of the court the only defence Winter could give was that he was 'in drink'. The prisoner was sent down for 14 days, and a further 14 if the costs of 19s were not paid.

7 JULY **1865** The death of Sarah Hunnabell – the woman who almost burnt down Great Yarmouth Tolhouse. Married to William Hunnabell, a local butcher, and mother of one child, her profession was listed in the Gaol Book as 'prostitute'. Admitted to the Tolhouse on several accounts of petty crimes including 'attempting to strike her husband', 'stealing two shifts' and 'running away from workhouse with apparel not hers', she was incarcerated in February 1856 on suspicion of stealing money. At 10.45 on the night of 19 March 1856, after she had been administered to by the doctor and was believed to be settled for the night, the gaoler, Mr Giles, was summoned to Hunnabell's cell by a bell and discovered it on fire. The fire could have easily spread if not for the presence of mind of Mr Giles, who extinguished it. On 21 March Hunnabell was recorded throwing her food about, and shouting that she hoped she would be in hell by 10 o'clock. Staff were fearful for her state of mind, so her hair was cropped and cooled to soothe the pain in her head and a nurse was placed to watch over her. Confessing on 31 March to firing her bed with a Lucifer and a piece of paper, Hunnabell was removed to Norwich and tried for setting fire to the gaol. Found guilty, sentence of death was ordered, but the judge insisted that she should be detained 'at Her Majesty's Pleasure' instead. She died back in Yarmouth Tolhouse Gaol aged about 45, nine years later.

1908 **8 JULY** The inquest upon the body of Lily Eliza Gooke (aged 41) at Great Yarmouth Town Hall was reported on this day. Wife of William George Gooke, carter of Elsie Terrace, Cobholm Road, she had died after a premature birth (the child was born dead) on the morning of Sunday 5th. A registered midwife, Mrs Snowling, had been sent for; she did not arrive in time for the birth but attended to the deceased. The concluding comments give an insight into mortality and the reasons for large families in this period: 'The deceased had had 18 children counting the last, only five were now alive.'

1836 **9 JULY** Mr J. Gotobed, one of the proprietors of the Lynn coach, was fined £50 for driving away the coach after it had been seized by HM Officers of Excise for conveying contraband spirits.

1888 **10 JULY** *Not Again!* Everson Lovett, a bricklayer of Bird Yard, Heigham Street, was charged before the Norwich Guildhall bench with being drunk and disorderly and with assaulting PC Brown on Barn Road. The officer found Lovett drunk and surrounded by a crowd, and asked him to go away. Lovett refused to move, struck PC Brown across the face and threw him to the ground. The constable produced his handcuffs to restrain the man but these were ripped from his grasp by the crowd. PC Brown then took out his truncheon, which was also taken from him. While on the ground, poor old PC Brown was kicked in the ribs by one of the crowd and the prisoner, rescued by the mob, proceeded to make his getaway. Brown got up and gave chase, but on apprehending Lovett a second time Brown was thrown to the ground again and kicked in the legs. Making his getaway he ran into PC Watts, who managed to restrain the violent man Brown made the arrest and, despite the crowd of about 50 people's attempts at intervention, Lovett was taken into custody with the assistance of a further four constables. Lovett was sentenced to two calendar months' imprisonment with hard labour, and a further seven days if he failed to pay fees of 8s 6d.

11 JULY   **1587**   Of uncertain date, from the ancient court records of King's Lynn in 1587. 'Carted' as common prostitutes were one Widow Porker, 'A Hoare', and another woman described as 'the wife John Wanker'. Her husband was suggested not to be true master of his house or bedchamber. I wonder if this led to a term of derision still familiar today?

12 JULY   **1851**   The Yarmouth Magistrates issued a warrant 'to apprehend the bodies of George Danby Palmer and James Cherry, charged on the oath of William Norton Burroughes with being about to commit a breach of the peace by fighting a duel'. The incident arose out of an extraordinary scene at a public meeting where 'Mr Palmer gave the lie to Mr Cherry.'

13 JULY   **1806**   Two servant girls tied themselves together with ribbon, walked into the sea at Great Yarmouth and were drowned. They were the wives of privates in the Shropshire Militia who had come to see them the previous day and refused to permit them to return with them, after which the girls committed 'the rash act'.

14 JULY   **1835**   A handbill was circulated in Norwich announcing that 'the Dutch Hercules, Mynheer Kousewinkeler van Raachboomstadt, professor of gymnastics and Maître des Armes to the 5th Regiment of Royal Jaagers', would give his 'celebrated series of gymnastic exercises' in Chapel Field. Some 1,000 people turned up to see this spectacle, finding much to their displeasure it was all a hoax!

15 JULY   **1828**   William Sutliffe appeared at Norwich City Sessions indicted for assaulting Lydia Bugg of Ber Street. Miss Bugg's account told of how she had visited the Marquis of Granby in Bishopgate and the King's Arms on the day of the fair and had had a drink with the accused. Going home with her friend

Ruth Blyth she saw the accused and another man running towards them when passing through St Pauls. She reassured her friend that 'they won't hurt us', but when Sutliffe drew near her he knocked her down 'and wished to take liberties'. When Miss Bugg refused he said 'Blast you then I'll drown you!' and rolled her into the river. She crawled out and called for help and held out her hand to a passer-by but Sutliffe struck her again, backwards into the water. She cried for mercy and called out 'Murder' as he threw her in again head first, saying 'there you B–, I'll drown you.' She then passed out, but was rescued by two passers-by and came to her sense kneeling in the water. Constable Bullard, who lived nearby, called his wife and they took the girl in to recover. With the assistance of another the constable then carried her to her home, as she was soaked through and could not walk. Found guilty but pleading he was drunk, Sutliffe was sentenced to two years' imprisonment.

1887 The new prison opened on Plumstead Road, Norwich, on this day. Built in 1886–7 by the government to replace Norwich Castle and the old City Gaol, this was to be a prison for both the county and the city. Standing in extensive walled grounds, the building was built on the approved system of one long building with three floors of cells, the upper floors reached by galleries so that complete supervision could be exercised. It housed most categories of prisoners, male and female, and executions were carried out here until 1951. Norwich Prison is still in use today.

16 JULY

Staff and Warders of Norwich Prison, *c.* 1905. *(Norfolk Constabulary Archives)*

17 JULY   **1841**   John Self (aged 20) killed Jemima Simpson (aged 15) of Wymondham by striking her on the head with a spade, and afterwards threw her body in a duckpond. Brought to account at the Norfolk Assizes on 28 July and found guilty he was sentenced to death, a penalty he suffered on Norwich Castle Hill on 14 August.

18 JULY   **1816**   *Trial for the first recorded instance of machine-breaking in Norfolk.* Four labourers were found guilty for riotously assembling with 100 other persons at Hockham on 19 May and destroying a thrashing machine, the property of William Burlingham. Two of the prisoners got 12 months, the others three months, and all were required to find sureties for their future behaviour.

19 JULY   **1951**   *The last execution in Norfolk, carried out behind closed doors at Norwich Prison.* This occasion saw two men executed side by side for similar but unconnected crimes – they had both killed their pregnant sweethearts. Dennis Moore was 22, two weeks away from marriage to his fiancée Eileen Cullen. They had rowed, and he had strangled her in a cow shed at Catton, near Norwich. Instantly regretting his foul deed he telephoned the police. Thinking the call a stupid prank, a police officer arrived at the scene poorly prepared to deal with the situation that confronted him. The officer told Moore to 'Wait there' at the shed while he went to the nearest house to summon assistance. Moore was still there when he returned, and went very quietly. Alfred Reynolds was 24: he had shot his girlfriend, 19-year-old Ellen Ludkin, at Dereham five days after the Cullen murder. Reynolds claimed it was a suicide pact gone wrong. Having thought it over he confessed all. The jury took just 40 minutes to decide, and he was on his way to the executioner too. Public executioners Albert Pierrepoint and Syd Dernley assisted by Harry Allen and Les Stuart were engaged to dispatch Reynolds and Moore respectively. Syd Dernley recorded the event in his memoirs as 'a completely unremarkable execution, about which I was extremely thankful, as no doubt were the prison authorities at Norwich'.

20 JULY   **1833**   A duel was fought on the North Denes, Great Yarmouth. 'The combatants were Mr. H. B– and Mr. C. W–, the former seconded by Mr J. B– and the latter by Mr W. C–, of the medical profession in Norwich. At the first shot Mr W's pistol missed, and his antagonist fired in the air. At the second Mr B again fired in the air and Mr W missed his aim. Another try took place, Mr W missing and Mr B shooting skyward. On the fourth and last, Mr W's ball just grazed Mr B's thumb, when the parties appeared to have been satisfied, for they shortly after left the ground. The cause of the meeting arose at Maxim's Marine Hotel on the beach.'

21 JULY   *A poaching case at Norwich Shirehall.*
George Bunn of Arabian Horse Yard, St Martin's, was summoned for having game in his possession at Rackheath. Inspector Eagling stated that early on

Trial, Execution, and Confession, of John Self, For the wilful Murder of Jemima Stimpson, which took place on Saturda Aug. 14, 1841.

JOHN SELF, aged 20, was placed at the bar charged with having on the 17th of July, in the parish of Wymondham, Murdered Jemima Stimpson, single woman,

The prisoner on being arraigned, was found guilty. and received the awful sentence of Death.

CONFESSION OF JOHN SELF.

About nine o'clock in the morning of the day of the murder, Jemima Stimpson passed him on her way from a neighbouring cottage to her work. A few words passed between them of only common import. At his dinner hour he walked to her and found her seated on a bank. He sat down by her side. She had a knife in her hand. He asked her to let him look at it. He took it and put it into his pocket, and said he should keep it. He began to play with her, and after a time took hold of her clothes in a manner that she much resented, threatening to tell her mother of it and to expose him. He desisted, and denies having at any time violated her person. He returned to his work, and brooding over the threat, first thought of murdering her if she would not retract it. At four o'clock he left off work, and met her near the fatal spot after they had got over the gap he enquired whether she still intended to tell her mother. She replied yes, and that she would mob him for it wherever she met him. He said then she would tell nothing but lies, and he took her by the throat. She said she would tell her mother that he graned her. Upon this he threw her down and struck her with his spade, and repeated the blows till he supposed he had killed her. She shrieked after the first blow, he believes but once. He then took her by her heels and dragged her on her back to the pond, and threw her into a part of it that was not deep. He returned to the place of the murder, and finding there her hat and apron, in which she had tied up some sticks, he took and hid them in an adjoining field, and then returned for his spade. When he came back, he saw to his great surprise the poor girl sitting on the margin of the pond, about two yards from it, The blood was running from her wounds. She fixed her eyes on him, but neither cried out nor spoke. He again took her by her heels and dragged her as before. On the way she caught hold of the grass and clinched it in her hands. He threw her into another part of the pond, and put his spade upon her neck to keep her under the water; and after a short interval he pushed her with it into the middle of the pond, and left her with her head and mouth more especially above the surface. The whole of this latter scene of the horrid transaction did not occupy according to his account much more than a minute. He denies having struck her in this second attack, except in thrusting the spade upon her neck, and say that he saw the wound which was described as more immediately causing her death, when she was sitting on the side of the pond. On being asked whether he was sure she did not shriek during this part of the murder, he hesitated and said he did not remember that she did, which might be the case in the hurry, confusion and agitation that must necessarily have accompanied the whole of this horrid deed The bloody cloth which was found, was what it was sworn to be, a nd the stocking was his father's. The blood on his trowsers belonged to the poor girl, but the stain on his hat was not the stain of blood.

JOHN SELF was a labourer at Wymondham and bore an excellent character as a kind-hearted and industrious youth, up to the time of his committing the dreadful crime of murder, at all times an appalling offence; but rendered still more horrible in his case, by the reckless cruelty with which he treated his innocent and unoffending victim Jemima Stimpson; and which he expiated with his life this day upon the scaffold— The prisoner was led from his Cell to the drop at the usual hour, calm, and resigned to his fate; and after the ordinary time spent in fervent prayer with the excellent Chaplain of the gaol, the fatal bolt was withdrawn and the unhappy youth after a short struggle ceased to exist— thus ignominiously perished in the dawn of manhood, one who might have been the stay, comfort, and protector of his parents. after hanging the usual time his body was taken down and buried within the precincts of the prison.

Thus we see the evil of sin, by the death of another of our fellow creatures, who allowed Satan to rouse his worst passions to destroy every humane principle, and by one act of almost unexampled atrocity and wickedness he brutally sent a fellow creature unprepared to meet her God with all her sins upon her head—Dear Reader beware of sin! remember "do unto others as you would they should do unto you" is the great moral, safe guard against the tempter of mankind—had the Criminal John Self sufficiently studied this divine command he might still have been happy in the affections and regard of his family and friends. It is Sin, and Satan that are the principle ringleaders in this dreadful affair, Sin naturally breeds distempers, and destruction in the soul—what a continual tempest and commotion is there in a discontented mind! what a baneful evil and inordinate care! What is passion but a very fever of the brain? What is pride but a deadly tyranny? or covetousness, but an insatiable, and insufferable thirst? or malice an envy but venom in the heart? And how can that soul have true comfort that is under so many diseases? Cursed is that peace that is maintained in a way of sin!—Sin, O the work that sin hath made in the world! this is the enemy that hath brought in death, and hath robbed and enslaved men, that hath backed the Devil, that hath digged Hell; and sown dissension between man and his creator;

The prisoner was visited on Monday last by his heartbroken and weeping relations—He said mother—do not weep—I know I have shortened your days—but mother I trust in the merits of our blessed Redeemer that we shall meet in heaven—you will stay but a short time behind, I have made my peace with God. I have seen both you and my Saviour in my lonely Cell—(The mother now wept bitterly) Do n t cry mother for we shall meet I trust in the arms of our blessed Saviour—when turning to his father—well father how are you?—Do not weep for me—bring up my brothers, and sisters in the love and fear of the Lord—I pray that my poor murdered victim may meet the forgiveness of Christ—the wretched man parted with his unhappy parents for ever in this world—The mother more dead than alive was conveyed from the prison. supported by her sorrowing husband—Thus reader you see the amount of misery inflicted by one living mortal—again, Beware of sin!

Sinner stop! I pray take heed
A lesson learn from this my wicked deed,
Which with shuddering frame I tell,
Whilst laying in my mournful cell.

Although I doomed another not to live,
And brutally took a life the Lord had pleased
   to give,
In this my dismal cell I humbly crave,
My Saviour will a repentant sinner save.

It was in misfortune's darkening hour,
Satan triumphed, and o'er me gained power,
My senses gone, the fell fiend succeed,
Madly did I committed this dreadful deed.

A guilty conscience accuses me,
In frightful dreams I think I see,
My tortured victim writhing on the ground
Whilst crimson gore pours from every
   wound.

Again I see her with imploring eyes,
And hands outstretched pointing to the Skies
She piteously implores her life to spare,
And cries Oh Self! think of our father there.

How shall I meet my Saviour dear,
When before him in awful judgment I appear,
Let my last moments to earnest prayer be
   given,
That our prayers Lord may pardon me in
   Heaven.

Justly denied all mercy by my Judges here,
I humbly crave a pardon there,
Kind Christians all I pray forgive,
The wretch by law doom'd not to live.

God grant these verses may a warning be,
Unto all them that hear of me.
Dare not to take that which you cannot give,
Think of John Self—be warned—and happy
   live.

Walker, Printer, White-Hart St. Miles's, Norwich.

(Norfolk Local Studies Library)

the 8th he was in the company of Sgt Chambers at Rackheath when they met Bunn, another named Smith and a third man driving a cart. Having his suspicions aroused by the three dogs in the back, he stopped the cart. The third man ran for it and his obedient dogs followed. On searching Smith, Inspector Eagling found in his pocket two old partridges and a rabbit, all of which were quite warm and had the appearance of being recently killed. Smith's legs were wet and muddy. A pouch containing shot was found on Bunn, and in the cart was a single barrel gun loaded and capped. The gun seemed to have been fired recently. Smith did not account for his possession of the game but Bunn said the gun was his property. Bunn was fined £5 with 1s 6d costs, or one month if in default; the gun was ordered to be sold. Bunn was removed to custody, remarking that he could not pay 6d if they killed him.

22 JULY **1868** The last day of a ten day show of Chang, the Chinese giant. At the time aged 22, he was claimed to stand nearly 9 ft in height and was publicised as 'the largest man in the world'. He was accompanied by his wife King-Foo, and they were exhibited at the Old Corn Hall, Great Yarmouth.

23 JULY **1803** Two men named Denny and Allen were placed in the pillory at Norwich, in accordance with the sentence passed on them at the Assizes for conspiracy against Mr F. Latham. Over their heads was hung the inscription 'false conspirators'. Allen wept bitterly when he was put in but Denny, with great effrontery, continued to nod and smile at the numerous spectators until the people, by a shower of rotten eggs and potatoes, convinced him of their detestation and abhorrence of his character and crime. After an hour of such abuse Denny appeared to faint, and was removed on the advice of a medical man back to gaol. The gaol surgeon decreed that he found him to be in a fit state to stand in the pillory, but on his return he apparently fainted again. All efforts to reinstate him failed so they laid him over the pillory for an hour 'amidst the execrations of the enraged multitude'. Once time was expired both men were removed to the Bridewell to undergo two years' imprisonment.

24 JULY **1665** A triple event: convicted felons Thomas Peirson, George Thornton and Thomas Voucher were hung on this day in the Norwich Castle ditches.

25 JULY **1776** *A miracle cure!* 'Sutton's Alternative Pills for various Chronic Complaints which from several years of practice, and numerous repeated Trials have been found an effectual Remedy for the following diseases: The Leprosy, scurvy, King's Evil, Cancer, Contractions in the joints, pains in the bones, whether Rheumatic, Venerial, Gouty or Scorbutic, Flour Alous and Female Obstructions; they greatly promote the healing of ulcers, Fistulas and other Wounds and are of great service in the Gravel and most obstinate Chronic Diseases. . . . By appointment of the proprietor they are sold at the following places viz. Chase at Norwich; Eaton in Yarmouth; Hollingworth and Son at Lynn and Shave at Ipswich in bottles at half a guinea, five shillings and three pence each with proper directions.'

1788 Thomas Hardy was executed in the Norwich Castle ditches for murder. 26 JULY
Once his life was expired he was cut down and his body delivered to surgeons
for dissection.

Hogarth's observation
of a body delivered to
the surgeons.

1886 Reported today a case of squalor at Great Ryburgh at Fakenham 27 JULY
Petty Sessions. This is an account of an all too familiar scenario reported to
petty sessions across Norfolk at the time. Robert Nelson of Great Ryburgh
was summoned by Charles Swann of Fakenham, Inspector of Nuisances
of the Walsingham Union, with allowing a nuisance to exist: cottage was
so overcrowded as to be injurious to the health of the inhabitants. The
complainant said the defendant's cottage was in Fenn's Yard. The family,
consisting of the wife and five children, lived and slept in one small lean-to,

THE FAKENHAM GHOST,

By ROBERT BLOOMFIELD.

THE lawns were dry in Euston Park;
  (Here truth inspires my tale)
The lonely footpath, still and dark,
  Led over hill and dale.

Benighted was an ancient dame,
  And fearful haste she made,
To gain the vale of Fakenham,
  And hail its willow shade.

Her footsteps knew no idle stops,
  But follow'd faster still;
And echo'd to the darksome copse
  That whisper'd on the hill;

Where clam'rous rooks, yet scarcely hush'd,
  Bespoke a peopled shade;
And many a wing the foliage brush'd,
  And hov'ring circuits made.

The dappled herd of grazing deer
  That sought the shades by day,
Now started from her path with fear,
  And gave the stranger way.

Darker it grew; and darker fears
  Came o'er her troubled mind:
When now a short quick step she hears
  Come patting close behind.

She turn'd; it stopt!—nought could she see
  Upon the gloomy plain!
But as she strove the sprite to flee,
  She heard the same again.

Now terror seiz'd her quaking frame;
  For, where the path was bare,
The trotting ghost kept on the same!
  She mutter'd many a pray'r.

Yet once again, amidst her fright,
  She tried what sight could do;
When, thro' the cheating glooms of night,
  A MONSTER stood in view.

Regardless of whate'er she felt,
  It follow'd down the plain!
She own'd her sins, and down she knelt,
  And said her pray'rs again.

Then on she sped: and hope grew strong,
  The white park-gate in view;
Which pushing hard, so long it swung
  That ghost and all pass'd through.

Loud fell the gate against the post!
  Her heart-strings like to crack:
For, much she fear'd the grisly ghost
  Would leap upon her back.

Still on, pat, pat, the goblin went,
  As it had done before:—
Her strength and resolution spent,
  She fainted at the door.

Out came her husband, much surpris'd:
  Out came her daughter dear:
Good-natur'd souls! all unadvis'd
  Of what they had to fear.

The candle's gleam pierc'd thro' the night,
  Some short space o'er the green;
And there the little trotting sprite
  Distinctly might be seen.

An *Ass's Foal* had lost its dam
  Within the spacious park;
And, simple as the playful lamb,
  Had follow'd in the dark.

No goblin he; no imp of sin;
  No crimes had ever known.
They took the shaggy stranger in,
  And rear'd him as their own.

His little hoofs would rattle round
  Upon the cottage-floor:
The matron learn'd to love the sound
  That frighten'd her before.

A favourite the ghost became;
  And, 'twas his fate to thrive:
And long he liv'd, and spread his fame,
  And kept the joke alive.

For many a laugh went thro' the vale;
  And some conviction too:—
Each thought some other goblin tale,
  Perhaps, was just as true.

THIS Poem, which the Artist has selected for the above Plate, is founded on a fact; and though the circumstance occurred, perhaps, long before the author was born, yet, he says, it is related by his mother, and some of the oldest inhabitants in the county of Norfolk. A desire of contributing, as much as is in his power, to the eradication of the ridiculous notions too often imbibed in early life, of ghosts, goblins, and such visionary beings, he hopes, will be a sufficient apology for his attempting to increase, if possible, the popularity of this pleasant tale.

Published 15th July, 1805, by LAURIE and WHITTLE, No. 53, Fleet Street, London.

A little tale on a broadsheet from the borders of Norfolk and Suffolk. (*Norfolk Local Studies Library*)

which measured 5 ft by 10 ft. The children were in a very dirty state, being completely covered in vermin. The Bench ordered the nuisance to be abated within 14 days and the defendant to pay 10s 6d costs.

1823   John Locke of Larling died today at the ripe old age of 110. He left behind him a total of 130 children and grandchildren.

28 JULY

1886   *Shocking boating accident on the Yare.* At the Coroner's Inquest at the Waterman's Arms on King Street witnesses gave accounts of the fatal incident. After viewing the bodies Frank Sabberton, engineer of *The Arrow*, a small steam pleasure boat, identified the bodies of Mr Moses Levine (owner of the boat) Mr George Woods and Mr Gay. He also recounted there were three other men on board including himself. Emphasizing they were not overloaded Sabberton stated they had set out on the river from Thorpe Station at two to go to Whitlingham to get up steam, then re-started from Thorpe Gardens to go to Bramerton – once they got through the bridge near the Marl Stage at Whitlingham the large pleasure boat SS *Jenny Lind* overtook them drawing the smaller *Arrow* into her side with the wash of water. Mr Nobbs, who was steering the *Arrow* put the tiller towards the *Jenny Lind* to keep the bows off but this simply drew the stern of *Arrow* under the bigger boat. The occupants in the fore part of *Arrow* attempted to push her off the large steamer but in doing so the little boat filled with water and went down dragging Levine and Woods with it while the rest of the occupants clambered on to the *Jenny Lind*. The river police were summoned and an hour later the drags were out and the bodies recovered. Other witnesses who were on board the *Jenny Lind* were called and more or less the stories tallied. After careful deliberation over 26 minutes the jury returned the verdict of accidental death on all casualties with no blame attached to anyone.

29 JULY

JENNY LIND STEAMBOAT COMPANY.

EXCURSION TRIPS

ON THE RIVER YARE.

FINEST SCENERY IN THE NEIGHBOURHOOD.

From YARMOUTH TO NORWICH AND BACK every Week-day except Saturday (unforeseen circumstances excepted), commencing July 26th until further notice.

A Special Trip every Sunday to BRAMERTON and BACK, leaving Yarmouth Bridge at 9·15 a.m., and returning at 4 p.m. FARE 1s. 6d.

The fine Saloon Screw Steamer CITY OF NORWICH, built expressly for this serpentine River, fitted throughout with Electric Light and every accommodation, the Saloon being upholstered and most spacious, leaves Hall Quay, Yarmouth, at 9·15 a.m. Returning from Norwich at 3·45 p.m.

RETURN FARE—2s. SINGLE—1s. 6d.

Monday, Tuesday, and Friday, August 2nd, 3rd, and 6th, EXCEPTED.

Refreshments of First-Class quality on Board.

Advert for the Jenny Lind Steamboat Co, 1886.

1907   In the early hours of this morning in Edgefield one William Jacobs was discovered by off duty Parish Constable Walter Ford in his neighbour's back garden. A man who had been displaying 'erratic and unexplainable traits', Jacobs was humoured by the constable who joined him in the adjoining garden to be 'converted'. Suddenly and without warning Jacobs threw Constable Ford to the ground and repeatedly stabbed him 'like a man possessed'. Mrs Ford, who had observed this, screamed for assistance. The neighbour, George Batchelor, rushed into the garden when he heard the call. Batchelor grappled with Jacobs but was beaten back, suffering slash cuts to his head. Constable Ford, although mortally wounded, crawled across the garden to help, but he collapsed before he could further intervene. By now other villagers had rushed to the scene and made his escape but not before further stabbing attacks on the dying constable. Constable Ford died of his wounds at 6 o'clock that morning. Inspector

30 JULY

Robert Flint and Constable Moore were summoned from Holt, and shortly afterwards Jacobs was found hiding in a garden shed; he was taken into custody without incident. They visited Jacobs' home where he lived with his father to find the old man with his head cleft through by a meat cleaver. Placed on the conveyance to Holt police station Jacobs laughed heartily and threw his cap in the air. Taken to Beckham Workhouse, he was placed in custody as being insane.

30 JULY *The Revd Harold Davidson, 'The Prostitutes' Padre'.*
Harold Francis Davidson was born on 14 July 1875 in the dreary Southampton suburb of Sholing where his father Francis was long-time vicar. Twenty-seven members of his family had taken Holy Orders, and it was almost assumed that young Harold would follow suit. After graduating from Exeter College, Oxford, Harold served as curate at Holy Trinity, Windsor, and as Assistant Chaplain to the Household Cavalry. Transferring to St Martins-in-the Fields he left after only a year and at the age of 26 became rector at Stiffkey. He married Molly Saurin, daughter of a rich Irish landowner, and they had four children (two boys and two girls) in quick succession, but sadly married bliss turned sour and they argued as Harold increasingly spent more time in London than at home.

Harold was a dapper little man of 5 ft 3 in with piercing blue eyes. The people of Stiffkey by and large accepted his unusual lifestyle and affectionately knew him as 'Little Jimmy'. Their only jibe was that it was best not to die on a Monday, especially in the summer, for one's remains got pretty high by the time the rector returned from London the following weekend to take the funeral! Appointed chaplain to the Actors' Church Union, he was given access to every dressing room – and every actress. His desire to help young prostitutes put him in danger from their ponces when he stood up to their fists and flick knives. Some of the saved fallen women were even brought back to Stiffkey and treated as members of the family – much to the bemusement of the locals.

His work in this area eventually got him into trouble with Church hierarchy following a malicious complaint placed about his 'immoral behaviour', sent to the Bishop of Norwich. When he was banned from his parish churches people still came to hear him preach on vicarage lawns. Sadly, the legal snowball kept rolling and grew; a Consistory Court case which fascinated the country ensued, and ended with Davidson being defrocked in 1932.

Protesting his innocence, Davidson took his story on the road with fairgrounds and circuses, where he was to be found drawing large crowds arguing his case and reading the Bible from a barrel. His death was as dramatic as his life. He had a side show called 'A Modern Daniel in the Lion's Den', a popular display in which Harold put his head in the lion's mouth. One day the act went wrong and Freddie the lion mauled Harold; removed to hospital, the Prostitutes' Padre died of his wounds two days later on 30 July 1937.

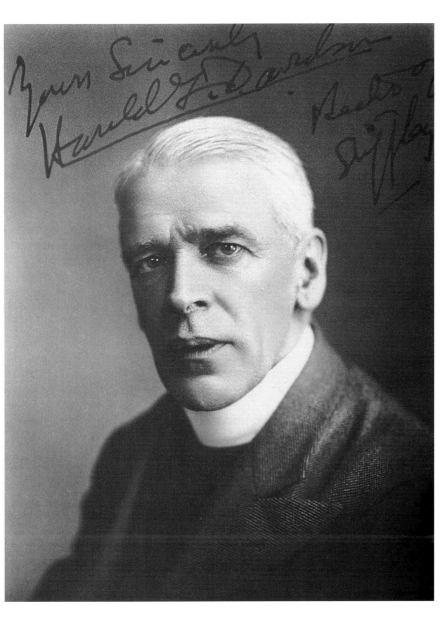

The Revd Harold
Davidson. *(Geoffrey
Scott Collection)*

1807 Martha Alden executed at Norwich Castle for the murder of her husband   **30 JULY**
on 18 July. The facts of the case given at her trial were that while her husband
was asleep in bed his wife inflicted terrible wounds on his head, face and throat
with a bill hook. The next day, with the assistance of a girl named Mary Orvice,
Mrs Alden deposited the body in a dry ditch in the garden. On the 20th they
carried it in a corn sack to the common and 'shot' it into a pond, where it was
subsequently discovered. Orvice was severely warned but was not prosecuted,
while Mrs Alden was given the ultimate sentence: 'to be drawn on a hurdle to the

place of execution, there to be hanged by the neck, and her body dissected'. The populace of Attleborough showed their detestation of the crime by destroying the prisoner's house. It was later reported that Alden's ghost 'walked' the Castle Hill, and in December 1807 a party of drunken men went to 'lay' the spirit, but were seized by the jailer and detained in prison for two days pending an enquiry into their conduct.

31 JULY Before the advent of fingerprinting as an effective means of proving a suspect was present at the scene of a crime or had held an incriminating weapon (Scotland Yard fingerprint bureau was founded in 1901, the first conviction based on fingerprints was in 1902) all manner of methods were employed to keep tabs on and identify criminals. Our subject here is Samuel Lodge, pictured in an early attempt at criminal photography in Norfolk. His head and profile are photographed simultaneously with the aid of a mirror. He holds his hands in a contrived position to show he has all his fingers; if he had any distinguishing marks on his hands these would also have shown

(Norfolk Constabulary Archives)

up. Lodge was a notorious Yarmouth rogue whose previous convictions were such that a page from the Assize 'Calendar' was cut out and pasted on the page with all his previous appearances in court and convictions to save time listing the deeds of this recidivist in the more traditional longhand. Over the course of 20 years Lodge amassed a catalogue of convictions which included furious driving, cruelty to animals, stealing turkeys, sporting with dogs on a Sunday, stealing watches and money, using obscene language, assault and poaching.

AUGUST

PC Charles Alger, fatally shot in the line of duty at Gorleston on 18 August 1909. *(Norfolk Constabulary Archives)*

Matthew Hopkins, Witchfinder General pictured on the woodcut which accompanied his book *The Discovery of Witches* written '. . . in answer to severall Queries lately delivered to the Judges of Assize for the County of Norfolk' in 1647. Prosecutions and punishments for witchcraft in Norfolk can be found recorded as far back as 1279 when John de Warham was fined 12d by the Court Leet at King's Lynn for scratching a witch's face. Although never as common as English popular history may infer, witch persecutions and trials grew in frequency in Norfolk towards the end of the sixteenth century. Typical of this case type was the prosecution of Elizabeth Butler and Celia Atkin. Found guilty of witchcraft in March 1582 by the Yarmouth Sessions Court they were sentenced to stand in the pillory in the market place until they confessed their guilt. Elizabeth was obstinate and would not confess and after several 'stands' in the pillory 'as an example to others' appeared again before the judges in April 1584 where she was sentenced along with another woman named Joan Lingwood to be hanged for witchcraft.

During war popular fears are far more easily stirred up into frenzies or 'scares,' ports and coastal areas are always more susceptible to notions from the continent so it is no surprise the mass persecutions of witches covens in the Germany would rub off on East Anglia. One name rises above all from this time, that of Matthew Hopkins the self-styled 'Witchfinder General' who claimed to have in his possession 'the Devil's list of all English witches.' Often targeting lonely old widows Hopkins and his small team of 'searchers' would prick the bodies of suspected witches to find 'The Devil's Tit' an area insensible to pain from which he alleged the witches' familiar would suckle blood. Physical torture was not allowed but every other means was used by Hopkins to extract confessions including severe sleep depravation, solitary confinements and tying those accused cross-legged for days. Although working mainly in Essex and Suffolk Hopkins worked in Norfolk on a number of occasions. One account states that during his employment at Norwich in 1645 he saw to it 40 witches tried at the Assizes, and King's Lynn paid him £15 for his services.

In September 1645 Hopkins concluded his Norfolk circuit with a visit to Great Yarmouth where he saw to it eleven people (two of whom were men) appeared before the Sessions Court charged on various accounts of witchcraft. From these prosecutions five were hanged together on the town gallows: Alice Clipwell, spinster, for practicing and exercising witchcraft and for having a diabolical pact with the devil, Brigetta Howard and Elizabeth Dudgeon (spinsters) and Maria Blackborne (widow) for 'practising witchcraft and feeding and entertaining spirits', and finally Elizabeth Bradwell who was not only found guilty of witchcraft, but was held personally responsible for the suffering of an infant child, one John Moulton, the son of local hosier.

(Johnson Collection)

1 August — **Lammas (Loaf-Mass) Day**

The festival of harvest's beginning, when the first cut sheaf of corn or bread made from it was blessed in churches. In the county we have the delightful neighbouring villages of Buxton and Lammas. In the village of Buxton once could be found Gallows Hill (now levelled). The village had the distinctive and ancient manorial right of executing its criminals and all criminals caught in its bounds. This may have been on the mind of Peter, the rector of Lamas in the thirteenth century who, so local lore tells, was informed by his parish clerk that Roger Kebebald was stealing beans from his orchard. Peter went out with a spade to tackle the thief but killed him in the struggle. He then took the body and buried it by the church door. The secret could not be kept, and Peter soon left the area and, it is believed, the country.

2 August — **1838** A foot steeplechase was held at Whitlingham. This event was attended by thousands from far and wide, but it was made remarkable because of the amount of 'base coinage' put in circulation by the swell mob from London. The landlord of the Whitlingham Gardens public house alone took £4-worth of bad silver.

3 August — **1888** Report of another case at Cromer Petty Sessions against one of the most slippery of all the poachers – John Farrow of Gresham. Charged by Police Sergeant Lovick under the Poaching Prevention Act with unlawfully having in his possession one rabbit on 25 July, with William Dunning and Edward Gray of the same place, labourers, charged with aiding and abetting. All pleaded not guilty, Dunning stating he was not aware Farrow had a rabbit. Sgt Lovick stated he was on the Felbrigg Road at about 11.30 on the night in question with PC Watson. Lovick had his suspicions aroused by the defendants. He approached them enquiring 'What have you got?'. They raised their arms and sticks and Lovick searched them. Farrow had on gaiters which were quite wet, he also had 'some sort of covering about his head to make him look like a woman.' Searching Farrow Lovick found a rabbit and confiscated the mens' sticks – all of which were produced in court. George Allen, a labourer on Cromer Hall estate deposed in court that he turned two dogs off the estate where he met the three defendants. Farrow's defence was he had brought three rabbits to Cromer to sell to his father, disposing of two he was taking the one found on him home again. Farrow's father was called and backed up the story. The bench under the Chairman H.R. Upcher Esq had no option and addressed the defendants saying there was a 'very strong suspicion they were out to catch rabbits but the evidence was not strong enough to convict.' Warning the men he hoped they would take warning by these preceedings. Farrow slipped through the law again.

4 August — **1914** War was declared with Germany at 11 p.m. on this night. Propaganda began to circulate, describing outrages such as throwing babies on to bayonets, cutting breasts off mothers and the rape of nuns, all claimed to have been committed on Belgians by the Germans marching through their country, and anti-German feelings were stirred up across Britain. Shops and businesses with German-sounding names had their windows smashed and vulgar slogans daubed on their walls. Even pubs like the King of Prussia on Ipswich Road in Norwich were attacked, and their signs torn down and smashed. 'Blue spectacled' German spies were thought to have infiltrated English communities and were considered to be working to bring down Britain from within; so under the Defence of the Realm Act all German citizens were rounded up and incarcerated 'for the duration'. One incident in those opening months of the war occurred at the Hotel de Paris in Cromer, where the German waiters employed for the benefit of the German royal family who visited before the war were arrested at gun point by locally billeted members of the Essex Regiment. These poor waiters were removed to Norwich and placed in a 'cage' of barbed wire and wood in the Market Place. Guarded by troops, they were observed to be 'standing morosely in a ring of bayonets'.

Defence of the Realm (Consolidation) Regulations, 1914.

PART OF THE
COUNTY OF NORFOLK.

Order as to Registration of
NEW RESIDENTS AND VISITORS.

WHEREAS an Order under Regulation 53 of the Defence of the Realm (Consolidation) Regulations, 1914, has been made by General Sir H. L. SMITH-DORRIEN, G.C.B., G.C.M.G.. D.S.O., a Competent Military Authority under the said Regulations.

NOTICE IS HEREBY GIVEN that:—

1. (a) Every person in the area specified in the first Schedule hereto who at the date hereof is not a permanent resident therein, and (b) every person who at any time after midnight on the 6th day of August, 1915, shall arrive in the said area, whether to reside permanently or stay temporarily therein, shall, as to (A) forthwith, and as to (B) within twelve hours after his or her arrival in the said area, fill up one of the prescribed forms in accordance with the directions stated thereon, and transmit the same to the nearest Police Station.

2. The owner, occupier, or manager (as the case may be) of any premises at or on which any such person as aforesaid shall be residing or staying shall take all necessary steps to ascertain that every person residing or staying at or on his or her premises to whom this Order applies has complied with this Order, and shall forthwith give information at the nearest Police Station if he or she shall have reason to believe that this Order has not been complied with.

3. Any person who has filled up and transmitted one of the prescribed forms in accordance with this Order may apply at the Police Station to which such prescribed form was transmitted for a permit, which, if granted, shall exempt such person from further compliance with this Order for such period as is stated in such permit.

Any person claiming to act under any such permit as aforesaid shall, if at any time required to do so by the Competent Military Authority or any person authorized by him, or by any soldier engaged on sentry patrol or other similar duty, or by any officer of Customs and Excise, officer of police, or aliens officer, produce the permit for inspection, and if he refuses or neglects to do so he shall be guilty of an offence against the said Regulations. Any such permit as aforesaid may at any time be revoked.

4. The prescribed form hereinbefore referred to shall be that set forth in the Second Schedule hereto, and may be obtained at any Post Office or Police Station within the said area.

5. This Order shall remain in force during the period of the War unless previously altered or revoked.

5 AUGUST **1827** A duel took place on Yarmouth Denes 'between J– B– Esq, and W. M– Esq, in consequence of a dispute the previous day at the Bath Rooms. Both were to fire at the same time but on the signal being given Mr M's ball did not take effect, and Mr B's pistol missed fire. The second then interfered and the affair was adjusted without much difficulty.'

(Great Yarmouth Museums)

BOROUGH OF GREAT YARMOUTH PRISON.

DIETARY, SCALE FOR MALE PRISONERS.

CLASS	TERM OF IMPRISONMENT.		EVERY DAY. BREAKFAST BREAD	GRUEL	MONDAYS, WEDNESDAYS and FRIDAYS. DINNER. BREAD	MEAT	POTATOES	SUET PUDDING	MEAL PUDDING	TUESDAYS, THURSDAYS, and SATURDAYS. DINNER. BREAD	POTATOES	PEA SOUP	BARLEY	SUNDAYS. DINNER. BREAD	CHEESE	EVERY DAY. SUPPER. BREAD	GRUEL
			ozs.	pints.	ozs.	ozs.	ozs.	ozs.	ozs.	ozs.	ozs.	pints.	pints.	ozs.	ozs.	ozs.	pints.
1	SEVEN DAYS AND UNDER.	WITH OR WITHOUT HARD LABOUR.	6		6				6	6	8			8		6	
2	AFTER SEVEN DAYS, AND UP TO THE FIRST CALENDAR MONTH.	WITH HARD LABOUR.	6	1	6				8	6	12			8	2	6	1
		WITHOUT HARD LABOUR.	6	1	6				8	6	12			8	1	6	
3	AFTER ONE MONTH AND UP TO THE THIRD CALENDAR MONTH.	WITH HARD LABOUR.	8	1	4	3	12	8		8	8	¾		10	3	6	1
		WITHOUT HARD LABOUR. Prisoners for Trial or Remand, Debtors, and Prisoners from County Court, and Misdemeanants of the 1st division, up to the 1st calendar month.	8	1	4		12	8		8	8		¾	10	2	6	1
4	AFTER THREE MONTHS AND UP TO THE SIXTH CALENDAR MONTH.	WITH HARD LABOUR.	8	1	4	4	16	12		8	8	1		10	4	8	1
		WITHOUT HARD LABOUR. Prisoners for Trial or Remand, Debtors, and Prisoners from County Court, and Misdemeanants of the 1st division, after 1st month and up to the 2nd calendar month.	8	1	4		16	12		8	8		1	10	3	8	1
5	AFTER SIX MONTHS.	WITH HARD LABOUR.	8	1	4	4	16	12		8	16	1		12	4	8	1
		WITHOUT HARD LABOUR. Prisoners for Trial or Remand, Debtors, and Prisoners from County Court, and Misdemeanants of the 2nd division, for any term after the 2nd calendar month.	8	1	4		16	12		8	16		1	12	3	8	1

Prisoners sentenced by the Court to Solitary Confinement, to be placed on the Progressive Scale of Diet, in accordance with the duration of their sentences.

Prisoners under Punishment for Prison Offences, the diet of Class 1 for the first seven days, and after that two ounces of Bread extra per diem. Debtors or Bankrupts, committed by any Court of Law for Fraud, or any serious legal offence, and Deserters, *en route*, the Diet of class 3.

* Meat to be issued on Mondays and Fridays in lieu of Suet Pudding. One ounce of Molasses in the Gruel for Breakfast on Sundays, in Class 4, and one ounce for Breakfast and Supper in Class 5.

I hereby Certify the foregoing Dietaries, as proper to be adopted in the Prison for the Borough of Great Yarmouth.

G. GREY.

Whitehall, 4th August, 1864.

6 AUGUST **1759** *The execution of Eugene Aram.* Coming to King's Lynn in 1759, Aram soon settled in as a popular tutor at the local grammar school, the only hint of anything untoward being his frequent bouts of melancholy and 'an

odd habit of turning his head shiftingly over his shoulder as if to discover someone following him'. Fate caught up with Aram (right) when he was recognised by a Yorkshire horse dealer at the market as a man wanted for murder in his home county. Constables John Barker and Francis Moor (more like bounty hunters than policemen) were dispatched from Yorkshire with a warrant for Aram's arrest. Marching into the school with local magistrates, Constable Barker, who was acquainted with Aram, identified him; he was arrested and charged with the murder of flax dresser Daniel Clarke at Knaresborough in 1744. Motivated by money troubles, Aram had committed the murder with Richard Houseman. The pair had tried to hide their wicked deed by burying their victim's body in a cave; the body had only come to light when a sweep came in to dig stones for his lime kiln. Aram's accomplice had turned King's Evidence, and following arraignment at York on 3 August Aram was found guilty and sentenced to death. Gibbeted by the roadside at

Knaresborough, where the murder was committed, his body is said to have been attended by his wife until her death in 1774. The gibbet was destroyed during land enclosures in the area 14 years later. Aram's skull was presented to the Royal College of Surgeons and is on display today in the Tales of the Old Gaol House Museum, King's Lynn.

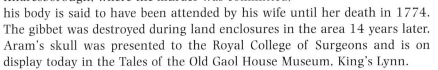

1826 Prisoners were removed from the old city gaol near the Guildhall to the new gaol outside St Giles Gates. The old city gaol was in the rooms at the end of the Guildhall until 1597, when it was removed to a former inn known as the Lamb, on the site of what became the old public library off Guildhall Hill. Here it remained until 1826 when the City Gaol and House of Correction opened at St Giles Gates, technically in Heigham hamlet. This prison was begun in 1824 and fully completed in 1827. It was built to the plans of Philip Barnes, a local architect. It cost about £30,000 and enclosed an area of just over an acre. Conducted on the separate system, it contained 120 cells and 8 airing yards. The treadwheel was used to pump water into the cisterns of the four towers and thence to the various apartments. The prison was built with exercise yards at varying levels so the governor could command a view of the whole from the inspection gallery in his residence. The old city gaol closed in 1881. Nothing may be seen of it today, as its entire site is occupied by the Roman Catholic cathedral, built between 1884 and 1910.

7 August

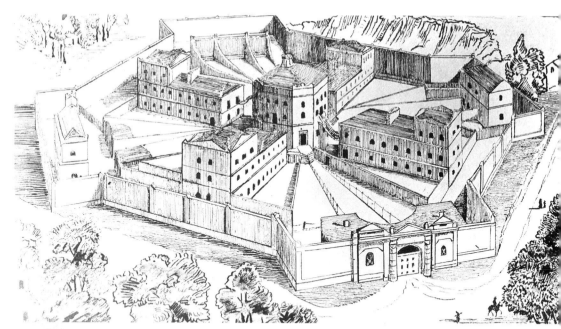

Norwich City Prison
stood outside St Giles
Gates from 1826 to
1881.

8 August   **1744**   Robert Capps was executed in Norwich Castle ditches for murder.

9 August   **1880**   A case was reported in the Norwich Mercury of four soldiers who attempted to murder one of their colleagues at the old cavalry barracks. From the evidence given it is apparent that while the soldier was in sick quarters the four accused stuffed up the chimney with straw, closed the windows and door and placed plates of burning sulphur on the floor to 'kill or cure' him; he died a few days later. After several remands the four prisoners eventually appeared at the Assizes on 12 November 1880. The jury considered the victim would have died anyhow, from the 'loathsome disease' (probably VD) from which he was suffering, and acquitted them all.

10 August   **1835**   The execution of Frances Billings (aged 46) and Catherine Frary (aged 40) on Norwich Castle Hill. They are found guilty of the murder of Mary Taylor of Burnham Westgate, by administering arsenic to her. They were also found guilty of murdering Robert Frary, husband of Catherine. Frary was in deep mourning for her husband and wore a widow's cap; both women held each other as they walked on to the scaffold. The silence which had hitherto pervaded the immense assembly that stood intently gazing on this dreadful exhibition was broken by a piercing shriek when the drop fell; then all was still again. Mrs Billings had 11 children, eight of whom were living at the time of the execution. The report concluded: 'Both women had been in the habit of consulting reputed witches at Burnham and Sall.'(See also 23 April 1836)

The Trial and Execution,

Of Frances BILLINGS, aged 46, & Catherine FRAREY, aged 40,

Who were Executed on the Castle-Hill, at Norwich, on Monday, Aug. 10, 1835, Billings for the Murder of Mary Taylor, wife of Peter Taylor, of Burnham, by administering Poison, and Frarey for the Murder of her own Husband, by Poison, also in the same place.

THE Trial of these two miserable Women who have been so long in Prison, excited such a degree of interest, that the Court on Friday morning was crowded to excess. The cruel and diabolical nature of their Guilt inspired such universal horror and detestation, that Country People from the parts where these Culprits dwelt flocked in numbers to witness their trial. The Children and other Relations of the Prisoners stood trembling in the court in awful expectation of the event, that would tear these miserable Mothers from their sight for ever. The unhappy woman Billings have been the mother of 14 Children, 9 of them now alive, most of whom were in the court in a fainting state during the greater part of the trial of their miserable Parent. The trial of these wretched women lasted many hours, during which 17 witnesses were examined whose testimony brought the Guilt of the Prisoners so forcibly home to them, that the Jury after a most impressive charge from the Learned Judge found them both Guilty of their separate crimes. The verdict was received in the profoundest silence, and the moment the Foreman of the Jury pronounced the word Guilty, the Paleness of Death overspread the countenances of both Prisoners, and they were with difficulty kept from falling. And when the Judge proceeded to pass the dreadful sentence of Death Shrieks of Horror were heard in different parts of the court proceeding from the Friends and Relations of the miserable condemn'd Women, who were both taken out of court in a senseless state, and convey'd back to their Cells. On Saturday the children and other relations of the Prisoners were permitted to visit them, to take their last farewell, and the scene that took place on this melancholy occasion, it is not in our power to describe; two fine young women the daughters of the prisoner Billings hung round the neck of their miserable Parent in speechless agony. Whilst the wretched Mother, who although in other respects so Guilty, was always infinitely fond of her children exclaimed " Oh my dear, dear children, tis for you I shall feel, as for myself I have merited my Fate, but to be torn from you by an ignominious Death, to part from all my dear children, to end my Life on a Scaffold, tear my very heartstrings asunder, Oh wretched Mother, & is this to be the last time, I shall fold you to my miserable bosom, what cruel Fate could tempt me to commit the horrid Deed that have brought me to this dreadful End! again she clasp'd them in her arms, whilst the voices of all three were chuoked by their Sobs in silent anguish, the daughters clung to their miserable Parent, and groan'd in anguish, those who were permitted to witness this Scene, could bear it no longer without giving vent to their feelings by a Shower of Tears! The woman Frarey who have always been nearly in a state of distraction ever since her first being taken to Walsingham, now appear to feel in a tenfold degree, all the horrors of her situation. She could scarcely recollect her nearest Friends, but continually kept exclaiming in a frantic manner, Oh my Murdered Husband! Soon shall I appear at that Bar where thou wilt confront me with the diabolical act of thy cruel murder. Oh! then wilt thou reproach me with thine untimely death. My Judges were merciful and gave me time to prepare for Death, but I wretched woman shew no mercy to thee, but sent thee to an untimely Grave, without allowing thee one hour to make thy peace with God; but soon shall my writhing and suffering frame be expos'd to the Gaze of the multitude who will witness without regret the miserable Death of so wretched a Murderer as myself: And Oh, may my awful End be a warning to all who see and read of me.

After these afflicting scenes their Friends and Relations took their last and Final Leave of the unhappy Women, and were with difficulty separated for ever from their heartbroken and Forlorn Culprits, who passed the rest of their time till the period of their Execution, in unfeigned repentance, every opportunity was afforded to them for the Spiritual assistance so necessary to their unhappy condition, and their last hours were devoted to offering up the most fervent prayer for their Guilty Souls! On Monday morning at an early hour the Spectators began to assemble, and by the time the unfortunate women ascended the Drop, it was computed that not less than 10,000 People were assembled. At the sight of the unhappy Culprits, who were both comely women, an universal feeling of commiseration pervaded the breasts of the Spectators. At the sight of the awful preparations for their dreadful Doom, they were with great difficulty kept from fainting, and were obliged to be supported to the Fatal Drop, which after a few moments spent in prayer fell, and the wretched Culprits were Launched into Eternity !!!

AH you that these poor Wretches end behold,
One hour ago in health now Dead and Cold;
Their vicious passions brought them to their end,
And to the warning of their fate attend.

Two Guilty Murderers, many years it have been
Since a woman Executed here have been;
An awful dreadful sight that none behold,
But at the Spectacle, their blood ran Cold.

What anguish must that wretched Billings feel,
For 'though loose in Life she lov'd her Children well;
Nine of them in their prime to mourn her Fate,
Who loved their mother 'though her crime was great.

Two of them smiling Babes of tender years,
Who not as yet have thought of worldly cares;
Whose artless innocence, but little know
The Crime that work'd their mother's overthrow.

Who can their tender wants so well supply,
Or where's the stranger like a Mother's Eye;
That wretched mother who Alas is gone,
And to her offspring never can return.

This other wretch that suffer'd by her side,
The woman Frarey deep in Guilt was dy'd,
Or else she had never mix'd the fatal Dose,
That in the Grave her Husband's life did close

Ah what could tempt her guilty murderous hand,
Thus unprepar'd her Husband's Soul, to send
Before his Maker! that she might live in Sin,
Which at last brought her to this untimely end.

Ah who can view their Bodies after death,
That lately saw them full of Life and Breath;
Now for dissection laid, and Public Shew,
Oh awful warning dreadful sight of woe!

May such a Spectacle a Lesson be,
To shun the Paths of Vice and Misery,
And though with crimes their Guilty Souls are stain'd,
May both in Christ's redeeming arms be screen'd

[*Walker, Printer, Orford-Hill, Norwich.*]

11 August   **1809**   Joseph Bexfield, 'unfortunately drowned', so reads the grave stone at Thurlton. The story tells of how wherryman Bexfield was warned not to cross the marshes to Thurlton Staithe when the jack-o'-lanterns (believed by some not mystically inclined to be flickers of self-igniting marsh gas) were visible. Many believed these flickering lights were mischevous and would lure travellers to their death on marshy ground. Bexfield was having none of 'that old squit', and he knew the marshes too well to be led astray by any jack-o'-lantern. He was never seen alive again; his body was washed up between Reedham and Breydon a few days later.

12 August   **1812**   On or about this date William Flaxman of Gorleston was placed in a pillory erected in Great Yarmouth Market Place, and after 'the usual time' was removed to the gaol to complete a term of three months' imprisonment. An effective and humiliating punishment for seditious speech and sexual crimes dating back to the statutes of the thirteenth century, pillories were considered so essential by the authorities that towns risked forfeiting the right to hold a market if they didn't have one. Set up in the market place, the pillory was where the miscreant was pelted with rotten fruit, mud, excrement and dead animals to varying degrees, depending on the crime the culprit had committed and the mood of the crowd. Pillories were in regular use until the end of the eighteenth century. Great Yarmouth's permanent pillory is

A Victorian artist's impression of standing in the pillory, seventeenth-century style.

recorded as being 'removed' in 1729; thus Flaxman saw his erected for the purpose. He was probably the last man to be pilloried at Great Yarmouth. The last man pilloried in England was Peter Bossy, for the old pillory favourite of lying under oath. His punishment was carried out on Tower Hill, London on 22 June 1832.

1829   Ireland and Robert Watts were brought before the County Assizes charged with obstructing custom-house officers in the discharge of their duty. Captain De Lafosse, the officer at Mundesley, traced the goods to the house of the defendants at Antingham. Having obtained a writ of assistance he proceeded to the house with Lieutenant Lee, several of the coastguards and a peace officer. Admittance was demanded but the Watts boys offered resistance. The captain then drew his pistol and threatened to fire when Robert Watts appeared, bared his breast, and cried 'Fire and be Damned!' Captain De Lafosse, fearing he could not enter the house without bloodshed, withdrew his men. At the trial the defence submitted that the captain's authority did not permit him to search the house, but the special jury returned a verdict of guilty. Mr Kelly, for the defence, moved that there should be a new trial on the grounds of invalidity of the officer's writ. The case reached the Court of the King's Bench, where Lord Tenterden held that this might be a question of great importance on public grounds, although in the individual case it was of little consequence. The rule was granted, and there is no further record of action in this case.

13 August

1851   *The murder that wasn't.* News reports in America revealed the particulars of a confession of a private soldier named Thomson serving with the 1st Royals, in Halifax, North America. He stated that when in Norwich eight years previously he was on terms of intimacy with a woman named Anna Barber. A quarrel had occurred between them and he had thrown her into the river. The crime had so played on his mind that he determined to give himself up to justice and allow the law to take its course. On 13 September it was announced that Thomson had been brought to England and committed to Winchester Gaol, pending inquiries by the local police. Two officers came to Norwich to investigate, and uncovered the remarkable tale of James Taylor. He had been fishing for eels in the river near Blackfriars Bridge when he heard a scuffle, a shriek, a splash and the sound of quickly retreating footsteps. He immediately rowed to the place and assisted a young woman out of the water; she refused to give him her name. She went away, and no report was given to the police. It also transpired that Anna Barber had been seen in Norwich as recently as 1851. Thomson was free to go, but I wonder if his conscience was ever completely clear?

15 August

1819   John Pycraft was executed on Norwich Castle Hill for administering arsenic to an infant, 'when the platform fell his chest expanded at intervals during the space of 7 or 8 minutes . . . after dissection had been performed his body was exposed to public view at the Shirehouse for 1 hour.'

16 August

17 AUGUST   **1829**   John Stratford (aged 42) was found guilty at Norwich Assizes of the murder of John Burgess, an inmate of the Norwich Workhouse, by poisoning with arsenic on 2 March. He was to be the first man executed on the roof of the new city gaol, just outside St Giles Gates, on 17 August. A cast of his head was made after death for phrenological examination.

Trial and Execution,

LIFE, CHARACTER, and BEHAVIOUR of JOHN STRATFORD, who was Executed at the City Gaol, of Norwich, on Monday, August 17th, 1829, for the wilful Murder of John Burgess, by Poison.

The Trial which commenced on Friday Morning last about nine o'clock and lasted till five in the afternoon, excited the most extraordinary interest in the minds of the inhabitants of this City, as the wretched culprit was a man generally known, and (until the fatal connexion between him and the infamous woman, Briggs, the wife of another man) was respected as an industrious, careful man, and much esteemed by his employers as an ingenious workman, he being a Whitesmith by Trade. At one time he kept the sign of the Swan, in King-street, which after a year or two he left, and continued to follow his business as a Smith, by which he supported a wife and six children, that he was infinitely attached to, till the unfortunate connexion that he formed with this woman, when so infatuated did he become by his criminal attachment to this disgrace to her sex, that he sacrificed, without remorse, the peace and happiness of his family, to prefer the embraces of this wanton; and not satisfied with the degree of guilt in which he was thus involved, he formed the diabolical plan of taking away the life of the poor afflicted creature, her husband, who was a pauper in the Workhouse, in this City, who for this last year has not taken any thing but thick milk through a tube on account of his having a cancer in the throat, for which purpose he procured some arsenic, and mixing it with some flour, left it with a servant girl in the Work-house, to be delivered to Briggs, the injured husband of the object of his attachment; but it pleased the Almighty to disappoint his intention in this respect, as the flour remained untouched by Briggs for three weeks, but unfortunately he requested his Nurse [Rhoda Burgess] to take it for her own use, as he had no occasion for it, and thought it a pity the flour should be spoiled, she accordingly took it, and made it up into dumplings, of which she and her husband [the deceased John Burgess] did eat, as did also her son and two other persons, who were all soon affected with vomitings, and other symptoms indicative of their having taken poison. Medical assistance being called and every assistance offered which the case demanded, they all recovered, except the unfortunate husband John Burgess, who lingered in the greatest agony for a few hours and then expired, it being ascertained by the Surgeons, that his death was occasioned by arsenic being mixed with the flour of which he had eaten.

The Prisoner was immediately apprehended, and the girl swore to his being the person of whom she received the flour in the Work-house kitchen, and he was in consequence committed to the City Gaol till the Assizes, and when put on his Trial, pleaded "Not Guilty."

A number of witnesses were then called, whose testimony tended so clearly to convict the Prisoner, [more especially the woman who was the original cause of his guilt] that no doubt remained of his culpability, and although he had assistance of two Counsellors from London, with the well-known professional abilities of Mr. Palmer, St. Stephens, Norwich, the circumstances were so clear against him, and the crime so clearly established, that Lord Chief Justice Park in summing up the evidence, pointed out to the Jury, how every part of the evidence corroborated to criminate the Prisoner beyond the possibility of a doubt. Notwithstanding which, the Jury after retiring, remained five hours in consultation, before they returned a verdict of Guilty.

The Learned Judge immediately passed the awful sentence of the law, and the people from the windows of the Court-room proclaimed the event of the Trial to the anxious multitude outside, who had waited the result with the most intense interest till 11 o'clock at night.—We understand, that since his condemnation, he has confessed his Guilt, and no one knew what he did.

He was therefore, pursuant to his sentence, brought out for Execution, on Monday, amidst a vast concourse of spectators, being the first that has suffered at this place of Execution.

With what earnestness might he say,
BEWARE OF INFIDELITY.

How truly awful must be the situation of that man who denies the truth of God's Holy Word.—He who can be so daringly wicked must shut himself out of all happiness in both worlds.—All is dark in this, and in the next, blackness and darkness for ever. It is this unbelief which has proved the ruin of thousands, and for this numbers are fearfully anticipating the day of Judgment, when all unbelievers shall be cast into the land of anguish, from whence the God of their idolatry can never deliver them. It is unbelief which leads mankind to the perpetration of those crimes which render them a pest to society, and brings them to an untimely end.

If men would believe the Bible, they would not continue to practice those sins which are too prevalent in this our highly favoured country. The Sabbath breaker would obey the command and keep holy the Sabbath day. The Thief would remember God has said, Thou shalt not steal. The whore-monger, the idolater, and the liar, would stop in their mad career, knowing such must have their portion in the lake of fire and brimstone, and the Murderer would immediately drop his arm which was raised to take away his brother's life, knowing that God has said, Thou shalt do no Murder.

(Norfolk Local Studies Library)

1802 A duel was fought on Mousehold Heath, Norwich, between Robert Alderson, a well-known barrister, and a Mr Grigby. The latter conceived that he had been unfairly treated in cross-examination by Mr Alderson at Suffolk Assizes and, refusing to accept his explanation, sent him a challenge. 'Mr Alderson was attended to the field by Mr Mackintosh and Mr Grigby by Mr Turner. Two shots were exchanged, with no effect than that of Mr Grigby's first ball passing through the skirts of Mr Alderson's coat. A cordial reconciliation was afterwards effected.'

1909 Constable Charles Alger of the Great Yarmouth Borough Police was summoned to 12 St Andrew's Road, Gorleston, the home of Thomas Allen (aged 53), vermin catcher, petty thief, poacher and habitual wife beater, who was once again reported to be assaulting his wife. Arriving at the scene where quite a crowd had gathered Constable Alger enquired about the disturbance, to which Allen replied 'Come into the garden and I will tell you about it.' Upon entering the garden Allen picked up a sawn-off double-barrelled breech-loader shotgun he had hidden in his potato patch and discharged it at point blank range. Alger received the charge in the right side of his head, face and neck. Although terribly disfigured and mortally wounded, he managed to retreat some 20 paces before collapsing. Concerned neighbours, Mr Warner, Miss Popay and Miss Lancaster, were injured by a second shot as they approached Allen. Inspector Moore was summoned to the scene where he cordoned off the area, sending the injured to the local cottage hospital. Engaging Allen in conversation, the inspector gradually moved closer and, picking his moment, sprang forward, pinning Allen's hand holding the gun to the wall. Allen was overpowered, and the gun was wrenched from his grasp. Allen was lodged at Gorleston police station until a four-man escort removed him to Great Yarmouth lock-up. Found guilty of the murder and sentenced to death, he was subsequently reprieved and sent to Broadmoor for the rest of his life.

PC 37, Charles Alger. *(Norfolk Constabulary Archives)*

1796 Following the events in France, which had led to bloody revolution in 1789, combined with bad harvests and the increasing price of corn, agitators began to band together into seditious societies and hold public meetings to muster support for their controversial views. One agitator, a 'political lecturer' named Thelwall, became particularly notorious across East Anglia. On this date he was 'declaiming' in Great Yarmouth, his main aim being to 'seduce the military from their allegiance'. A party of armed sailors broke in, and in their attempts to seize the orator knocked down every person that opposed them.

Upwards of 40 people were wounded or bruised in the scuffle, during which the orator escaped.

This was not Thelwall's first escape; on the preceding 26 May he arrived in Norwich and began organising public meetings. On the 29th a party of the Iniskilling Dragoons proceeded to his lecture room, drove out everyone there, and destroyed the tribune and benches. The soldiers then proceeded to smash up the Shakespeare public house where agitators had caused a disturbance, and receiving intelligence that Thelwall was in the Rose Tavern began smashing the windows and furniture in that pub as well. At this juncture the Officers of the Dragoons and the city magistrates called a halt and the soldiers retired to their barracks. Thelwall had escaped in the affray. Davey, the master of the Shakespeare, had been pursued by soldiers to his garret, where he threw himself on to the street, receiving considerable injuries. At the subsequent Assizes Luke Rice, a tailor of the city, was indicted capitally for aiding and encouraging the soldiers to demolish the Shakespeare. Rice was fortunate. He got off on a rare technicality: 'the offence with which he was charged did not come within the meaning of the statute on which the indictment was founded'.

20 AUGUST **1698** A duel was fought on Cawston Heath between Sir Henry Hobart of Blickling Hall and Oliver Le Neve of Great Witchingham Hall as the result of a quarrel following the election of Hobart's rival, Le Neve, to be member for Norwich in his place. After the opening formalities swords were drawn and the duel commenced. Sir Henry had the best of the fight until a carefully delivered thrust saw Le Neve run him through his belly. Retiring from the field Sir Henry died of the wound the following day. Support for Hobart was so strong that Le Neve fled to Holland, but subsequently returned, stood trial and was acquitted. A stone pillar and urn (right), carved with the initials HH still stands on the site about a mile from the village where the duel took place.

21 AUGUST **1828** The inquest on the body of Thomas Jones before Mr Pilgrim, the coroner at Somerton. It appeared from the evidence given that Lord Braybrook, owner of a large nearby estate, came over for the purpose of meeting friends at Admiral Stevens's house. On his Lordship leaving the village he sent the fishermen a handsome present to drink his health; they immediately put a large swivel gun in a conspicuous situation and discharged it several times in a salute to His Lordship's honour. They had nearly finished when Jones wanted another firing. On firing the gun burst, a part of it striking

the deceased on the head, killing him on the spot. Although many people were standing in the vicinity and the pieces flew in various directions no one else received any injury. The verdict was a clear cut accidental death.

1891 *Man in a whale's stomach – rescue of a modern Jonah.* This incredible story appeared as fact in the *Great Yarmouth Mercury* on this day. The preceding February the whaling ship Star of the East was in the vicinity of the Falkland Islands when whales were sighted. Two boats were manned and a harpooner was enabled to send a spear into the larger of the two whales. His boat was dragged away at a fearful speed, but on a return pass the second boat speared the whale. The poor beast dragged the boats for about three miles, then in its death throes upturned one of the boats, drowning one man while another, one James Bartley, apparently disappeared. The dead whale was brought alongside the ship and the crew began their grim work with axes and spades to secure the blubber. They worked all day and part of the night, then resumed the next forenoon and were soon down to the stomach, which was hoisted on to the deck. 'The workmen were startled while labouring to clear it to discover something doubled up in it

The Modern Jonah.

DISAPPEARING VIEW OF JAMES BARTLEY, AN ENGLISH SAILOR, WHO WAS RESCUED ALIVE, AFTER BEING IN A WHALE'S BELLY THIRTY-SIX HOURS, AS VOUCHED FOR BY THE SCIENTIFIC EDITOR OF THE JOURNAL DES DEBATS, THE WELL-KNOWN PARIS NEWSPAPER.

22 August

that gave spasmodic signs of life . . . [it was] cut open, and inside was found the missing sailor doubled up and unconscious.' Revived by a salt water bath, he spent the following two weeks delirious in the captain's cabin. Carefully nursed back to health, Bartley regained his senses and by the end of the third week had entirely recovered from the shock and resumed his duties. 'During the brief sojourn in the whale's belly Bartley's skin, where it had been exposed to the action of the gastric juices underwent a striking change. His face and hands were bleached to a deathly whiteness and his skin wrinkled giving the appearance of being parboiled.'

1695 On this day Frances Spore, the murdered servant of Mr Buckenham, a Haddiscoe farmer, was buried at Toft Monks. Miss Spore was engaged to one Mr Gymer, a carpenter of Aldeby. Gymer had gone the preceding Sunday to borrow about 30*s* from Mr Buckenham. When he arrived he found Spore the only person in the house – she was cooking the dinner. Knowing the money was kept in the kitchen, Gymer decided to steal it. He enticed Spore away, saying the hogs were loose in a piece of wheat outside. Following her outside, Gymer possibly revealed his intentions and a row ensued. Poor Frances Spore was found the following day by men harvesting with her throat cut with the kitchen knife. Gymer made off with the money and allegedly hid it in part of the village known afterwards as Money Grove. His sudden disappearance was suspicious and when he was tracked down he was presented before a

23 August

Trial and Execution,

LIFE, CHARACTER, and BEHAVIOUR of JOHN RANDALSOME, who was Executed at the Castle of Norwich, on Saturday, August 22nd, 1840.

This unfortunate man has just expiated his life on the scaffold for the Wilful Murder of his own wife, on the night of the 18th of June, 1840. The evidence on which he was convicted, was entirely of a circumstantial nature, but the circumstances though each in itself trivial and apparently unimportant; when brought together presented such a mass of evidence, as could not be held consistent with the Prisoner's innocence. He had been married to Mary Barnaby, of Thwaite, at St. Julian's Church in the city, on the month of April, 1839, but the marriage had never been known, and she continued from that time to keep her father's house until the night of the murder; but was to have left the following morning to live with her sister in the same village. Within the last few weeks of her life an attempt had been made to poison her by mixing arsenic in the water in a tea kettle, but by a providential interference she escaped this base and cowardly attempt on her life. Her own father was suspected, and was several days in custody, but the Magistrates believing him to be innocent set him at liberty, remarking that no suspicion attached to him. This was no doubt an attempt of John Randalsome to get rid of his wife; his mother had observed poison in his room, which she found on the day of the murder, bid him take away. Added to this, he had for five years been acquainted with a girl of the name of Elizabeth Punchard, who lived maid servant with Mr. Margarson, an Attorney, at Ditchingham: this girl he had promised to marry after seducing her three years, during which time they had often gone out together and sometimes passed as husband and wife. Besides he had got £14 of this girl's money, and upon the whole, like too many stolen embraces, he seemed to enjoy the company of Punchard, much better than that of his own wife. To this wife however, he would frequently go in the night, and she suspecting no evil, and knowing that he was her husband, no doubt gladly consented to meet him. They no doubt frequently spent hours together in the straw-house and stack yard, when all the rest of the family was in bed, and the woman because pregnant, Randalsome found he could keep this from the world, and consequently from Bet Punchard no longer, and he formed the desperate resolution to murder her. The poison not succeeding he determined on effecting it by violence, the last night she had to be at her father's house. She was seen to be setting up for him at 11 o'clock, and was heard to say that he was coming. When all was silent he came, and the poor confiding wife walked out as usual with him. He no doubt inveigled her to the side of the pond, and then unexpectedly plunged her into the water, with the intention of keeping her down with a stake he had provided. Finding some difficulty in this, and that she shruck MURDER, he beat her over the head with it, and that is no doubt the way in which her gown became torn, and her hair hanging about her shoulders. He succeeded in murdering her, and she was soon after found in this state by her brother John and brother-in-law

Stowards? Randalsome had gone off unseen by any person but his murdered wife who now could tell no tales, and he managed that his poor old mother and his sister's daughter were brought up to swear that he was at home and in bed at the time. They told this tale before the Coroner, and again presisted in it before the Magistrates at Loddon; but now since confessed that it was false, and were not called on his trial at the Assizes. Many other circumstances besides those mentioned above were spoken to by different witnesses, and amongst the rest he gave two different accounts of himself, as to where he was that night. The Jury having heard the whole of the case, and after a trial which lasted 13 hours they found him guilty of the murder, and Mr. Justice Patteson sentenced him to die, and his body to be buried within the Precinct of the Castle. He stood firm during the whole time, and again denied all knowledge of the affair. When taken to the Castle he for several days refused to eat, but nature not being able to hold out any longer he afterwards took his food; but stubbornly adhered to his statement of innocence, and expressed an opinion that after all he should not be hanged. He could not bear to lie alone; and occasionally was heard still to say what he would do when he got out, but he would not go back to Thwaite, he said, but would go to a distant place and take a farm and live alone. Thus he passed his time between hope and despair till the last morning arrived.

If men would believe the Bible, they would not continue to practice those sins which are too prevalent in this our highly favoured country. The Sabbath breaker would obey the command and keep holy the Sabbath day. The Thief would remember God hath said, Thou shalt not steal. The whore-monger, the idolitar, and the liar, would stop in their mad career, knowing such must have their portion in the lake of fire and brimstone, and the Murderer would immediately drop his arm which was raised to take away his brother's life, knowing God hath said, Thou shalt do no murder.

Randalsome, guilty as he was of one of the worst of crimes that can disgrace Humanity, still hoped on, but without knowing that any attempt were made to delay the Execution. Such however were made. A Patition was sent to the Prime Minister, Lord Melborne, who handed it to Mr. Justice Patteson. His Lordship declined to interfere, and Randalsome was brought to the Scaffold erected by the bridge leading to the Castle on Saturday morning. The Hill being crowded with thousands of Spectators. The Bell announced the solemn procession and at 12 o'clock the unhappy man appeared outside the Castle doors, pinioned, and in company of the Officers of the law, and the Rev. Chaplain of the Castle. He mounted the scaffold, no doubt convinced at last that his sin would fine him out. The Chaplain read the funeral service, and in a few seconds the drop fell.

Tremendous sound, what do I hear!
O Lord receive my soul,
For I'm condemn'd and death is near,
Which puts an end to all.

How have I lived and spent my time;
Great God awake my fears,
And in thy bosom close confin'd,
Safe number all my tears.

My thoughts to men I now reveal,
But tongue can't utter what I feel,
The dire remorse within my breast,
May be conceiv'd but not express'd.

O that I had been wise in time,
And kept my hands from every crime,
This sin ne'er would me attend,
Nor had I known this shameful end.

O that my crimes may be forgiven,
Before the gracious throne of heaven,
May mercy there appear in store,
To save me when life's storm is o'er.

The clock now strikes, the dismal bell,
It seems to sound my passing knell;
I know for me it soon will toll,
May God have mercy on my soul.

(*Walker, Printer, White Hart, St. Miles', Norwich.*)

(Norfolk Local Studies Library)

magistrate, where he confessed his guilt. Sent to Norwich Castle, Gymer escaped before his Assize trial and was found at Yarmouth seeking passage across the sea. He was sent back to Norwich for trial, was found guilty and executed on Norwich Castle Hill. As grim remembrances of this deed, the field where the deed was done was later known as Cut-Throat Close and the lane adjoining it Cut-Throat Lane.

1822 The execution of James Smith (a member of the notorious Cossey Gang) and Henry Carter at Norwich. The Cossey Gang had been active in January 1822, breaking into the Half Moon pub and stealing 16 gallons of spirits and other property.

24 August

Tiring of 'foot depradations', they found stables belonging to those in bed by 10 o'clock and stole their horses in order to steal game, poultry or sheep, returning the horses in the early morning 'almost jaded and harassed to death'. Smith was found guilty of the theft of liquor and a purse containing £8 in notes plus silver and copper coin, and was sentenced to death. Carter was found guilty of entering the house of John Clarke of St Pauls and stealing diverse articles therein, and was sentenced to death. Leaving their gaol at St Giles in procession headed by the under sheriffs on horseback, the sheriffs were accompanied by the chaplain and a Wesleyan minister in the mourning coach followed 'by a cart covered with black cloth on which sat the two malefactors each with arms pinioned, neck bare and head uncovered, each sitting on the coffin destined to receive his lifeless body'. Smith was well behaved, but Carter behaved with great levity during the progress of the procession through the market place to the scaffold erected near the weighing machine on Castle Meadow. On the very drop itself 'he seemed to evince perfect indifference to the fate which awaited him'. After hanging an hour 'the bodies were carried by twelve bearers to the house of Carter's parents in St Margaret's and were buried in the churchyard of that parish'.

1829 A singular marriage took place at Fakenham. The bridegroom was Thomas Hudson, aged 79 and the bride was Martha Frary, aged 21. They were followed to church by an unfortunate cripple driving his curricle of dogs. Immediately after the knot was tied the bridegroom was torn from his fainting partner, thrown into an open cart decorated with rams' horns, and drawn through the principal streets of the town, amid the firing of guns and the shouts and ridicule of the people.

25 August

1867 Hubbard Lingley (aged 22) was executed by public executioner William Calcraft on Norwich Castle Hill for the murder of his uncle, Benjamin Black. Performed before a crowd of thousands this was to be the last public execution in Norwich.

26 August

1737 Charles Grimmer was executed on Norwich Castle Hill for horse stealing.

27 August

THE SORROWFUL AND HEART-RENDING
Lamentations
OF

HUBBARD **LINGLEY**

Who was tried on the 8th and 9th of August, 1867, was found Guilty, and is now lying in Norwich Castle, under Sentence of Death, for the wilful Murder of his Uncle, Mr. Benjamin Black, at Barton Bendish, in Norfolk.

Sinner attend and hear the prayer
Of one condemned to die ;
The sorrows of a guilty wretch,
Who loud for mercy cry.

'Twas envy's venom'd canker, which
Did cause me for to sin ;
And shed my victim's precious blood,
Some sordid pelf to win.

Oh ! may the all atoning Lamb,
Plead for my guilty soul ;
And cleanse me with the purple stream
Which makes the wounded whole.

My Uncle dear I did waylay,
And secretly did kill ;
Just like a Tiger in his lair,
His life's blood I did spill.

But the all seeing eye of God,
With anger viewed the crime ;
For which I soon this world shall leave,
Though scarcely in my prime.

To view me in my gloomy cell,
Would make your heart to bleed ;
The anguish of my soul is great,
When I think on that deed.

But in the gloom of dark despair,
A ray of light is given ;
On Calvary's mount my Saviour pav'd,
The Sinner's road to Heaven.

Oh ! Lamb of God pray intercede,
For me on that dread day ;
And let the fountain with Christ's blood,
Wash all my guilt away.

For thou my Saviour didst forgive,
The thief upon the cross ;
Lord let me thus thy mercy share,
And think this life no loss.

O pray for me my loving wife,
With friends and neighbours dear ;
Pray to the throne of heavenly grace,
My wretched soul to spare.

My weary eyes through sleepless nights,
Of mournful thoughts remain ;
O may my bursting heart be freed,
From sin's internal pain.

Lord grant that I in the short time.
On this earth have to spare ;
May seek salvation, and obtain
From Christ, the prize so dear.

Oh ! Lord my Saviour may it prove,
The cloud I so much dread,
Is big with mercy and will break,
In showers upon my head.

So when I quit this mortal frame,
Which gives the weary rest ;
Oh ! may I rise to heaven above,
And lodge in Jesus' breast.

When on that awful vengeful morn,
The sombre bell it tolls ;
May feeling hearts its warning take,
Strike pity on their souls.

My fleeting moments soon will pass,
This world to bid adieu ;
May holy angels waft my soul,
To Paradise in view.

And when beneath the dreadful beam,
Convulsively I stand ;
Oh ! God my fainting spirit cheer,
Hold out a saving hand.

Whilst I thus agitated wait.
The awful moment near ;
May Christ with succour to me come,
And whisper in my ear.

Poor Sinner now thy race is run,
My Father hath forgiven ;
Thy robes are now wash'd purely white,
Join the whole choir in heaven.

Where the redeem'd for ages have,
Their Saviour's praises sung ;
And all the holy Saints with harps,
Loud Hallelujahs ! rung.

And when the fatal bolt is drawn,
May hosts of Angels sing ; [flies !
" Lend, lend him wings ! he mounts ! he
Oh ! Death where is thy sting.

W. U. Norwich.

W. UPCROFT, PRINTER. WRIGHT'S COURT, ST. SIMON'S, NORWICH.

28 AUGUST 1819 Edward Fisher was executed on Norwich Castle Hill for stabbing William Harrison to death.

County Bridewells and Gaols visited by Prison Reformer John Howard

Walsingham Bridewell, visited in 1779, described as 'A room 15 feet by 8 in the keeper's court, with two dark lodging rooms about 7 feet square, and straw on the brick floors. The walls of the court not secure. Prisoners in irons.'

1701   Robert 'Gaffer' Watts was executed before his own house in St Augustines, Norwich, for murdering his wife on the previous 7 January. A weaving trade 'throwster', Watts was a drinking man. On the morning of the murder he went for a drink at the local, the Globe, where his drinking companions wanted to really 'chaff him up'. To top all previous jocular stirrings of Watts's infamous jealousy, one man claimed he had bedded Watts's wife. In the words of a rhyme that embroidered the tale, 'there isn't much from me she wouldn't stand – I'd get the wedding ring from off her hand!' For the wager of a gallon of beer he said he would go and fetch it and bring it back to the pub. After a lot of persuasion, and telling her he was acting on 'Gaffer's behalf', and that the ring was required to settle a bet, the innocent Mrs Watts gave the ring to the man, so she wouldn't 'put him [Watts] in a passion'. The man returned to the pub with the ring, and Watts stormed out before the prank was revealed. Drunkenly stumbling into his house, he picked up a knife and stabbed his wife, after the first minor blow.

> Trembling and bleeding, up again she flies,
> Unto the window, where she vainly tries,
> To call assistance; but no help was near,
> And so he cut her throat from ear to ear.

£3 Reward!

Whereas, some evil-disposed Person did early this Morning, (the 28th instant,) wilfully and maliciously assault, batter, and otherwise ill-treat and alarm Mr. G. BLYTH, Reporter to the 'Norfolk News,' whilst that gentleman was engaged in prosecuting some important Archæological Researches in the South Tower, otherwise called the Black Friars' Tower, and situate in, near, or adjoining to and upon the precincts of the Priory appertaining or belonging to the Order of Monks known as the Predicant or Dominican Friars. The said party was attired in a white nightcap and white trowsers, his face whitened, and his body covered with a man's shirt, a portion of which was torn off by Mr. BLYTH whilst struggling upon the ground with the pretended Ghost or Apparition, and the portion of that article of wearing apparel was this morning exhibited to the Bench of Magistrates, before whom Mr. Blyth did lay information of the above occurrence, proved by the evidence of several respectable witnesses.

This is to Give Notice,

That the sum of Three Pounds will be paid to any Person or Persons who will give such information as will lead to the discovery and conviction of the Party who played the above infamous trick upon the said Informant.

N.B.   The said portion of wearing apparel is now lying at the Police Station.

Great Yarmouth, August, 28th, 1851.

(Norfolk Constabulary Archives)

31 AUGUST 1728 *A good day for hanging about?* James Cannon or Canhan was the unlucky member of a gang of six horse thieves sentenced to death. All the others got reprieves while he was left to swing in the Norwich Castle ditches. Not far from him on the Castle Hill Deborah Harris was hanged for firing a house. Almost 90 years later on this same day in 1816 Thomas Moy was executed on Norwich Castle Hill for sheep stealing. A 33-year-old farmer of 100 acres, he left a wife and seven young children.

The hempen noose with hangman's knot used for executions in England from the Middle Ages until the late ninetenth century, when the more efficient spliced ringle and washer were introduced by executioner Marwood.

SEPTEMBER

A FULL AND PARTICULAR ACCOUNT OF A MOST

CRUEL MURDER

COMMITTED ON THE BODY OF A MALE

INFANT BY HIS MOTHER,

AT THE DOVE,

St.George's Colegate Street

NORWICH.

On Wednesday last, an inquest was held at the DOVE, St. George's at Colegate, on the body of a male child, which had been found that morning under the bed in the above house. It appears from the evidence that a woman about 29 years of age, named Lucy Thorpe, hired a ready furnished room of Mrs. Roll, about a month since, when she asked Thorpe, if she was not pregnant, but she denied it. Thorpe was a single woman, but had a little boy about 2 years old, who slept with her. On Wednesday, Emily Roll, daughter of Mrs. Roll, (who had for the last two or three nights, slept with Thorpe), went and told her mother she saw a child's head under the bed, and that she heard it cry about six in the morning, but had not heard it since. Mrs Roll went into the room, and from certain appearances she observed, induced her to ask if she had not got a child there under the bed, and Thorpe said, " Yes." Thorpe after her confinement got up and dressed herself and put the breakfast things on the table, got some water from the pipe, and began to wash the room up, when the child was heard to cry, upon which Thorpe went to the place from where the noise proceeded and drew the curtain so that Emily Roll could not see what she was doing. The child was then heard to make *gurgling* noise in the throat, and was heard no more. There was a slight external injury on the throat on the left side; in internally there were marks of the fingures on the child's throat, which had caused an effusion of blood, partly to the nose and extending to the stomach There was no sort of indication by the preparation of linen, on the appearance of the body of the child, of there being any intention of preserving its life. There was a *post mortem* examination of the body, Mr. Dashwood having examined it in the company of Mr. Firth, they both agreed that the child died from strangulation. Such injuries could not possibly have occurred by the woman's attempting to relieve herself. The jury accordingly returned a verdict of WIL-FUL MURDER against Lucy Thorpe but as may be expected, is yet too unwell to be removed to the City Gaol.

Robert Walker, Printer, St. Martin at Oak Norwich.

Sept. 13. 1844

Norwich broadsheet, September 1844. (*Norfolk Local Studies Library*)

1 SEPTEMBER **1764** A double event on Norwich Castle Hill: John Carman was executed for returning early from transportation, alongside Samuel Creasey, who swung for robbery with violence.

2 SEPTEMBER **1756** Following a naval engagement between HMS *Hazard* and the French privateer *La Subtille* carrying 12 guns and 86 men, after six hours the French ship fled. It ran aground off Winterton, and the French were captured on this day, landed in Great Yarmouth and lodged as prisoners in the Tolhouse Gaol. By undermining the prison wall 14 of these prisoners broke out, but only four were retaken. There appear to be no records about what happened to the rest; maybe their descendants are still among us!

3 SEPTEMBER **1791** A double event involving two young men drew the crowds to throng around Norwich Castle Hill. William Bales (aged 26) was hanged for horse stealing and beside him dropped the well-known thief John Turner (aged 25), who could evade ultimate justice no longer.

4 SEPTEMBER **1829** The body of Ann Coe, buried two days previously in Fincham churchyard, was discovered to have been disinterred from her grave and stolen by bodysnatchers. The resurrectionists no doubt made their escape by the nearby turnpike road. The empty coffin was found in the churchyard 'superficially covered with mold'.

5 SEPTEMBER **1747** Jeered to his death by an angry crowd, disgusted by his crime, 18-year-old John Cooper was hanged on Norwich Castle Hill for 'the rape of a girl under 10 years'.

6 SEPTEMBER **1794** A young highwayman Cook March (aged 24) was executed in the Norwich Castle ditches for highway robbery and assault. Often drawing the sympathy of the crowd and large numbers of curious folk, highwaymen had a certain mystique and attracted a following because their attacks were normally directed against those better off in society – those wealthy enough to have carriages.

6 SEPTEMBER **1813** The last man to be hanged in Great Yarmouth was John Hannah. In a house on the north side, towards the end on Row 91, lived this 'wretched old man upwards of 70 years of age'. He murdered his wife during a quarrel, and was the last man to be tried and executed for a capital crime in the borough of Great Yarmouth. The story goes that Mr Jodrell, the town recorder, was a man of quiet and obliging disposition; rather than condemn a man to death, he resigned his office, leaving the disagreeable duty to his successor. No tenant could be found for the Hannahs' old house. His neighbours were happy to assist in its demolition, and a stable was erected on the site.

A FULL & PARTICULAR ACCOUNT OF THE

LIFE, CHARACTER, TRIAL, & BEHAVIOUR

TOGETHER WITH THE

CONFESSION

OF

John Hannah,

WHO WAS EXECUTED ON YARMOUTH DOWNS,

FOR THE

WILFUL MURDER,

OF

Elizabeth Hannah, his Wife,

On Monday, September, 6th. 1813.

It appeared from the evidence produced upon the trial of this unhappy man, that on Wednesday Morning April the 14th, between the hours of three & four o'clock the neighbourhood were alarmed by a violent outcry of Murder proceeding from the Dwelling-house of the Prisoner, but from the frequency of such alarms, altho the noise continued for a considerable length of time no particular notice was taken thereof, until all became suddenly quiet, which occasioned an apprehension that all was not right, and on some persons attempting to gain admission into the house, no one appeared to answer the call made and therefore after trying in vain for a considerable time, they at length broke open the door and found the unhappy man seated by the fire and smoaking a pipe, with his wife dead, and lying near him ; on the following morning the Coroner requested to have HANNAH brought before him for examination over the Body, as it appeared the deceased had come by her death from violence as her body was bruised in various places, particularly the hard pressure of a thumb on one of her Arms, & a general appearance of having been strangled ; in the course of this examination he uncautiously acknowledged himself guilty, by declaring he did not intend drawing the cord so tight, and also that he did not know what he had done untill it was past recovery ; after he had committed the rash act he washed the deceased's Hands and Face, and laid her forth ; in which order she was found when the door was broke open ; various evidence also proved that he had for many years been frequently ill treating her, which ill treatment of her he gradually increased till it terminated her existance, he had been frequently advised to check his ungovernable temper to no purpose, as he seemed rather to indulge it, till at the age of near threescore and ten it led him to commit the horrid crime for which he suffered ; they had been many years married, and it appears in the early part of the time to have been tolerably comfortable together, during which period they accumulated some property, which he has willed during his confinement and previous to his trial.

The day after he was committed to Prison he endeavoured to end his miserable existance by forcing an iron skewer through his throat, however he did not succeed in the attempt, and after that time every caution was used to prevent his depriving the law from bringing him to public justice.

EXECUTION,

Confession, & Prayer.

About eleven o'clock, he was conveyed from the place of his confinement to that of execution on a cart, he appeared sensible of his awful situation, and previous to his being turned off, & after the cap had been drawn over his eyes, he requested to be indulged by addressing the surrounding multitude, which he did to the following effect. Good People, you are here assembled to witness the just sentence of the Law put in execution against me ; and I here acknowledge myself guilty of the crime for which I am going to suffer, which I did with my own hands, by forceably and wickedly stopping her breath ; I hope all present will take warning by my Fate, and not give way to the diabolical influence of passion ; I trust I am so far brought to a sense of my own iniquities, that through God's infinite mercy I feel a lively hope of future happiness.

PRAYER.

O ALMIGHTY and most righteous Judge, I meekly receive my sentence, as the just reward of my sins ; but, as my iniquity bring on me this untimely and shameful death, O let my true repentance secure me a forgiveness of my sins, and bring me to everlasting life. O blessed Lord who didst not disdain to cast an eye on the penitent thief on the cross, despise not me who am now to suffer a like ignominious death, and I hope truly repent me of my sins, and fix all my hopes on thee in my distress, as he did in his.

Thou, who for the sins of others thyself suffered, O Lord save me, who am justly condemned for my own sins. In thy mercy do I trust ; into thy merciful hand I commend my spirit : O rescue my departing soul from eternal misery: forgive me in the abundant riches of thy mercy, and save me, great and wretched, but penitent and contrite sinner. Let the example of my fall be a warning to others, and tho' I taste thy justice in suffering an ignominious death, trust and hope hereafter to find the sweetness of thy mercy.

Stewardson, Printer, Norwich.

(Great Yarmouth Museums)

7 SEPTEMBER **1783** John Fox (aged 18) was executed on Norwich Castle Hill. On the Wisbech Road at Hardwicke Common, South Lynn, Fox set upon a poor itinerant Jew, robbed and beat him to the ground. This was described as a 'barbarous atrocity' by the court, which showed no mercy to his pleas for mitigation – that he had been drunk at the time and that this was his first and sworn last crime. The court ensured it was by executing him, and then by carting his body to the spot where he committed the crime on Hardwicke Common and gibbeting the remains to act as a stern warning to others.

8 SEPTEMBER **1560** Amy Robsart, Lady Dudley, was found at the bottom of the stairs at Cumnor House, Oxfordshire, with her neck broken. Raised on her father's various estates, principally Syderstone, she met her husband, Robert Dudley, when he accompanied his father to Norfolk in the royal army to put down Kett's rebel army in 1549; they married a year later. After a few years out of favour at court, following their support for Lady Jane Grey's abortive claim for the throne, the Dudleys were back in favour when the Protestant Elizabeth I ascended the throne in 1558. Robert and Elizabeth became very close friends, and court gossip implied they were lovers. There was also speculation about plans to marry, and even Robert becoming king – the only snag being that Robert was already married to Amy. She was sent to live at Cumnor House. On this day all the servants, having been given leave to visit the fair, returned to find Amy's body at the foot of the stairs. Some claimed she was killed on Robert's orders, while others suggest suicide, or it could have been an accident. The enigma still remains: was she pushed or did she fall?

9 SEPTEMBER **1837** Mr Jonathan Whitely-Cooper, an attorney practising at Norwich, was accosted while being driven in his gig through Catton by Cornelius Moor. Cooper drew a pistol, discharged it at Moor severely wounding him. Moor was removed to the Norfolk & Norwich Hospital where he died later that night. Cooper was taken into custody for murder and for shooting with intent to murder another man named Ford at the same place and time. Despite inference the shooting arose out of an election dispute there was no real evidence for this. The public had got this idea into their head and that a miscarriage of justice had occurred when the verdict of manslaughter was passed on Cooper. It was with great difficulty the jurymen were kept from the mob as they left the Coroner's court.

10 SEPTEMBER **1874** *Thorpe railway disaster.* This was described as 'one of the most appalling accidents that ever happened in English Railway travelling'. It occurred on the Great Eastern Railway between Norwich and Brundall on this day shortly after 9 p.m. The mail train from Great Yarmouth, joined at Reedham by another train from Lowestoft, had to wait at Brundall station (because the line is single) until the arrival of the evening express from Norwich to Great Yarmouth, or until permission was given to proceed. A mistaken order from the night inspector at Norwich station allowed the down express to leave Norwich, and the mail train was allowed to proceed from Brundall. The

doomed trains met head on at Thorpe, about 2 miles from Norwich. It was a wet slippery night and neither train saw the other, so had no time to apply effective braking. Thus 'a pyramid was formed of locomotives, the shattered carriages, and the wounded, dead, or dying passengers'. Eighteen people were killed and four died of their injuries; one, Mr G.R. Womack, clothier of

Engraving of the Thorpe railway disaster, 1874. *(Norfolk St John Ambulance Collection)*

Clearing the wreckage of the disaster, 1874. *(Norfolk St John Ambulance Collection)*

Norwich, 'lasted some hours'. This was undoubtedly one of the incidents which inspired the foundation of the St John Ambulance Association in 1877 to train workers and members of the public in first aid skills.

11 SEPTEMBER

1840 On or about this date the remains of the famous Norwich physician and philosopher Sir Thomas Browne were discovered during the preparation of another grave in the sanctuary of St Peter Mancroft Church. Author of a number of books, most notably *Religio Medici*, the explanation and justification of the physician's craft, and *Hydriotaphia or Urn Burial*, the contemplation of Roman cremations – 'To be gnawed out our graves, to have our skulls made drinking-bowls and our bone turned into pipes to delight and sport our enemies, are tragical abominations, escaped in burning burials.'

Poor Sir Thomas (left) was not 'burned and urned' but had his grave opened 160 years after his death in 1682. 'The bones of the skeleton were found to be in good preservation, particularly those of the skull. The brain was considerable in quantity but changed to a state of adipocere resembling ointment of a dark brown hue. The hair and beard remained profuse and perfect though the flesh of the face as well as every other part was gone. With respect to the formation of the head, we are informed that the forehead was remarkably low but the back of the cranium exhibited an unusual degree of depth and capaciousness.'

Most of Sir Thomas was respectfully reburied, apart from his skull, hair and coffin plate, which were removed by local chemist Robert Fitch. Later presented by Dr Lubbock to the Norfolk and Norwich Hospital, where it remained until after an undignified squabble over the cost, it was returned to St Peter Mancroft in 1922.

It was reinterred in a specially made casket with full burial rites which referred to it being 317-years-old!

12 September

1917 Norwich lad, Private John Abigail, 8th Battalion, the Norfolk Regiment, was shot at dawn. Following action on the first day of the Somme (1 July 1916) Private Abigail deserted, but was captured and sentenced to ten years' penal servitude, which had then been suspended.

Events on the Ypres salient the following year proved too much for the soldier, and he was once again brought before a court martial. Either indifferent to his fate, arrogant, or doubtful of the likelihood of an acquittal, he declined the assistance of an officer to defend him. The capital sentence was passed on him and this 20-year-old soldier was shot at dawn at the remote village of Esquelbecq, France. He is one of only two British soldiers to be buried in the village cemetery.

13 September

County Bridewells and Gaols visited by Prison Reformer John Howard

Acle Bridewell, visited by Howard in 1779 and 1782: no prisoners present on both of his visits. Above ground the Bridewell consisted of a day room with two rooms over it. Down nine steps were two dark dungeons 8 ft by 5 ft by 10 ft. Dating from 1633, by the time of Howard's visit it was in a poor state of repair. It had no courtyard, no water supply accessible to prisoners, no allowance and not even any straw.

14 September

Norfolk Old Dame's Leechcraft

Diarrhoea and similar disorders are allayed by the gratings of cakes or bread baked on a Good Friday. Nose bleeds are treated by the sufferer wearing a skein of scarlet silk round his neck, tied in nine knots by a maiden. Typhus fever may be drawn out at the feet of the patient by placing the skirt of a fresh killed sheep on the soles.

15 September

1885 Robert Goodale, 'the Walsoken Murderer', was executed at Norwich Castle for the murder of his wife. A big man by all accounts, he had lost a lot of weight through his incarceration and trial, but still tipped the scales at over 15 stones. James Berry, the public executioner, worked the drop that he should give Goodale from Marwood's table of drops – 7 ft 8 in – but, uneasy about such a long drop on such a big man, he reduced it to 5 ft 9 in. Berry recorded what happened next in his memoirs:

A Victorian artist's somewhat fanciful impression of the last beheading (albeit an accident) at a British execution. Robert Goodale, the Walsoken murderer, after the most infamous 'drop' of Public Executioner, James Berry's career, Norwich Castle, 15 September 1885.

The whole of the arrangements were carried out in the usual manner and when I pulled the lever the drop fell properly and the prisoner fell out of sight. We were horrified, however, to see the rope jerked upwards and for an instant I thought the noose had slipped from the culprit's head or that the rope had broken. But it was worse than that for the jerk had severed the head entirely from the body and both had fallen into the bottom of the pit. Of course death was instantaneous so that the poor fellow had not suffered in any way; but it was terrible to think such a revolting thing should have occurred. We were all unnerved and shocked. The Governor, whose efforts to prevent any accident had kept his nerves at full strain, fairly broke down and wept.

Berry was haunted by the fear of a repetition of this incident for the rest of his career. By 1892 he could take no more, and he retired. After a brief lecture tour he found religion, and toured evangelical churches as a respectable speaker who declared he 'gave himself to Jesus'.

1769 Elizabeth Martin, the last woman to be hanged at Great Yarmouth, was executed on this day in 1769. A domestic servant in Custom House Row (Row 103), she paid the ultimate penalty for the murder of her illegitimate child.

16 September

Old Punishments: Whipping and Birching

By an Act of 1530 the use of whipping as a judicial punishment was clearly outlined: delinquents were 'to be tied to the end of a cart, naked, and beaten with whips through a market town till the body be bloody by reason of such whipping'. By the time of the Elizabethan Poor Law, when decree was made that 'sturdy beggars' be whipped and sent back to the parish from which they came, whipping posts were set up alongside stocks in every town and most villages. An example is still to be found under the ancient market house at New Buckenham. So easy to administer, so clear the warning to others, whipping became the judicial panacea for most minor crimes. Ruffians and vagabonds, rioters, drunkards and receivers of stolen goods provided a rich harvest for the flailing lashes. The lash was used in Norfolk up to the nineteenth century but birching, a common punishment used on younger criminals convicted of petty thefts and persistent bad behaviour, continued well into the twentieth century.

17 September

1583 John Lewes, heretic, burnt in the Castle ditches for blasphemy, probably the last man in the city to be punished so for his beliefs. Norwich has a long and tragic history of religious persecution. Near the site of the old Bishop's Gate is Lollard's Pit. In the fifteenth century Lollardism began to be seen as a disturbing element in the episcopate of Norwich. William Wyatt, William Waddon and Hugh Pye were probably the first to be burnt 'outside Bishop's Gate' in 1427. William White, a very popular preacher in the city and

18 September

William White awaiting his fate as they pile the faggots round the stake at Lollard's Pit, 1428.

probably the most famous of all the Norwich Martyrs was brought before Bishop Alnwick and condemned to be burnt in Lollard's Pit. One tale tells of how White made an attempt to preach to the people as he was being brought to the stake but one of the Bishop's servants struck him on the mouth to prevent this. The early sixteenth century saw about six people were burnt here for heresy or expression of Lollard ideas such as refusing the sacraments of the Roman Catholic Church, denial of the 'special' role of priests or shunning of religious images. Of these few one was Thomas Bilney 'an eminent martyr'. He was convicted of heresy before the Bishop of London in 1527 and returned to Norwich to be burnt as a lapsed heretic in 1531.

19 SEPTEMBER **Old Punishments: The Stocks**

This was probably the oldest and most widely used punitive device for punishment of minor offenders, and such as beggars, drunkards, louts, prostitutes and scolds. In the close-knit communities of the past retribution against those who transgressed social or moral codes was both public and humiliating. The simple construction of the stocks had changed little since their earliest appearances in Anglo-Saxon books. They consisted of two sturdy uprights fixed in the ground, with grooves in their inner surfaces in which were slotted two solid timber boards, one above the other. Each plank had semicircles cut in it, which when aligned formed holes which encircled the culprit's ankles. With the upper plank held in position by a padlock there was no escape for the victim until he or she was released by the parish constable, beadle or similar appointed official. The authorities considered it so important that villages should have stocks that acts decreeing this were passed in the fourteenth and fifteenth centuries. The absence of stocks in a village after 1405 would downgrade a village to a mere hamlet. Used heavily into the eighteenth century, stocks were known to be used for drunken miscreants up to the late nineteenth century.

The old stocks at Haveringland, *c.* 1905.

1720 A mob in Pockthorpe, Norwich, rioted 'under pretence of destroying calicoes'. It was dispersed by the local artillery company.

20 September

1863 James Naylor (aged 51) of Elsing murdered his 81-year-old wife Charlotte. From the time he was admitted to Norwich Castle to await trial at the Assizes he endeavoured to convince all he met that he was not sound of mind. He was however, to cheat the gallows: he died from cancer of the stomach on 23 November.

21 September

22 SEPTEMBER   **1900**   *The Great Yarmouth Bootlace Murder.* On 15 September Mary Jane Bennett, estranged wife of John Herbert Bennett, took lodgings with their baby child Ruby under the assumed name of Mrs Hood at Mrs Rudrum's, 3, Row 104, South Quay. Mary Jane even created a fictitious history in which she claimed she was a widow with a brother-in-law infatuated with her. On the 22nd, saying she was going to meet someone for a drink, Mary Jane left the child in Mrs Rudrum's care and went out. Mrs Rudrum next noticed her standing outside the town hall at 9 p.m. That was the last recorded sighting of Mary Jane alive. The following morning John Norton, a young lad of 14, discovered her body in a lonely scrubby dip on South Beach. She was lying on her back, skirt above her knees and strangled with a bootlace from one of her shoes.

The photograph of Mary Bennett with daughter Ruby on the beach at Yarmouth with chain found on Bennett – key evidence at the trial.

As soon as Mary Jane's identity was confirmed, her husband was identified as the first suspect. He was arrested in Woolwich. The most damning clue against him was the gold chain found in his possession – identified by Mrs Rudrum as the one Mary Jane was wearing, and shown on a photograph of the mother and child taken by a strolling beach photographer. Marshall Hall, the eminent defence counsel, argued that the chain shown on the photo was of a different link to that found in Bennett's possession. A Mr Sholto Douglas, a stranger to Bennett, came forward to identify Bennett as a man he had met in Eltham

Bennett in the dock.

at a time that would have made it impossible for him to have been in Yarmouth at the time of the murder. This could only be corroborated by Bennett's appearance in the witness box – considered out of the question by his defence counsel on his past performance. There had been too many lies: why did Mary Jane assume the false identity? Were they working a scam together, possibly blackmail – foiled by murder of which Bennett was innocent? Bennett was found guilty and silently went to his execution at Norwich Prison on 21 March 1901 carried out by father and son public executioner team James and Thomas Billington.

There is a strange postscript to this odd case. When the black flag was hoisted to proclaim the execution the flagstaff snapped, an event construed by some as a sign of Bennett's innocence. Twelve years later, on Monday 15 July 1912, the body of 18-year-old Dora Grey was discovered on almost the same spot where Mary Jane was found – strangled with a bootlace from one of her own shoes. Her murderer was never identified.

1895 Mr W. Le Neve, a Tunstead farmer, drove through Neatishead in the company of another man and a young lad. On reaching the White Horse Inn the two men got out, leaving the lad in charge of the cart. Almost immediately afterwards one of the horses shook its head, partly threw its halter and bolted down the road towards Irstead. Mrs Mary Ann Barber, an old lady aged about 70 who was very deaf and almost blind, was walking up the road when the runaway horse struck her and knocked her several yards, killing her instantly. According to the newspaper article, the elderly lady had married a man considerably younger than herself the previous year.

23 September

1827 An inquest was held by Mr Bell, the Norwich coroner, on the body of James Bailey, one of the persons forcibly carried away to prevent his voting at the alderman's election on the 12th. He had been taken to the Castle public house at Wroxham on the 10th and next morning taken to the Swan at Horning, thence to Smallburgh and on the same night removed to the Plough at Ridlington. Bailey, being very ill, suffered from being moved about. He was engaged on his return to sell programmes at the music festival between the 18th and 20th, but on the 22nd he 'broke a blood vessel and died'. His attendance at the music festival took the onus off his 'captors' and the jury returned a verdict of 'Died from the visitation of God'.

24 September

1866 Minnie Stratton, daughter of 'General and Mrs Tom Thumb' (a famous midget couple who toured with the legendary Barnum & Bailey Circus) died at the Norfolk Hotel, Norwich. Buried on the 26th at Norwich Cemetery Mr and Mrs Stratton were chief mourners 'many attended the funeral but there were more spectators than mourners.'

25 September

1815 Died this day aged 50 a Mrs Holland at Great Yarmouth. 'Her death was occasioned by her being frightened by the stories of a Mrs Spaul who pretended to tell fortunes.' Mrs Spaul was committed to gaol by the Mayor.

26 September

1766 A dreadful riot in Norwich occurred on this day on account of the great scarcity and price of provisions, especially corn. The mob damaged the houses and destroyed the furniture of several bakers, pulled down part of the new mills and destroyed a large quantity of flour. A large malthouse outside Conesford Gate was burned and a baker's house on Tombland was totally destroyed. The mob is even recorded as storming as far as Trowse Newton Hall, where they destroyed or damaged much of the furniture and fixtures. Once the riot was quelled by 'magistrates and citizens' 30 ringleaders were taken and tried by special commission on 1 December. Eight were given death sentences but only two were executed, more to provide a warning than for any other reason, on 10 January 1767.

27 September

1659 Anne Cowstad, a woman considered by many to be 'out of her wits' who murdered her two children, was executed on Norwich Castle Hill.

28 September

29 September **1708** Michael Hamond and his sister Ann, children aged 7 and 11 respectively, were hanged outside the South Gate, King's Lynn, on this day for theft. The people of Lynn were appalled; it was said that the sky turned black and there was thunder and lightning after the children were left to dangle. It is said that Antony Smith, the hangman, was filled with such remorse at this judicial killing that he died within a fortnight of this execution.

30 September **1757** Richard Taylor was executed on Norwich Castle Hill for felony and burglary.

(Norfolk Local Studies Library)

THE TRIAL CONFESSION

AND LAMENTATION.

Of

THOMAS, A, STURLEY

AGED 39 now under sentence of **DEATH**, in **NORWICH CASTLE**, For willfully **SHOOTING** at his **UNCLE**, Samuel **PAGE**, of Cawston, **FARMER**, with intent to Murder him,

Thomss A. Sturley, aged 39, was charged with having shot and wounded Samuel Page of Cawston, farmer, with intent to murder him. He pleaded not guily.

Mr. Evans appeared for the prosecution, and stated the partiulars of the case to the Jury. Mr. J. W. U. Browne also appeared for the prosecution, and Mr. Druery for the defence This case excited considerable interest, which was evidenced by the crowded state of the court.

Samuel Page, of Cawston, the prosecutor, was first called. He gave the following evidence, in a very indistinct manner, in consequence of the injury he had received. He remembered being in his yard on the 16th of November last, when the prisoner came to him and said, " I am come to see you again." I answered, " So I see you are." He said you have done nothing for me, I said I should do nothing till I had seen Mr. Keith, my attorney. Very little more passed between us, he put his hand into his breast pocket, and said, " I have two little things here, one for yon and one for me. He pulled out two small pocket pistols, and took one in each hand; he put them on the cock, they were both capped ready to fire. He said " are you prepared to pay lbs200 in two minutes for you have only two minutes to live." He said, are you ready are you ready to go. I had a half-peck measure in my hand, which I waved about my head to protect myself. He fired the pistol and said off she goes. It missed fire He then fired the second pistol, the charge from which hit me in the right hand corner of the mouth and knocked out two or three teeth. He had thrown down his stick before he fired, and then he picked it up and struck me with it. The surgeon, he said, had extracted one shot from his face, and the wadding from his mouth The prisoner was only arm's length off when he fired.

Samul Douglas deposed, that he was employ'd by Mr. Page, He saw the Prisoner fire the Pistol, he went up to take hold of him.

The prisoner flourished his stick and said, D—n you, keep your distance, He struck his master on the head with the stick,

Sturley walked away, he went after him & found him at the Rat-Catchers public house, Soon after he gave him into the custody of Ralph, the policeman.

Edward Ralph deposed, that he took the Prisoner into custody on the 16th, of Novem ber, & found a brace of pistols, some powder and shot on him, The Prisoner turned round and cried and said he was sorry he(Mr Page) did not fall dead on the spot, he would then have shot himself, He said he had not done his duty, as he did not shoot him dead,

Walter Harsant said he was a surgeon of Reepham, he had been called in to attend the prosecutor, and found a shot and wadding in his mouth, and several teeth gone, He attended him for five weeks.

The police Ralph said that the pistol which had missed fire was found to contain a charge the shot corresponding to that found upon the prisoner.

Mr. Druery then briefly addressed the jury on behalf of the prisoner. The assault had been committed under strong provocation and excitment, which he had no doubt they would take into consideration, and give their verdict with their usual justice.

The Learned Judge then summed up, and the jury having considered for a time, returned a virdict of guilty on the first count of the indictment, and recommended him to mercy. A death-like silence reigned throughout the vast assembly while the judge put on the black cap— fatal omen !—and thus addressed the prisoner at the bar. You have been found guilty of wounding this relation of yours, to whom you are much indebted. In point of moral guilt it is not in any respect short of the offence of having actually destroyed life for it was contrary to your intention; that he should escape. He fortunately has escape ; but, as far as your guilt is concerned, that circumstance makes no difference. It is my duty to pass upon you the extreme sentence of the law and, in adverting to that sentence—although I certainly think it right to trans mit to the Secretary of State the recommendation of the jury—I am not in any respect warranted in saying that your sentence is like ly to be mitigated ; that will be entirely for him to decide. So far as I am concerned, I can only exhort you to take the best means you can to reconcile yourself to your offended maker. The sentence of the law is, that you be hanged by the neck till you be dead,

OCTOBER

Police Sergeant Slater keeping order among the crowd at the spot (to the right of the photograph) where the murdered body of Nellie Howard was found on the Spixwoth Road, Catton, 29 October 1908.

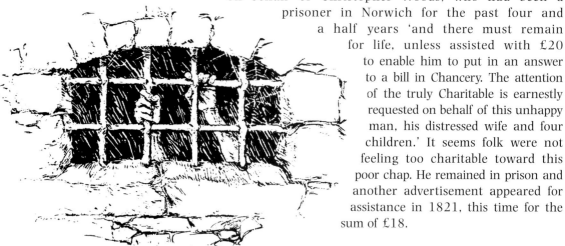

1 OCTOBER   **1817**   An advertisement appeared in the *Norfolk Chronicle* appealing on behalf of Christopher Woods, who had been a prisoner in Norwich for the past four and a half years 'and there must remain for life, unless assisted with £20 to enable him to put in an answer to a bill in Chancery. The attention of the truly Charitable is earnestly requested on behalf of this unhappy man, his distressed wife and four children.' It seems folk were not feeling too charitable toward this poor chap. He remained in prison and another advertisement appeared for assistance in 1821, this time for the sum of £18.

2 OCTOBER   **1907**   *'Never seen a worse record'*. John Cooper (aged 37), a stoker and Lynn-based habitual criminal, was arrested by PC Walden for stealing a pint of whisky, a bottle of cider and two bottles of ale from the Anchor of Hope, Norfolk Street, King's Lynn. He had been observed by the constable with these bottles sticking out of his pockets, and PC Walden made enquiries in the pub. The goods were not accounted for, so he tracked down Cooper whom he came across in the early hours of the morning. There was no trace of the whisky to be found, except the smell. Cooper was tried and found guilty at the Norfolk Assizes. The judge said that considering the prisoners age he 'had never seen a worse record. The prisoner would have begun a life of crime about the age of 10 and he had steadfastly kept it up ever since.' Cooper had been punished as a boy by six strokes of the birch rod, convicted of stealing money the next year and was sent to a reformatory. That was in 1881 and in 1885 he was again before the magistrates for stealing money. In 1886 he was given three months for stealing and the following year was convicted yet again. In 1888 at Plymouth he was convicted of larceny, and in the same year sentenced to five years for burglary at Exeter. 'That did not seem to do him any good' for in 1898 he was convicted of highway robbery at Maidstone. In 1897 Cooper was convicted for warehouse-breaking, and on his return to Lynn in 1900 was convicted of stealing iron, in 1901 at Norwich for stealing brass and in 1902 at Folkestone for burglary. Since then he had not been convicted, but the judge could not assume that with such a record he had been living an honest life. 'The public must be protected from such a man', and he was sentenced to penal servitude for three years.'

3 OCTOBER   **1776**   Almost a year after his escape, renewed appeals were posted for the capture of an escaped Norwich prisoner. 'Broke out of gaol, between

the hours of 8 and 9 o'clock in the evening of 31st October 1775 James Benstead, charged on an Exchequer Process. He formerly kept a publick house, known by the sign of the hospital out of St Stephen's Gates, situated between the Wymondham and Scole turnpike roads; is about 26 years of age, about 5 ft 6 in high, fresh complexion, grey eyes with eyebrows inclining to be sandy, flaxen hair, tied up behind and very thick curl'd behind the ears, remarkably thick upper lip with scar upon it and is supposed to be lurking about the area of Southwold and Halesworth. Whoever apprehends and secures the above J. Benstead and gives immediate notice to the Keeper of the said gaol shall receive a reward of Twenty Pounds to be paid by Benjamin Fakenham, Gaoler.'

County Bridewells and Gaols visited by Prison Reformer John Howard

4 OCTOBER

Norwich City Bridewell: 'Four rooms, 21 feet square and 10 high, with fire places, and two warehouses for wood. The dungeons are down 15 steps: in one part, four for the men and in another part three, more close and damp, for women. In these and in other rooms are cribs. But it is to be hoped the gentlemen, who have made many improvements in their gaol, will be so considerate as to order these cells to be barred to all, unless to such as are very refactory and disobedient. Only one court: river and pump water. Allowance two pennyworth of bread daily, two hot dinners in a week, and firing from Michaelmas to Ladyday. The sick have four pence a day and firing when wanted. Employment, cutting logwood, of which in 1782, there were 15 or 16 ton in the warehouses. This employment is too laborious and severe, where most of the prisoners are women.'

5 OCTOBER

1840 George Edward Seales, known as a common police informer, procured the conviction of a coach proprietor at the Norwich Police Court for carrying more than the regulation number of passengers. On leaving the Guildhall Seales was violently assaulted by the mob, and was escorted to his home by 20 police officers.

6 OCTOBER **1799** During the Napoleonic Wars the detached tower of East Dereham church was used as a lock-up for French prisoners of war when they were being marched from Yarmouth to the prison at Norman Cross. One such prisoner was a nimble French lieutenant named Jean de Narde, the 28-year-old son of a St Malo notary, who contrived to escape and made off, pursued with alacrity by a sentry. Taking refuge in a tree, the lieutenant refused to come down when challenged, whereupon he was 'shot out of the tree like a crow'. He was buried in the churchyard without a mark until the noble nineteenth-century vicar and historian the Revd B.J. Armstrong was so moved by the story that in 1857 he and two friends had a stone put up.

7 OCTOBER **1801** Elizabeth Manship of Ormesby was at the Norfolk County Sessions for committing an outrage upon the Revd Eli Morgan Price, when he was officiating at divine service at the parish church. It appeared that while Mr Price was reading a new form of Thanksgiving 'for the late plentiful season' the defendant rushed out of her pew and snatched the paper out of his hands, to the very great disturbance and alarm of the congregation. The jury found the defendant guilty and she was sentenced to pay a fine of £20 – a considerable amount to labouring folk in 1801.

8 OCTOBER **1842** At a late sitting of the Litcham Magistrates to hear appeals against assessed taxes, Mr Beck, one of the appellants accused Mr Lynes, the surveyor of taxes, of partial conduct. Incensed by comments made, Beck jumped up and got hold of Lynes' nose, which he held for some time. Lynes retaliated by striking Beck several blows on the head and face, and a battle ensued. The police interfered and Captain Fitzroy ordered the parties into custody. It was stated that there had previously been a quarrel between Mr King, the magistrates' clerk, Beck and Lynes, and King had challenged Lynes to a duel. All three were bound over for the affray in the court. Lynes sued Beck for assault at the Assizes and was granted 1s damages, the judge remarking that the assault 'was of a very degrading and contumacious character'.

9 OCTOBER **1776** The wall of Haddiscoe church bears a remarkable memorial tablet erected in memory of William Salter, aged 59, Yarmouth stage coach man, killed on this day when his horses skidded on the icy Haddiscoe hill and his coach overturned near the church. Part of the inscription reads:

> His up hill work chiefly done
> His Stage is ended Race is run
> One journey is remaining still,
> To climb up Sions holy hill
> And now his faults are all forgiv'n
> Elijah like drive up to heaven
> Take the Reward of all his Pains
> And leave to other hands the Reins.

1834 One Robert Cutting, aged 75, died about this day at Swainsthorpe. Commonly known as 'Blind Bob', he could find any place to which he was sent in Norwich to such accuracy that he was postman from Swainsthorpe to the city to for more than 50 years.

1823 One of the most popular means of keeping prisoners occupied while serving their 'hard labour' sentence was the treadwheel or treadmill. Introduced in Suffolk County Gaol in 1819, by 1860 it had been adopted by many prisons across the country. Prisoners walked up hill on this turning wheel going nowhere at a rate of 50 steps a minute, up to 19,000 feet each day. Often this was a meaningless waste of energy which produced nothing but never to waste motive power the larger Norfolk and City prisons used their treadwheel for pumping water around the prison. The treadmill was not without its dangers. On 11 October 1823 William Burton Peeling, a prisoner at Swaffham Gaol was endeavouring to have a conversation with a prisoner in the adjoining division or 'stall' while treading the wheel. Accidentally, Peeling caught his head in the wheel which drew him in and crushed him to death.

11 OCTOBER **1817** Mr Robert Baker, glover and breeches maker of Wells-next-the-Sea, was found murdered, his head beaten and his throat cut, in Market Lane, about 200 yards from the town. The county magistrates assembled for other business in the Shirehall in Norwich ordered the printing of 3,000 handbills giving notice of this foul deed. These were taken by constables to every coach, fish cart and other conveyance leaving Norwich. A 29-year-old man named James Johnson was apprehended on suspicion at the King's Head Inn, Hethersett on 15 October. The prisoner was tried at the Norfolk Assizes, held at Thetford on 19 March 1818, when, after a trial lasting seven and a half hours, the jury returned a verdict of guilty. Johnson was sentenced to death by Mr Justice Dallas, 'his body to be afterwards delivered to surgeons to be anatomised'. Full sentence was duly carried out on Norwich Castle Hill before 5,000 spectators. 'Mr Wilson, a gentleman from London and Mr Austen, a pupil of Mr Dalrymple's, performed the dissection and prepared the subject for lectures which have been daily delivered by Mr Crosse.'

12 OCTOBER **1915** Nurse Edith Cavell, Norfolk's greatest heroine, was executed by a German firing-squad. Born the daughter of the vicar of Swardeston in 1865, from her earliest years she dedicated her life to caring for others. Working in a clinic in Brussels that she had established before the outbreak of war, she treated Allied and German casualties without discrimination. She set up routes via the Dutch border by which recovered Allied soldiers could escape. Eventually she was betrayed, and condemned to death under the charge of 'conducting soldiers to the enemy'. Her name became a *cause célèbre* in British patriotism and recruitment during the war, but her message lives on and is far more profound. Her words recorded on the plaque above her grave at Life's

Green, in the precincts of Norwich Cathedral, sum up her final thoughts: 'I have seen death so often it is not fearful or strange to me, and this I would say, standing as I do in view of God and Eternity. I realise that patriotism is not enough. I must have no hatred or bitterness against anyone.'

13 OCTOBER

1835 At the Three Turks public house, Charing Cross, Norwich, one William Cork, an artisan, was singing the well-known song written on the death of General Wolfe. After repeating the words 'And I to death must yield' fell down, and much to the consternation of the company, instantly expired.

14 OCTOBER

1895 *'I'm Jack the Ripper!'* Michael Barker, a labourer, was summoned for being drunk and disorderly before the Norwich Guildhall. PC Burgess stated that on the previous Friday night he heard the smashing of glass while in George Street. He went to the spot and saw the prisoner standing in the middle of the street with a shovel in his hand calling out 'I'm Jack the Ripper'. He also used obscene language. On catching sight of the constable he ran down a row and met PC Wharton, who stopped him. He was drunk, and had smashed the windows of Mr Page's public house. In court Barker said 'I was drunk and could not help it'. Inspector Hardesty said that the prisoner had been before the court four times, three times for drunk and disorderly behaviour and once for larceny. Barker was fined 10s and costs or 14 days.

15 OCTOBER

1843 Sarah Martin, prisoner reformer, died. Without doubt the most well-known person connected with the Tolhouse Gaol in Great Yarmouth, her work has often been compared with Elizabeth Fry but there were significant differences. Unlike Mrs Fry, Sarah made no attempt to change or improve

Sarah Martin reading scriptures to prisoners in Yarmouth Tolhouse.

conditions, but stressed how wicked the prisoners were and that they fully deserved their sentences. Her concern was for the moral welfare of the prisoners, for which she strove with missionary-like zeal, reading scripture to them and organising Sunday services. She taught prisoners new skills so they could earn money before they left – women learnt how to sew and mend while the men learnt how to make straw hats and how to carve buttons and spoons from mutton bones. Living on the interest of money left to her by her grandmother and gifts from friends, it was only hardship when this money ran short that persuaded her to accept an annual income of £12 from the corporation for her labours. Poverty and strain took their toll on her, and after a gradual decline since the spring she died after a short illness on this day. She is buried next to her beloved grandmother in Caister churchyard.

16 October **1793** Queen Marie Antoinette, wife of King Louis XVI of France, went to her death on the guillotine. This event did not happen without a number of attempts to rescue her. Charlotte Atkyns was one who tried: she was the Norfolk Scarlet Pimpernel. The daughter of Robert Walpole and a fine actress, she was appearing at Drury Lane when Robert Atkyns of Ketteringham Hall saw her. Falling in love, they were soon married and travelled the continent, where, at Versailles, Charlotte met and became a friend of Marie Antoinette. On the French Queen's imprisonment under sentence of death, Charlotte attempted to help her escape, disguised as a soldier of the National Guard. Sadly her efforts were in vain, but undeterred – and unrestrained following her husband's death – she spent her fortune on wild schemes to get the dauphin out of France. She died in 1836 in poverty, and is buried in Paris in an unmarked grave. It was only in 1907 that 'a few who sympathised with her' erected a plaque to her memory in Ketteringham Church.

17 October **1890** Mrs Semmence, wife of Mr William Semmence, landlord of the Jolly Farmers Inn at Watton, was going upstairs when near the top she stumbled and fell, head foremost, to the bottom. The teeth of a large ornamental comb she was wearing stuck deeply into and broke off in her head. Dr Mallins was immediately sent for and he carefully extracted the broken teeth of the comb, but expressed great fear for her recovery owing to the depth of the wounds and the severity of shock to the system. After suffering much pain, Mrs Semmence died within 24 hours of the fall.

1730 Christopher Burraway of Martham died on this day. His stone is unique. It reads: 'Here lyeth The Body of Christ. Burraway who departed this life ye 18 day of October Anno Domini 1730 aged 59 years. And here Lyes Alice who by hir life was my Sister, my Mistres, My Mother and my Wife Dyed Feb ye 12, 1729. Aged 76 years.' The tale that explains this is that Burraway was unwittingly guilty of incest. Alice had had an illegitimate son by her father. Unaware of his parentage, Christopher left home as a boy and returning in manhood found work as a steward with Alice, who did not recognise him. He took her as his mistress, married her, and only then did the story emerge when Alice identified him by some distinguishing mark on his body. The Burraway stone is still in Martham church, but it has been hidden for many years by the organ.

18 OCTOBER

1842 At the Norwich Quarter Sessions Johnson Hemnell was sentenced to fifteen years' transportation for stealing promissory notes, gold and silver to the amount of £150, the property of Mr Harrison Wells of Dilham. On the night after his conviction the convict accompanied two of the prison warders to Seething, where he showed them a green garden bank in which £108 of the stolen money was found concealed.

19 OCTOBER

1739 Twenty people were robbed between Norwich and Honingham by two highwaymen.

20 OCTOBER

1897 A shocking tragedy occurred on this day at the home of Captain G. McIlwaine, RN, (Commander of the Coastguard), Beach House, Gorleston, at about 5.30 a.m. The perpetrator of the deed was a smacksman named William Moore (aged 34), and the victim was his wife Emma, a domestic servant in the employ of Captain McIlwaine. During a quarrel, while having an early meal together, Moore struck the fatal blows with a common dinner knife, but on discovery of the terrible scene Mrs Moore's head was found nearly severed from her body. Moore was brought to trial on 15 November where he was sentenced to seven years for manslaughter.

21 OCTOBER

The new sign for the Wild man pub on Bedford Street, Norwich. It shows Peter the Wild Boy with his animal friends in the forest in Germany.

1751 Fire broke out, destroying the Norwich Bridewell and several adjoining houses. Peter the Wild Youth was confined here at this time. This young man was lost in a

22 OCTOBER

wood in Germany when he was a small child aged about 6 years. After a space of some six years he was found naked and quite wild. Taken on by a travelling showman, he was toured around Europe as a curiosity. Peter was remembered for many years on the sign of the Wild Man on Bedford Street, which showed an apparently demon-like youth among flames.

23 OCTOBER **1919** Report of the trial at the Assizes of Hugh Stanley Jolly (aged 26) for the murder of Gladys Mary Lupton at Great Yarmouth on 15 May. Having been for a drink with a girl named Holmes in a local pub they left for home. Having bought some chips, they passed three girls, Ruby Quinton, Lily Chambers and Gladys Lupton. One of the girls, believed to be Chambers, called out 'Oh, Gussie!' which was taken by Jolly and Holmes as referring to them. Jolly went over to the girls: two ran off but Lupton remained, and Jolly asked the other girls' names.

Lupton said she did not know, and a heated exchange took place. 'The next thing known was that the girl Lupton fell to the ground with her throat cut by a razor.' The account then states that Holmes and Jolly ran off to Holmes's house, where Holmes said 'I shall get the blame for this.' And Jolly replied 'No, you won't; I'll take all the responsibility on my shoulders.' The mental stability of Jolly was brought into question. His war record showed that he was discharged from the army on three occasions with epilepsy and was finally certified with a congenital mental condition in 1917, after which he should have been taken into care.

Dr Starling, the prison doctor, was also called and confirmed the prisoner's insanity. The jury decided the prisoner was guilty but not responsible for his actions. The judge ordered the prisoner to be kept in custody during his Majesty's pleasure.

24 OCTOBER **1832** A reported general court martial at the Cavalry Barracks against certain privates for disobeying the lawful commands of the Colonel of 7th Hussars. Colonel Keane, gave the order of 'Attention', but to his surprise not a man obeyed his command. Seizing one of the men, a Private William Pitman, the colonel marched to the officers' quarters and tried him on the spot for insubordination. He was sentenced to 200 lashes, which were administered immediately in the presence of the whole regiment.

This action restored discipline, but a selection of men on parade who had disobeyed the order were court martialled and had to write a written defence of their actions. The principal complaint was that they were overworked. The court martial concluded its sitting on 10 November and the sentences, approved by His Majesty, were as follows: Private John Martin, transportation for life; Thomas Almond, seven years' transportation; Henry Bone, seven years, Charles Edwards, 12 months; and John Clason, 14 years' transportation. Five NCOs were reduced to the ranks and the RSM was suspended.

County Bridewells and Gaols visited by Prison Reformer John Howard

Thetford Town combined Gaol and Bridewell, visited in 1774, 1776, 1779 and 1782. 'The ground floor for the keeper. On the first storey are four rooms for debtors, and two for delinquents. For felons, a dungeon down a ladder of 10 steps 18 feet by nine and a half. At Assize once a year, from sixteen to twenty prisoners brought hither from Norwich Castle are confined in this dungeon for five nights. . . . Each felon is allowed one penny per day at the expense of the town, and each debtor the same. A clergyman to attend the felons while under sentence of death. Debtors and felons are to wash themselves every day, and are to be let into the yard where a trough is fixed with fresh water for the purpose. And they are to sweep and sprinkle their rooms every morning.'

1882 *A Somnambulist.* A girl of 17 employed as a general servant by a shopkeeper at Felthorpe, after retiring to rest at 9 o'clock got out of bed, put on a dress and a pair of boots, climbed out of the bedroom window and had walked the 5 miles to Cawston without waking. She was found fast asleep on her father's doorstep in the village at 4 a.m. in the morning. Stiff, cold and speechless when restored to warmth and comfort, she swore she had no recollection whatever of having left her bed.

1834 The 'Pilot' coach was on its journey from Norwich to Lowestoft with eight outside and two inside passengers when the lead horse from the team of horses changed at the Unicorn became restive on Bracondale Hill, and while turning sharply into Martineau Lane overturned the vehicle. Several of the passengers were injured; the one who came off worst was Mr Beeton Rathbone of Geldeston, who sustained a fracture of the skull from which he died an hour afterwards at the Pine Apple public house at Trowse.

1821 The New County Gaol opened on Castle Hill, Norwich.

1814 Charles Pegg stood in the city pillory for an hour as part of his sentence for an attempted felony. When his time was completed 'the hoary-headed culprit' was taken back to the City Gaol.

1908 Newspapers were hit today with the news of the murder of Ellen Elizabeth 'Nellie' Howard, whose body had been discovered the previous day at Old Catton. A young man by the name of Horace Larter (aged 19) was apprehended for the crime and brought to trial at the Assizes on 27 January 1909; he pleaded guilty to the crime. Sentence of death was passed, but was later commuted to penal servitude for life.

The funeral of Nellie Howard, victim of Horace Larter, the Spixworth murderer, 1908.

31 October

GREAT YARMOUTH, 31st October, 1809.

FELONY.
5 Guineas Reward

WHEREAS,

A Seaman, called JOHN MORRIS, belonging to His Majesty's Sloop of War the ONYX, and the Servant of JOHN PARISH, Esq. her Commander, on Saturday last, deserted from His Majesty's Service, and stands charged with stealing 130 Spanish Dollars, £25 in Bank of England Notes, 6 Tablespoons, and 6 four-pronged Silver Forks, marked J.P., 1 Dozen Teaspoons, marked P., and a Silver Nutmeg-Grater, the Property of Captain PARISH.

Whoever will apprehend the said JOHN MORRIS, and lodge him in any of His Majesty's Gaols, will, upon his Apprehension, be paid by Captain PARISH the above Reward, and will be entitled to His Majesty's Bounty for apprehending a Deserter.

JOHN MORRIS is a Native of America, 22 Years of Age, is a good-looking Black Man, with Woolly Hair; has a round Face, and a particular Cast in his right Eye; is in stature 5 Feet 3 Inches; speaks good English.

KEYMER, PRINTER, YARMOUTH.

On the night of 'Ghoulies, Ghosties and long-leggedy beasties' in 1809 John Morris was on the run. (*Great Yarmouth Museums*)

November

Eliza Chastney, a maid wounded in the murderous attack at Stanfield Hall in November 1848, is conveyed in a covered litter by a team of police constables to give evidence at Norwich Shirehall during the trial of James Blomfield Rush.

1 NOVEMBER **1812** James Parsons, a farrier in the employment of Richard Watson, veterinary surgeon, Norwich, was buried with full 'veterinary and Masonic' ceremonies at St Gregory's Church in the presence of 2,000 people. The procession was headed by two farriers in white aprons with their implements bound with white ribbons and reversed. The corpse was carried by six brethren of Stags Lodge in their full regalia, the sword, middle apron, and collar laid on the pall. Parsons's favourite horse, which he rode for many years, was covered in black velvet. The head stall and bridle were adorned with white roses and facings, as he had died a bachelor. At the conclusion of the service 'a solemn dirge was sung which much gratified many hundreds of persons'.

2 NOVEMBER **1896** At North Walsham Petty Sessions Richard Lovell and Frederick Brown, men on the tramp, were brought up in custody and charged by PC Oakley with begging at Sutton the previous day. The prisoners appeared in court in 'grotesque costumes'; having torn up all their clothes in their cells during the night, both greeted their gaolers in the morning in a nude state. The bench sentenced each to 14 days.

3 NOVEMBER **1828** Early on this very cold winter morning in Tunstead a Chelsea Pensioner about to marry a widow 'repaired to a cross roads where the intended bride crossed the road *in puris naturalis* to be received by her bridegroom'. By enacting this unusual rite, according to local lore, the old lady freed her bridegroom from the debts of her previous husband.

4 NOVEMBER **1851** Mrs Knights was widely publicised to give a lecture on 'Bloomer Costume' at St Andrew's Hall on this night. A large audience comprising many young men who claimed to be shop assistants and milliners' apprentices was assembled, possibly expecting a very different show altogether. When poor Mrs Knights appeared in an 'essentially ugly and unfeminine dress' known as 'the bloomer', ideal for ladies' outdoor pursuits such as bicycling and riding, she was greeted with such derision and laughter that she left the stage, leaving the orchestra to face a storm of groans and disapprobation.

Bloomer costume as seen at St Andrew's Hall on 4 November 1851. *(Housego Collection)*

1788 As part of the Norwich City celebrations for the centenary of the Glorious Revolution, a travelling menagerie was brought for display at the Bear Inn near the city centre. A large tiger which was exhibited broke loose and could not be secured again until he had devoured two monkeys and brought horror to all assembled. The tiger did not, however, live much longer, because the collar and chain he had swallowed to escape 'gangreened within him and killed the beast'.

5 NOVEMBER

1776 William Goodens of Thurlton was committed to the city gaol this day. He stood charged with being found at large in the city of Norwich before the expiration of the term for which he was sentenced to be transported. He had been tried at the Lent Assizes of 1775, where he was convicted of stealing a silver watch from a farmer at Swanton Morley, for which he was branded and discharged. The following year's Lent Assizes saw Goodens return, charged with breaking into the dwelling house of John Norton of North Tuddenham and stealing various goods, for which he was capitally convicted. This sentence was commuted to transportation for seven years, and accordingly he was shipped on 12 September. During the voyage Goodens and nearly forty others secured the crew in a cabin and made their escape. Goodens chanced his luck by returning to Norwich, where he was recognised while attempting to join the East India Company. While being sworn in he was identified by a person reading John Fielding's *Hue and Cry*, where all the escapees were advertised as 'Wanted' with a reward of £20 each. Confessing to the whole story, Goodings went to gaol again. History does not record his fate.

6 NOVEMBER

1906 James George Bell (aged 54), farm labourer, was indicted at Norfolk Assizes on a charge of killing and murdering Susannah Haynes of Wendling on 22 June. Found guilty, he was sentenced to death on 8 November but his sentence was commuted to penal servitude for life.

7 NOVEMBER

1886 Arthur Riches, fish hawker, murdered his wife in a fit of anger on the Walk near the Haymarket, Norwich. Immediately arrested and tried at the Assizes on 23 November, he was found guilty and sentenced to death, commuted to penal servitude for life. He died at Parkhurst Prison, Isle of Wight, in April 1898.

8 NOVEMBER

Mrs Riches and Arthur Riches. (*Norfolk Constabulary Archives*)

9 NOVEMBER **1808** A woman named Mary Hudson, aged 35, escaped from Norwich City Gaol under extraordinary circumstances. She made a hole through the wall of the cell in which she was confined and crept out into the street, taking her six month old infant with her. The wall was 2 ft in thickness, and she must have spent several nights in making the aperture. The bricks were concealed beneath her bed and the loose rubbish in the pillow case. Another bed served to conceal the hole in the wall. In the advertisement for her recapture a reward of ten guineas was offered for her recapture. It further named one Thomas Cocks, a Yarmouth hawker and peddler and a frequenter of the Norfolk and Suffolk cock pits, as the suspected accomplice 'on the outside'. There is no record of her recapture.

10 NOVEMBER **Old Punishments: The Cauldron**
The punishment of boiling to death was on the British statute books between 1531 and 1547. The sentence was normally carried out on those who had poisoned food – a grim notion of a cook stewing in his own juices. This horrible punishment was inflicted on a maidservant at the Tuesday Market Place at King's Lynn in 1531. A fire was lit below the cauldron and the terrified victim plunged in and out by means of a chain on the gibbet, until life was extinct.

11 NOVEMBER **1830** Machine-breaking riots and stack firing across the county. The first fire occurred at Mr J. Hill's farm at Briston, and a reward of £1,000 was immediately offered by Sir Jacob Astley for the discovery of the offenders. On the 16th a mob destroyed the agricultural machinery of John Girling of Paston. The outrages became so numerous that the principal agriculturalists got rid of their threshing machines and magistrates were empowered to swear in special constables for every parish. An attack was planned on Melton Constable Hall on the 22nd, but gentlemen of the neighbourhood banded together in opposition, seizing the ring leaders from the assembling mob at Hindolveston and conveying them to Walsingham Bridewell. At Norwich on the 29th the mob destroyed the sawmills at Catton and the looms at Willett's factory in St Martins, and broke the windows of the silk factory. Magistrates were constantly in the Guildhall, and the 200 Chelsea Pensioners in the city were called out to assist in preserving the peace.

12 NOVEMBER **1925** Swaffham man Hubert George Bloy, known in the town as Whiteman, murdered his wife and mother-in-law with a spanner. Bloy was a man of low intelligence and prone to 'fitting'; concerns for his mental health should have been raised but he was deemed fit to stand trial. Found guilty he was executed by obscure public executioner Robert Baxter in Norwich prison on this day at 8 o'clock in the morning.

13 NOVEMBER **1801** Peter Donahue, a sergeant in the 30th Regiment of Foot, was executed at Lynn for uttering counterfeit Bank of England notes. A contemporary added, 'We are sorry that he appeared sensible for many minutes after he was turned off: [hanged] and a large effusion of blood gushed from his mouth and nose, which rendered the scene most awful, terrible and distressing'.

Déjà Vu? Of uncertain date but said to be in the closing months of 1788 Rowe's play 'The Fair Penitent' was being performed in Billy Scragg's converted barn Theatre (later part of the famous Fisher's Theatre Circuit) at North Walsham. In the charnel house scene at the beginning of the fifth act the heroine Calista, played by Mrs Barry places her hand on a skull but there the acting of the script ended, reeling back in horror Mrs Barry collapsed and was taken back to her home where she died a few days later from shock. The story which transpired was that Flaxman the local sexton had been asked to obtain a skull from a grave for the performance, the skull had a distinctive shard of metal

14 NOVEMBER

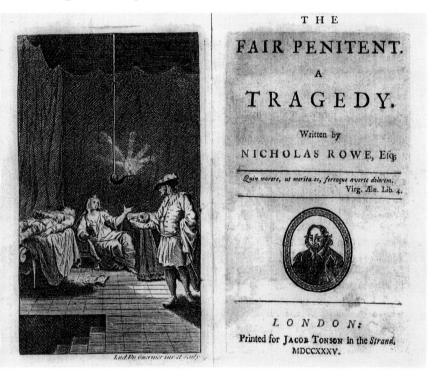

embedded in its skull some say from a sword blow he survived years before, others say it was a nail from the piece of wood used to murder him and the foul deed, known to Mrs Barry, was hushed up and the skull pulled purposefully out to confront her – either way that piece of metal, even in the dim lit stage made the skull unmistakeable as that of John Norris – her first husband!!

1887 The trial of Arthur Edward Gilbert-Cooper (aged 34), a clerk in Holy Orders. He was found guilty, having 'feloniously, wilfully and of his own malice aforethought killed and murdered one William Meymott Farley at the parish of Crettingham on 2nd October 1887'. The jury decided he was insane at the time he committed the offence, and was not responsible for his actions. Gilbert-Cooper was ordered to be kept in strict custody 'at Her Majesty's pleasure'.

15 NOVEMBER

16 NOVEMBER **1896** An inquest was held in the evening at the Town Hall under the Borough Coroner Mr E.M. Beloe into the death of a young man named Taylor, who worked in one of the Lynn factories. Playing football as outside right for the Rovers against North End (both local clubs), he was in a tragic collision with the inside left opposition player, Charles Hornigold, and received internal injuries. Taken home in a cab, he stayed in bed on the Sunday. He and Hornigold were friends, and he and others visited him during the day, but he died that evening. All witnesses agreed that the accident occurred in the ordinary course of the game. Charles Jackson, surgeon, said he could give no reason for the death beyond the fact 'that in violent sport of that kind such contingencies were always possible'. The jury returned the verdict of accidental death. The coroner observed this was the first fatal football accident that had occurred in Lynn.

17 NOVEMBER **1888** *Jack the Ripper threatens a visit to Norfolk?* On the week when the lurid headlines of the *Illustrated Police News* proclaimed 'The Seventh Horrible Murder by the Monster of the East End' and offered a £100 reward for

the capture of the Whitechapel murderer, a letter arrived on the desk of Great Yarmouth Borough Police Chief Constable William Brogden. Purportedly penned from Dorset Street in Spitalfields, the letter advised Brogden to 'Look out for me Thursday night by either of the two piers where I intend to rip up two Norwich women before closing time. So distinguish yourself better than the London coppers – Jack the Ripper.' News of this ominous and taunting letter leaked out and the people of Yarmouth reacted fearfully. A number of reports were filed with the police of sightings of Jack the Ripper, and a fellow went around the streets of the town with a bell, like a town crier, warning women to stay in at night because the Ripper would be on the prowl. Police vigilance was stepped up. No attacks occurred. Like many of the letters sent to the police in London it was probably a hoax, but we can never be sure that Jack *didn't* come on a little jaunt to the coast in search of another victim.

THE TRIAL, SENTENCE CONFESSION, AND EXECUTION OF

William Thompson.

Aged 21, who was Executed at Norwich, on Saturday April 8th, 1854, for the Wilful MURDER of LORENZ BEHA at TITTLESHALL, NORFOLK.

William Thompson, 21 was charged with wilful murdering Lorenz Beha at Tittleshall on the the 18th of November last and stealing from his person two 5lb bank notes two sovereigns four half sovereigns twenty shillings a sixpence, a four penny piece 3 silver watches of the value of £15 twelve watchkeys sixteen box keys of the value of 3s and one purse value 6d. his property.

Mr. Evans and Mr. Bulver appeared for the prosecution, and Mr. Cooper for the defence.

The prisoner appeared on the whole to be careless and indifferent as to the result of the proceedings against him.

The following evidence was then adduced.

Harriet Ewing said—I am the wife of Robert Ewing and live Wellingham On November 18th I saw Lorenz Beha he had a carpet bag with him, He was in the habit of coming to my house once a month. He generally came at noon on Friday's He stay ed at my house about five minutes on leaving my house he went on the Tittleshall road that road lead him past Mr. Norton's plantation.

John Roberson—I live at Tittlesham and am a butcher by trade Tittlesham is about a mile from Wellingham, On the 18th Nov. I was going from Tittlesham to Wellingham, when near Mr Norton's Plantation I observe some blood in the road This was about 3 o'clock in the afternoon I was the right side of the road In the ditch I observed a body and some more blood. I procured the assistance of four persons and soon after this the clergyman Mr. Digby came up. We examined the body, the face was very much cut The trousers pockets were turned inside out There was a box lying by and a bag, the box was locked, A stick laid on the right side of body and also an umbrella we also found in the ditch, there was a great deal of blood the body was the body of Mr. Beha, it was removed to the Griffin house, at Tittlesham.

COPY OF VERSES.

Oh how they flock from far and near
This wretched sight to see
A youth scarce twenty years of age
Suspended on a Tree,
My time is come my race is run
No longer I can stay
I see grim Death approaching me
To summons me away,

What a dismal sight to see
Exposed on Norwich fatal tree.

I Lorenz Beha did way-lay
There I in ambush stood
I with a hatchet did him slay
And robbed him of his goods
I took from him his property
And beat his body sore
Than dragged him to a lonesome spot
And left him in his gore

Mr. J. Jump. Surgeon, said—I am a surgeon, and live at Litcham. I was shown a body on the evening of the murder. It was shown me as the body of Beha. On the following Monday I examined it minutely.

William Webster,—I am a butcher, residing a Tittleshall, I left my home about half-past eleven on the morning of the day of the murder I passed the place about a quarter to twelve, I saw Thompson near the plantation, He had a slop and a cap on

Mr. Cooper, counsel for the prisoner, then made a very able defence

The jury, after a very brief deliberation, returned a verdict of GUILTY.

The Clerk of the Arraigns—w Thompson you have been found guilty of the wilful murder of Lorenza Beha what have you to say why sentence of death should not be passed upon you—

THE PRISONERS DEFENCE

I left my father's house, Tittleshall, on Friday, November the 18th, at about half-past eleven o'clock in the forenoon, and went for a walk up the Wellingham road, When I had got up to Mr. Riches' plantation it was about twelve. I saw a man get up from the bushes in the plantation. He asked me if I knew what time it was I told him that I thought about twelve. I then walked on and saw him either lying or sitting down in the same place When I got round the corner to Mr. Norton's plantation, which was about eighty or one hundred yards from the place where I first saw the man, I got over the fence to ease myself While I was doing so, Wm, Webster, the butcher, came past, There was a man standing in the ditch by the side of the dead body he was bent over it, I saw his hands was wet and daubed with blood I asked him what he was after he immediately got out of the ditch and got hold of me round my legs and daubed my trousers with blood he begged of me not to tell any one he said if I did he would chop me down I see him take out the purse some money he then put his hands into his waist coat pocket he pulled 5 watches 3 he gave me I said I would not have them he said I should he, is a dark person, I never saw him no more till I got to Roper, that all I can say about it.

Now I am cast and doomed to die
On Norwich Castle tree
And of the multitude around
No one does pity me
I see the hangman me approach
I see the awful spot
And as I feel the hangmans grasp
I tremble on the Drop.

Near Tittleshall I did reside
And happy might have been
And such a deed as I have done
Was scarcely ever seen
Farewell my friends a last farewell
No power can me save—
I now must go, in grief and woe
Unto the silent grave

The Judges Address

The Chief Baron then assumed the black cap, and proceeded to pass sentence of death Prisoner at the bar you have been found guilty of wilful murder, upon evidence as clear as conclusive, and as decisive as I ever heard in a court of justice—It is now my painful duty to pass the sentence of the court upon you, that you be taken to the place from whence you came , and from thence to the place of execution that you be hanged by the neck until you be dead. and that your body shall be buried in precincts of the prison.

EXECUTION

At an early hour, the space before the Prison was crowded to excess by persons of both sexes anxious to witness the execution of the wretched prisoner, which increased to such a degree, that a number of people suffered from the presure. The Sheriffs with their attendants arrived at the prison they then proceeded to the condemned cel, where they found the Rev. Ordinary engaged in prayer with the wretched culprit. After the usual formalities had been observed of demanding the delivery of the body of the prisoner into their custody, he was conducted to the press room where the executioner with his assistants then commenced pinioning his arms. During these awful preparations the unhappy man appeared mentally to suffer severely. All the arrangements having been completed, the prisoner, who, then trembled violently walked with the melancholy procession, preceded by the Rev. Ordinary who read aloud and in a distinct tone, the burial service for the dead. Whilst the executioner was adjusting the fatal apparatus of death, the prisoner was deeply absorbed in prayer, the executioner having drawn the cap over his face, retired from the scaffold and the signal having been given, the bolt was withdrawn, and the unhappy man was launched into eternity. He was seen to struggle for a few moments, after which he seased to exist.

William Thompson made a full Confession while lying under sentence of Death.

O God receive my wretched soul
Look on me from on high
And as I on the platform stand
Give me fortitude to die
And may my fate a warning be
To people old and young
I tremble when I think upon
The dreadful deed I done

Cursed Satan tempted me
Upon that fatal day
To meet my innocent victim
And barbarously him slay
I now must go for on this earth
I am not fit to live
Oh God above look down on me
And all my sins Forgive,

Gifford, Printer, Norwich

(Norfolk Local Studies Library)

18 NOVEMBER   **1948**   Stanley Joseph Clarke, a 34-year-old pig dealer, was hanged at Norwich Prison. Pleading guilty at his trial, he admitted stabbing to death Florence May Bentley, a chambermaid, at a Great Yarmouth boarding house. He was the first prisoner to hang in Norwich since 1945 and since the controversy which raged over the 'no hanging' clause. In his final hours he was attended by a condemned cell prison warder and the Bishop of Norwich.

19 NOVEMBER   **1820**   An eccentric person named Charles Archer, died in St Andrew's, Norwich, aged 81. 'It was his constant practice to be at his post every morning at 4 o'clock with his kettle of hot cocoa and saloop. His station was near the Two-Necked Swan and he was allowed half a pint of porter each morning for calling up the landlord at six. This custom he observed over 14 years, drinking an estimated 2,556 half pints or something more than 319 gallons. He had formerly been in the 12th Foot and lost a leg in the Siege of Gibraltar for which he received a pension for the ensuing 39 years of his life. But what most affected his mind next to the misfortune of having his leg shot away was to see a hog, a circumstance related by himself, snatch his lost limb up in his mouth and run away with it!'

20 NOVEMBER   **1881**   Hannah Brett was brutally murdered at Saham Toney by recently released convict Henry Stebbings. At the Assizes of February 1882 he was found guilty and sentenced to death, but was respited on the grounds of 'homicidal mania.'

21 NOVEMBER   **1877**   Henry March (aged 59) was executed on this day for the murder of his master Thomas Mayes (aged 76), veterinary surgeon, shoeing smith and farmer of Rothbury, Pople Street, Wymondham, and Henry Bidewell (aged 56), blacksmith, on 20 October. March was said to be a man of quarrelsome disposition and was jealous of Bidewell's influence with his master. Sarah Bailey, a servant girl, heard quarrelling in the smithy and through the open window saw March strike Bidewell with a piece of iron. Bidewell fell and March continued hitting him. Bailey called the master from his adjoining house and, attempting to intervene, Mayes received the same treatment. It is said Mayes then went for a pint in the nearby Feathers pub, leaving the men he clubbed to die. March stood trial and was found guilty at the Assizes before Mr Justice Hawkins. Capital sentence was passed and carried out in the walls of Norwich Castle by public executioner William Marwood.

22 NOVEMBER   **1863**   Robert Hales, the celebrated Norfolk giant, died on this day. In his prime he stood 7 ft 6 in tall, measured 64 in around the waist and weighed 33 stone. Received at Queen Victoria's court and introduced to nobility across the continent, he went to America in 1848 where he joined Barnum and Bailey's Circus as 'The Tallest Man in the World'. Returning to England in 1851 his fortunes declined, and he was reduced to selling the story of

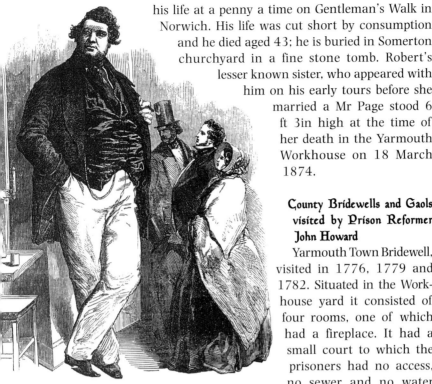

his life at a penny a time on Gentleman's Walk in Norwich. His life was cut short by consumption and he died aged 43; he is buried in Somerton churchyard in a fine stone tomb. Robert's lesser known sister, who appeared with him on his early tours before she married a Mr Page stood 6 ft 3in high at the time of her death in the Yarmouth Workhouse on 18 March 1874.

Robert Hales, the Norfolk Giant.
(*Johnson Collection*)

County Bridewells and Gaols visited by Prison Reformer John Howard

23 November

Yarmouth Town Bridewell, visited in 1776, 1779 and 1782. Situated in the Work-house yard it consisted of four rooms, one of which had a fireplace. It had a small court to which the prisoners had no access, no sewer and no water supply. 'Court of conscience debtors sometimes confined here, and discharged in three months: by the act (1758) they may be carried either to the common gaol, or house of correction.'

24 November

1950 Norman Goldthorpe was executed at Norwich Prison by Public Executioner Harry Kirk and his assistant Syd Dernley. Goldthorpe, frustrated and enraged by failure and by poor relationships, and fuelled by a heavy drinking session, hunted down an old prostitute he knew named Emma Howe to vent his spleen. Having checked in her usual haunt of the Great Eastern pub at Great Yarmouth he went to her one roomed home in Owles Court. Having used her, he strangled her in her own bed and quietly left. We will never know if he thought he would get away with it or if he was just stupid, but he was arrested, worse for drink, the next afternoon in Emma's pub – the Great Eastern. Found guilty at the Assizes, Goldthorpe took it gamely; asked if he had anything to say before sentence was passed, he replied: 'No, only that I thank my counsel and respect the prosecution – they had a rotten job.'

25 November

1831 Charlotte King stole a muslin cap, the property of one Jane Fox. There were two other indictments against Miss King, one for stealing a few items from Christopher Hill Smith, with whom she lived as a servant, the other for receiving stolen goods, the property of Mr Perowne. On the former she was tried in January 1832, and found guilty at the Norwich City Sessions.

In pronouncing the sentence the Recorder commented that it appeared to be the practice of the prisoner and other members of her family to let themselves out as servants and then to carry on a system of plunder. Her sister, he continued, was awaiting trial on a similar offence and two others were confined in Yarmouth Gaol for charges of like nature, while yet another had absconded under suspicion. Charlotte was given the stiffest sentence the law allowed – seven years' transportation for the first offence, a further seven for the second, the last to commence on the conclusion of the first period, 14 years in all. Her sister Elizabeth, just 15 years old, pleaded guilty to stealing a scarf, three books and a shirt pin and received a similar sentence to her sister. They were transported together.

27 November **1826** The Revd William Whitear, rector of Starston, met with his death. He went out with a party to apprehend poachers. After they had divided into two groups the Reverend was mistaken for a poacher and was shot by a young man named Thomas Pallant from the other group. He died from his wounds on 10 December and Pallant was tried at the Norfolk Assizes at Thetford for manslaughter on 26 March 1827. He was acquitted. 'He was so seriously affected during the trial that before its conclusion he became quite insensible and was taken home in that state.'

28 November

CLARK'S EDITION.

A FULL REPORT

OF THE

TRIAL OF JAMES BLOMFIELD RUSH

FOR THE

MURDER OF MR. JERMY AND HIS SON,

OF

STANFIELD HALL, IN THE COUNTY OF NORFOLK;

COMMENCING ON WEDNESDAY, MARCH 28, AND CONCLUDED APRIL 4, 1849, AT NORWICH ASSIZES.

PORTRAIT OF RUSH, SKETCHED IN THE COURT.

[TWENTY-SECOND EDITION.]

LONDON:

PRINTED AND PUBLISHED BY W. M. CLARK, 17, WARWIC

PRICE SIXPENCE.

1848 One of the most notorious murders ever committed in the county was perpetrated on this day. James Blomfield Rush had dallied on the wrong side of the law since his early life. In 1836 he became the tennant of Stanfield Hall Farm. When his wife died he went to London and adevertised for a governess. He brought a Miss Emily Sandford back to the farm and seduced her under the promise of marriage; he also took lodgings with her in London. By 1848 he was heavily in debt, was evicted and was removed to Potash Farm about a mile from Stanfield Hall. Bankrupt and seething with rage against Isaac Jermy (the recorder of Norwich), his landlord and owner of the Hall, who still demanded the arrears, Rush forged documents and deceived himself yet further into a morass

of debt. On this night at 8.30 p.m. Rush crept up to Stanfield Hall disguised with a bush of false hair about his head. Issac Jermy, standing near the front of the building, was shot dead by Rush from the porch. Rush then threatened the butler who ran to investigate, and when Jermy Jermy, Isaac's son, ran from the drawing room Rush shot again, killing Jermy instantly, and seriously wounding his wife in the breast when she ran to the body. The maid Eliza Chastney was also wounded as she went to aid her mistress.

Despite his disguise Rush was clearly identified and soon brought to trial. In what appeared a clear-cut case which received national exposure, Rush was found guilty and hanged on Norwich Castle Hill before a crowd of thousands, some travelling on a special train from London, on 21 April 1849. His bulky figure soon joined other notorious criminals in Madame Tussaud's Chamber of Horrors. Stanfield Hall received many visitors on account of this murder, even Charles Dickens, who was much affected by the sinister ambience of the old hall.

Eliza Chastney giving evidence at Norwich Shirehall. Rush is seen standing in the dock, far right.

1822 The inquest was held at Loddon on the body of James Dale, killed by a patient in the private lunatic asylum kept by Mr Jollye, a surgeon.

29 NOVEMBER

30 NOVEMBER *Baby Farming scare in Great Yarmouth.* A crime indicative of its time, word would be put about that a 'certain woman' would, for a fee, place unwanted new-born children in the care of another home without form filling or embarrassment – end of problem. It was one of the most sinister of crimes, the service was performed but Victorian hypocrisy turned eyes to the wall and ignored the crime. A number of babies' bodies had been found secreted about the town, the first appeared on the riverside ridge of the bridge on 4 September 1875. Enquiries were made but little was made of the other two babes recovered alive, found in side streets over the ensuing two months and sent to the Orphanage in Norwich. With a fast-running river and the sea a short distance away it is terrifying to think how many unwanted babies may have watery graves. No baby farmer was ever caught and brought to justice in Yarmouth. The last two tragic cases are probably not the work of a baby farmer but are none the less worthy of recording as a mark of their times. In 1877 a 5-month-old child was sent from Liverpoool Street Station to Yarmouth Vauxhall Station in a small black bag. No clue was ever found to the supposed murderers or of the gentleman to whom it was consigned. On 10 May 1879 the body of a dead female child was found in Row 48. Wrapped up in rags and weighing about 8lbs the culprits of this crime were never caught. The hideous underbelly of baby farming was exposed once and for all when the steely eyed Mrs Amelia Dyer who operated in London, Reading and Bristol was caught in 1896. She was not the only baby farmer but now the truth of the trade was exposed and regarded with due revulsion. This vile trade petered out after her appointment with the executioner at Newgate on 10 June 1896.

DECEMBER

Great Yarmouth Borough Police Force, December 1894. *(Norfolk Constabulary Archives)*

1 DECEMBER   **1896**   The report of the inquest held at Great Yarmouth Workhouse on the body of John Ridgson, a waif. PC Platten said he knew the deceased, who three months earlier had been brought before magistrates on a charge of having no visible means. Ridgson was discharged on the magistrate's recommendation that he sought shelter in the workhouse, a piece of advice he fatally ignored. he was known to loaf around the Fish Wharf, and on his last day of life he looked 'wretched'; he was advised to go to the workhouse, but the lad obstinately replied 'I shall be alright'. PC White said he found the lad seated on a swill at the Wharf, groaning and apparently dying. Procuring a cart, the good constable wheeled the lad to the workhouse, where poor John Ridgson died ten minutes after arrival. The jury returned a verdict of death by exposure. Attempts were made to contact his sister in London but with no response. Our poor waif lies lost and forgotten in a pauper's grave.

2 DECEMBER   **1908**   James Nicholls executed at Norwich by public executioner Henry Pierrepoint with Henry's brother Tom as Assistant (Henry's son Albert went on to become the longest-serving executioner of the twentieth century and was public executioner in overall charge at the last execution at Norwich Prison: see 19 July 1951.) Nicholls was identified by his clothing entering the cottage of the Wilson family at Feltwell between 2 and 3 p.m. on 8 October 1908. Nicholls was then seen dragging a woman out of the house, she cried for help and he pulled her back inside.

Charles Wilson returned to find the door to his house locked but after forcing entry found his wife on the floor battered to death. Nicholls walked to Magee's Farm where he broke the news that Wilson had murdered his wife but only Wilson could have known of Mrs Wilson's murder at that time. The evidence against Nicholls was a little circumstantial, much was made of the prosecution hinging on one witness, a 14-year-old boy's identification of Nicholls. After jury deliberation of 15 minutes Nicholls was found guilty at the Norfolk Assizes and was sent on his way to the gallows.

3 DECEMBER   **1826**   An advertisement appeared in the local press: 'Whereas a report was very generally circulated last week, and in a great measure obtained credit, that the body of William Tounshend, which was buried at Lakenham, on Sunday Nov 19th had been disinterred and taken away we the undersigned have investigated the matter and certify the following statement to be correct: The relatives of the deceased being much affected at such a report . . . made application to have the grave examined. The grave was opened on Saturday last in the presence of them, together with us, when it was discovered that the body reposed in its peaceful abode undisturbed. We consider it to be our duty to give this public contradiction to so groundless and scandalous report, in order thereby to satisfy the minds of the parishioners and the public at large. – George Carter, Vicar, Hunton Jackson, William Norman, Churchwardens; Lakenham Vestry.'

Guildhall, Norwich,

DECEMBER 4th, 1830.

The Mayor and Magistrates consider it to be a paramount duty which they owe to their Sovereign and their Country at this moment of general disturbance, to declare that, whilst in common with the rest of their Fellow Citizens, they are on the one hand ready to do all which sympathy and benevolence can suggest for the relief of distressed operatives in this populous place, so on the other hand it is their full determination to act with the promptitude, decision, and vigour, which circumstances imperatively demand, in prohibiting tumultuous assemblies, and suppressing riotous proceedings, in oppposing every kind of open outrage, and actively endeavouring to detect secret attacks, on either Person or Property.

The Mayor and Magistrates are anxious to impress on the minds of their Fellow Citizens, that persons who are guilty of these lawless proceedings, are liable on conviction to suffer Death, and that the loss incurred by Individuals by the destruction of their Property must be paid by the Public, and will consequently tend to the increase of the County Rate.---Taking the present occasion therefore to acknowledge and applaud the zeal of numerous respectable Individuals, who in voluntary compliance with the summons already issued, have meritoriously come forward as Special Constables, the Mayor and Magistrates renew their call on every well-disposed Person, capable of rendering assistance, to enrol himself on the same list, being firmly resolved upon an organized and efficient employment of the Civil power, supported, if there should be need, with such other aid as is authorized by Law, for the speedy restoration of public tranquillity.

W. SIMPSON,
TOWN CLERK.

J. IUNGIUS, PRINTER, ELM HILL, NORWICH.

(Norfolk Local Studies Library)

4 December   **1314** The Black Plague hit Norwich with 22 pestilential outbreaks between 1314 and 1665/66. Despite the city closing its gates when outbreaks were heard of in other parts of the country the plague still arrived in the city. First cases were removed to the Pest House. Humphrey Howlins and Stephen Chapman were appointed barrow men to cart of those infected to pest house but soon the St Benedict's area was riddled with plague, doors sealed and painted with white crosses. Dogs and hogs were to be hunted down as carriers of plague and killed and searchers employed to find other outbreaks. Plague raged on and a watch house, eight-hole stocks and whipping post was erected near the expanded St Augustine's Pest House to maintain order. Eventually the entire city saw outbreaks of bubonic plague and an estimated 2,251 bodies of city folks swelled the plague pits beyond the city walls before it was finally rid of plague for the last time in 1667.

5 December   **1896** At about 7.20 p.m. on this day a terrible accident occurred at St Mary's Silk Mills, Norwich, which resulted in the death of 15-year-old apprentice Leonard Delves, the son of Mr Joseph Delves who resided on the premises. It appeared the boy was at home attending to a lathe in motion when his clothes became entangled in it and he was drawn into the machine. His head was crushed by a pin projecting from the lathe. A man named Springfield who was working in the same shop heard the unfortunate lad's cries and ran to stop the machine; then with the help of Mr Kay, the manager, he extracted the poor lad who was quite unconscious. Dr Burton was summoned, but by the time he arrived all signs of life were extinct.

6 December   **1944**   Sir Eric and Lady Teichman were in residence at their home of Honingham Hall when they heard shots coming from their nearby wood. Sir Eric went out to investigate; despite it being late in the war there were still fears of German parachutists being dropped. The shots were actually from a couple of American servicemen, who had the mistaken idea that if they bought a shooting licence it would entitle them to shoot anywhere. As Sir Eric approached and asked them their names one of the servicemen, named George E. Smith, without making any reply, shot him. Arrested the following day, Smith was tried by US court martial. His defence attorney tried to build a plea for insanity, and described it as a 'purposeless, motiveless and idiotic act' but this was at best a weak excuse. Major Brockus, for the prosecution, said 'Smith had forfeited his right to live and by his calm, deliberate act of murder had become a cancerous growth on the world's surface and must be removed.' The insanity plea failed, and with a unanimous verdict of guilty Smith was sentenced to death by hanging on 13 January 1945. 'Smith was handcuffed and left the court with half a smile on his face.'

7 December   **1549**   *The end of Captain Mischief, the execution of Robert Kett.* The last major open rebellion in Norfolk began in June 1549 when bands of folk rose up after the feast of the translation of St Thomas Becket at Wymondham. After breaking down fences in the locality and obtaining a leader in the form of

Robert Kett they marched on Norwich to deliver their grievances about enclosure and public freedom, gathering much support on the way. While they were encamped on Mousehold Heath negotiations with the King's Army broke down, and the city was eventually stormed by the rebels. There was much bloodshed, one of the most horrible deaths being that of Lord Sheffield whose horse had floundered in a ditch near the Great Hospital. Overblown with victory, the rebels saw Sheffield remove his helmet to identify himself; rather than take him hostage they bludgeoned him to death. Some records name one Fulke, a butcher and carpenter by trade, as dealing the final blow, removing Sheffield's head with his cleaver.

A new Royal Army, including foreign mercenaries, was dispatched to join the retreating forces of the Marquis of Northampton to march on Norwich again under the overall command of experienced campaigner the Earl of Warwick. Warwick dispatched a herald who offered a free pardon to Kett at his encampment. Folklore tells of such derision being shown to the herald that the crowd's feeling was summed up by a small boy who stepped in front of the herald, bared his buttocks and defecated. Enough said: nobody could argue that Norfolk people weren't succinct! Warwick rapidly assembled his troops for action and attacked the rebels, driving them back to what were to become the killing fields of Dussindale. Despite skilful use of artillery by Kett's master gunner, Myles, the day was lost and the field 'ran red and blodie'. Those not slaughtered in battle were summarily tried by the Earl of Warwick over the

Robert Kett sits under the Oak of Reformation while the defecating boy steps forward to show his opinion of the Earl of Warwick's herald, Mousehold Heath, Norwich, 1549.

ensuing days. Justice was swift and harsh, many rebels swinging from the city gallows by Magdalen Gates. Myles and eight other leading rebels were specifically ordered to be hung from 'the Oak of Reformation' under which Kett had kept his 'court'. Before they were quite dead they were cut down, disemboweled, heads removed and bodies cut into four quarters, all of which were displayed on city gates or on poles around the streets. Robert Kett's older brother and rebel 'general' was executed and gibbeted from Wymondham church tower. Robert was saved to last, and hung from the walls of Norwich Castle and gibbeted there for many months afterwards as a final warning to all who might consider similar action.

8 December **1897** John George Foster killed Alice Maria Newby during an argument at their home, 60 Pottergate Street, Norwich, on this day. Found guilty of manslaughter at the following Assizes, he was sentenced to penal servitude for life.

9 December **1688** Clearing up begins in Norwich after two days of anti-Catholic riots. The mob destroyed the Catholic chapel at Black Friars' Yard, and many houses of known Catholics were pillaged. Such was the ferocity of the mob that trained bands were called out to disperse them.

10 December **1866** An extraordinary charge was preferred before Walsingham Magistrates against Miles Brown, a farmer of Houghton St Giles, and his brother William. It was alleged that they had exhibited in the window of their cottage 'an apparatus revolving before a light, and exhibiting in a glass behind an upright coffin, on the lid of which was a photograph of the Revd Septimus Henry Lee Warner. Such public exhibition being a threat on the part of the defendants to take away the life of the said complainant.' The defendants were bound over in the sum of £1,600 to keep the peace.

11 December **1821** An inquest was held at King's Lynn on the body of Robert Roberson, shot by Henry Pond, linen draper on the High Street, while Roberson was breaking into his premises. The jury returned a verdict of 'justifiable homicide'.

12 December **1806** On or about this date died Sarah Pickwood, aged 49 years. She was claimed to be one of the most enormous cases of dropsy on record. In the course of about 50 months she was tapped thirty-eight times and discharged 350 gallons of fluid, weighing 4,656 lbs. The greatest quantity discharged at one operation measured 11½ gallons and weighed 153½ lb.

13 December **1886** George Harmer (aged 26) – the last man hanged at Norwich Castle – was executed by public executioner James Berry on this day. On 14 August Harmer had been released from the castle following imprisonment of one month for assault on his wife. Within a few hours of release he visited Henry Last, an aged carpenter who lived in School Lane, Old Post Office Street,

Norwich, known today as Exchange Street. Concocting some pretence to be there, Harmer bludgeoned Last's skull with a hammer and robbed the man of what little money and possessions of worth he had. Covering the old man with sacks he made his escape to London. The poor old man lived on his own and was not discovered for some hours, but within four days of this horrible crime Harmer was under arrest. Police had been tipped off to the culprit and traced him via his luggage, which was forwarded to him, At the last Harmer was contrite, and left a full confession of his crimes.

George Harmer.
(*Norfolk Constabulary Archives*)

1908 *Brutal outrage at Feltwell.* Hardly two months after Nicholls murdered Mrs Wilson (see 2 November) an old woman named Georgina Rowe was attacked in her shop with a blacksmith's hammer by Ernest William Russell, a recently released convict who had just finished a six-month sentence for felony. The attention of neighbours was called by shrieks of 'murder' coming from the unfortunate old lady's house. Russell was seen leaving the house and a hue and cry was raised. PC Farrington gave chase but 'lost his quarry. The following day cries were heard by Mr Tibbett, an engine driver in the employ of Cock Brothers, who went to Tennis Hill farm to remove the thrashing tackle. Russell was found down an 85 ft well in about 5 ft of water. Hoisted out by the police, Russell was conveyed to the Methwold lock-up and brought before a magistrate later in the day. Appearing at the next Sessions Russell was sentenced to five years' penal servitude, despite claiming extenuating circumstances.

14 December

1887 In a case reminiscent of the Neale family in 1825, Esther Bacon a 41-year-old Great Yarmouth charwoman administered a quantity of precipitate powder to her children Bessie (aged 14), George (aged 10) and Ellen (aged 6) in an attempt to murder them. Tried on 14 February 1888, she was found guilty on all counts but was given a comparatively merciful sentence of 18 calendar months with hard labour.

15 December

1827 William Moore, a young lad of 13, was brutally murdered and horribly mutilated in a field at Brisley by 'loosed lunatic' John Kenny, aged 20.

16 December

1892 The report of the inquest on Harriet Edith Mary Rayner of Wensum Street was published today. A worker at the St Andrews Works of Harmer & Co, she died after her hair became entangled in the shafting of the sewing machine bench. She was drawn into the machinery and was killed instantly.

17 December

18 December **1875** The inquest was held into the actions of Robert Edwards of Marsham who, while a patient at the Norfolk and Norwich Hospital, attacked a group of children in a neighbouring ward with a pair of fire tongs, killing three instantly while a fourth died of wounds shortly afterwards. A verdict of wilful murder was returned. However, Edwards was found incapable of pleading and was committed to Broadmoor Prison at Her Majesty's pleasure.

19 December **1813** On or about this date a smuggling cutter with 600 casks of Geneva on board was captured off Salthouse by the Sheringham Revenue boat. The vessel was taken to Blakeney Harbour and her cargo was deposited in the King's Warehouse at Cley.

20 December **1800s** On or about this date in the early nineteenth century a band of poachers set out to 'walk by night' through the grounds of Breckles Manor. George Mace was elected their look-out, and they arranged to meet at the dilapidated hall to divide their spoils after a couple of hours' poaching. Mace was already at the porch of the hall as they walked to meet him. As they approached they were stopped in their tracks as a spectral coach swept up the drive. Rooted to the ground by fear, the men stared in horror as the coach halted in front of the porch, and the ghostly apparition of a ball gowned lady stepped out from the coach and was seen to stare straight into Mace's eyes. He slumped to the ground with a bloodcurdling shriek. The scream seemed to release his friends from their transfixed state, and they ran to the nearest house to get help – but could find no one willing to go near the hall until daylight. Next morning the vicar led a group of villagers to the spot. The body of poor George Mace lay stiff and cold, his face a mask of terror.

21 December **County Bridewells and Gaols visited by Prison Reformer John Howard**
Lynn Regis Town Gaol, visited 1774, 1779 (twice) and 1782. 'The rooms for debtors, felons and petty offender are convenient, and were clean at my first visit. Cribs with straw and two coverlets for the felons: the court is small, and has fowls kept in it.'

22 December **1909** The Votes for Women, or Suffragette Movement, was growing in momentum. Large protests and public meetings had been held across the country, but women seemed no closer to their goals or even closer to gaining credibility for their arguments. Direct action was decided to be the way forward; in Norfolk Suffragettes publicly smashed shop windows and infiltrated public meetings and church services, leaping up at key moments revealing concealed banners calling for 'Votes for Women'. One protest probably not intended to go as far as it did was the small fire they started in the Pavilion Theatre on Britannia Pier on this day. Fanned by high winds, fire rapidly spread through the structure, devastating the theatre and causing extensive damage to the pier.

1900 John Edward Casey, a young man of Stokesby, had become much enamoured, albeit from afar, of Thirza Kelly, a young widow with a baby who had recently moved to the village. Shortly after her arrival Casey had received a 'right ribbing' in the pub about events in his misspent youth and didn't handle it too well. Fired up about the relationship which only really existed in his mind, Casey went to Thirza's house, where she was asleep, and broke in. Waking, she feared this unidentified intruder was going to harm her baby, and she took hold of him. There was a struggle during which the hotheaded Casey stabbed at her wildly with a knife before fleeing. Thirza was found dying on the floor by her mother the following morning; with her last breaths she was able to tell what happened. Casey was brought to trial and surprisingly was not considered to be insane, but had his death sentence commuted to penal servitude for life on account of his age.

(Norfolk Local Studies Library)

20 GUINEAS REWARD.

WHEREAS on Friday evening last, between the hours of 7 and 8 o'clock, **JAMES UPCROFT**, late of the City of Norwich, Publican, charged with Felony, made his escape from the Bridewell of the said City;

The said JAMES UPCROFT is about 28 Years of age, *5 feet 8 inches high*, pale Complexion, dark or hazle Eyes, dark Hair, is much pock-pitted, and rather slender. Had on a blue frock Coat, Corduroy small-clothes, black Woollen Waistcoat, white Neck-handkerchief, and brown top boots.

Whoever will give such information as may lead to the Apprehension of the said JAMES UPCROFT, or shall cause him to be lodged in any of his Majesty's Gaols, shall receive the above Reward, by applying to GEO. BAMBRIDGE, Governor of the said Bridewell.

GEORGE BAMBRIDGE.

Norwich, Dec. 23, 1820.

PRINTED BY WILKIN AND YOUNGMAN, NORWICH.

24 December   **1899**   Horace Alfred Cox entered a café in St Benedicts Street and fired three shots at Ellen Parker. Missing his target completely, he turned the weapon on himself and died shortly after removal to the Norfolk & Norwich Hospital.

25 December   **1830**   *What better for Christmas time than a ghost story?* Many a fireside around the Worstead area was graced by this tale with a ring of truth. A white lady was believed to appear in the tower of St Mary's Church as the clock chimed midnight on Christmas Eve. It was then the custom for the senior bellringer or the sexton to ring in Christmas, usually accompanied by a few booze-fuelled folk who thought they might catch a glimpse of the White Lady. It is said that in 1830 one man boasted he would go alone, saying that if he saw her he swore he would give her a kiss. As his compatriots waited in the inn, they soon heard the church clock strike 12, but no Christmas bell rang. Rushing up the church tower they found him in the ringing chamber paralysed with fright. He only recovered enough to open his eyes and whisper 'I've seen her' before expiring. I claim nothing more, but add that the Worstead church burial register records one Green Potter, aged 65, who was buried in the churchyard on 3 January 1830.

26 December   **1863**   A revolting performance was given at one of the shows at the Norwich Christmas Fair. 'A man and a woman, said to be Kaffirs, actually fed on live rats, in the presence of continually succeeding audiences.' The Mayor, on being informed of the proceedings, prohibited the exhibition, after which raw flesh was substituted for live rats. At Walsingham, a few days afterwards, the show was visited by many hundreds of country folk; at Wells, the police expelled the performers from the town.

27 December   **1828**   The commitments to Walsingham Bridewell give an idea of crime and criminals in rural Norfolk almost 200 years ago: William Williamson – for refusing work, one calendar month to treadwheel; Matthew Edge – for disobeying an order of bastardy, three months; Samuel Lake – for leaving his wife chargeable to the parish of Bale, one calendar month to treadwheel; Catherine Watson – for misdemeanour, one calendar month hard labour; Thomas Smith, James Pigge and William Bullock – being found poaching in the night, two calendar months hard labour; John Chestney – for a misdemeanour, one month to treadwheel.

28 December   **1839**   The theft by persons unknown of the bell from Swardeston church. The rogues broke the bell to pieces on the spot, and although the blows must have made a great noise the villagers were not disturbed enough to investigate. The 'sacrilegious depredators' were able to carry off their booty unmolested.

29 December   **1827**   *Bodysnatching at Great Yarmouth.* George Beck, a local baker, was concerned to find his recently buried wife's grave apparently disturbed. Further investigation confirmed his worst fears – the body had been stolen by Resurrectionists, otherwise known as bodysnatchers! Recently bereaved

St Nicholas's Church, Great Yarmouth, *c*. 1830.

persons' fears were aroused, and upon investigation about 20 graves were found to have been tampered with. The bodysnatching gang was soon traced; identified among their number were father and son team William and Robert Barber. The son, Robert, turned King's Evidence in a plea for leniency, and told how he and his father robbed graves, packed bodies in boxes and sent them by wain to London to the notable and brilliant surgeon Astley Cooper (later appointed Professor of Anatomy to the Royal College of Surgeons and personal physician to the monarch, and made a baronet). The most adept member of the gang was a tall, strong Irishman named Murphy who handled the bodies – he was paid £12 12s for at least four of the bodies from Yarmouth. Their leader was a professional resurrectionist named Thomas Vaughan, who had his bail expenses paid by Cooper. Vaughan was found guilty and sentenced to the House of Correction for six months: bodysnatching was considered a mere misdemeanour. An intriguing footnote is to be found in the ultimate fate of Vaughan. After his release, while in Plymouth, he appropriated some of the clothes in which a dead body had been wrapped. Prosecuted for felony, he was transported to Australia.

Norfolk Old Dame's Leechcraft

30 December

This excerpt from John Hollybush's *The Homish Apothecary* of 1561 offers a cure for festive headaches. 'Set a dish or platter of tin upon the bare head filled with water, and then drop an ounce and a half or two ounces of molten lead therein while he hath it on his head. That helpeth wonderfully.'

'Now, are you going to come quietly lad?' A Norfolk Police Constable in about 1880. *(Norfolk Constabulary Archives)*

1733 The first New Year's Eve celebrated at Waxham Hall by the Brograve family. Many stories have become attached to this rustic gentry family, from the duels they fought to their pack of ferocious hounds, and even that Sir 'Barney' Brograve took a wager and mowed for his soul against the Devil himself. Every New Year's Eve, as long as the Brograves were at Waxham Hall, they would (allegedly) entertain their dead ancestors: Sir Ralph, who was killed in the Crusades, Sir Edmund in the Baron's Wars, Sir John at Agincourt, Sir Francis in the Wars of the Roses, Sir Thomas at Marston Moor, Sir Charles at Ramillies. This motley crew would disappear with the chimes at midnight, not to be seen again until the next year.

31 December

''Tis said they entertain the dead 'uns till midnight.'
(Derek Rogers)

The condemned cell.

A Calendar of Norfolk Executions, 1835-1951

Frances Billings & Catherine Frary (poisoning): 10 August 1835

Peter Taylor (accessory to the above): 23 April 1836

John Smith & George Timmins (murder): 29 April 1837

Charles Daines (wife poisoner): 27 April 1839

John Randalsome (murder of wife): 22 August 1840

John Self (murder): 14 August 1841

Lucy Thorpe (murder of child): 13 September 1844 (*Last woman executed in Norfolk*)

Samuel Yarham (murder): 11 April 1846

James Blomfield Rush (Stanfield Hall murder) :21 April 1849

James Flood (murder): 22 April 1851

Henry Groom (murder): 16 August 1851

William Thompson (murder): 8 April 1854

Hubbard Lingley (murder): 26 August 1867 (*Last public execution in Norfolk*)

William Sheward (murder of wife): 20 April 1869

Henry Webster (murder of wife): 1 May 1876

Henry March (murder): 20 November 1877

William George Abigail (murder): 22 May 1882

Robert Goodale (murder) :15 September 1885

John Thurston (murder): 10 February 1886

George Harmer (murder): 13 December 1886 (*Last man executed in Norwich Castle*)

George Watt (murder of wife): 12 July 1898 (*First man executed at Norwich Prison*)

John Herbert Bennett (Yarmouth Beach murder): 21 March 1901

James Nichols (murder): 2 December 1908

Robert Galloway (murder): 5 November 1912

Herbert George Bloye (murder): 12 November 1925

Walter Smith (murder): 8 March 1938

Arthur Heys (murder): 13 March 1945

Stanley Joseph Clark (murder): 18 November 1948

James Frank Rivett (murder): 8 March 1950

Norman Goldthorpe (murder): 24 November 1950

Alfred Reynolds and Dennis Moore (murder): 19 July 1951 (*Last execution to be carried out in Norwich Prison*)

A Grim Gallery of some of the Public Executioners who Worked in Norfolk

William Calcraft 1829–74

William Marwood 1874–83
(Mortons of Horncastle)

James Berry 1884–92
(Hulton Archive)

James Billington 1884–1901

Henry Pierrepoint 1901–10

Albert Pierrepoint 1932–56

Casts of executed criminals' heads used by phrenologists in their old display in the dungeons of Norwich Castle.

Acknowledgements

I am deeply indebted to the following, without whom this book would not have been so enriched or so grim.

John Mason and Peter Pilgram from the Norfolk Constabulary Archives, Maurice Morson, Hulton Archive Picture Collection, James Nice, Nick Arber, Peter Skiggs, Robert 'Bookman' Wright, Michael Bean, Great Yarmouth Library, Bryan McNerney, Chris Tracy, Geoffrey Scott, the late Syd Dernley, Lincoln Central Library, Mortons of Horncastle, Sheila Watson at Great Yarmouth Museums, Oliver Bone at Ancient House Museum, Thetford, the staff of Tales of the Old Gaol House at King's Lynn, Walsingham Shirehall and Bridewell, Norwich Castle Museum, the Norfolk Record Office, especially Freda Wilkins-Jones for her expert guidance, Andy Archer and the contributing listeners of BBC Radio Norfolk, the irreplaceable Clive Wilkins-Jones and all the staff at the Norfolk Local Studies Library, and the Galleries of Justice at Nottingham for their encouragement and inspiration.

Usual respects are paid to Terry Burchell for his photographic wonders also Tony Smith from Shutters Photographic for the studio reconstructions and Simon Pegg for superb artwork where no engraving existed.

During my research into this book of dark deeds and grim tales I have met some of the nicest people, who have directed me towards and suggested some of the most sinister stories for inclusion in these pages, or shown real interest and given encouragement to my research. To those too numerous to mention, I sincerely thank you all.

Every attempt has been made to contact the owners of copyright for images used in this book. If any omission has been made it is not deliberate and no offence was intended.

Finally, I thank my family for their love and support of this temperamental author, especially my mother Diane, who kindled my interest in folklore, crime, matters strange and occurrences anomalous from an early age. A master storyteller, she could send a shiver down my spine but never caused a sleepless night!

Please note: All pictures are from the author's collection, unless otherwise credited. All the modern photographs of monuments, gravestones and sites were taken by the author on his travels across Norfolk over the last ten years.

Places to Visit

Tales of the Old Gaol House
Saturday Market Place
King's Lynn
Norfolk
PE30 5DQ
(01553) 774297
(open daily Easter to end of October
November to Easter Friday–Tuesday)

Norwich Castle Museum
Castle Meadow
Norwich
NR1 3JU
(01603) 493625

The Tolhouse Museum
Tolhouse Street
Great Yarmouth
NR30 2SH
(01493) 745526

Thetford Ancient House Museum
White Hart Street
Thetford
IP24 1AA
(01842) 752599

The Walsingham Shirehall and Bridewell
Common Place
Little Walsingham
NR22 6BP
(01328) 820510
(open daily April to end of October
open weekends from end of October until Christmas)